CRITIQUE OF IDENTITY THINKING

CRITIQUE OF IDENTITY THINKING

Michael Jackson

berghahn
NEW YORK · OXFORD
www.berghahnbooks.com

First published in 2019 by
Berghahn Books
www.berghahnbooks.com

Library of Congress Cataloging-in-Publication Data

A C.I.P. cataloging record is available from the Library of Congress
Library of Congress Cataloging in Publication Control Number:
2019014069

British Library Cataloguing in Publication Data

A catalogue record for this book is available from the British Library

ISBN 978-1-78920-282-3 hardback
ISBN 978-1-80073-442-5 paperback
ISBN 978-1-78920-283-0 ebook

https://doi.org/10.3167/9781789202823

From my point of view, no label, no slogan, no party, no skin color and indeed no religion is more important than the human being.

—James Baldwin, "The Price of the Ticket"

Humanitas is never acquired in solitude … It can be achieved only by one who has thrown his life and his person into the "venture into the public realm"—in the course of which he risks revealing something that is not "subjective" and which for that very reason he can neither recognize nor control.

—Hannah Arendt, "Karl Jaspers: A Laudatio," from *Men in Dark Times*

We wait for our permission to be human.

—Postcard from an asylum-seeker in a Calais camp

❧ Contents

℘ Acknowledgments

Several friends, colleagues, and students read portions of this work while it was still in progress and offered helpful and encouraging comments. I record here my sincere thanks to Sidra Ali, Jiaying Ding, Joshua Jackson, Sejal Patel, and Devaka Premawardhana. I am also indebted to James Faubion, the reader of my manuscript, whose erudite insights and suggestions were singularly useful to me in writing the final version. I am grateful to Indiana University Press for allowing me to reprint, albeit in a much-revised form, two chapters ("The Witch as a Category and as a Person," and "Identification and Description: An Essay on Metaphor") from *Paths Toward a Clearing: Radical Empiricism and Ethnographic Inquiry* (1989).

✣ Introduction

Open thinking points beyond itself.
                    —Theodor W. Adorno, "Resignation"

When Hannah Arendt writes of "humanity in dark times,"[1] she is thinking mainly of the years between 1933 and 1945 and of the almost complete collapse of *humanitas* in Germany during this period. In singling out Karl Jaspers as someone who sustained a small space in which human decency was preserved, Arendt elaborates on what her mentor and friend called "the venture into the public realm." This venture is always fraught. There is no guarantee that one's words will be understood or that one's actions have their desired effect. Though one works to weave the strands of one's own life into the lives of others, one can never know the repercussions of what anyone says or does. "That is what is meant by a venture," Arendt explains. And "this venture is only possible when there is trust in people. A trust which is hard to formulate. But one which is fundamental. *A trust in what is human in all people*. Otherwise such a venture could not be made."[2]

This book echoes Arendt's concerns. It argues that contemporary academic and political discourses based on notions of fixed identity and radical alterity lose sight of what all human beings have in common, despite their idiosyncratic, ethnic, cultural, or political differences. When Arendt speaks of the paradox of plurality she is mindful that, as a species, human beings share the same evolutionary history and confront similar existential quandaries, yet no two individuals are alike and very different adaptive strategies and worldviews have emerged in the course of human history. If we are to resist essentializing and reifying traits that make us appear different, thus creating irreconcilable divisions among us, *or between us and non-human life forms,*[3] we must restore a sense of trust in what we and others have in common, even if it is the planet earth.

History brings home to us the fragility of this trust. Its presence is not only compromised by inequalities in wealth and power, as Zygmunt Bauman observes,[4] but it is exponentially tied to the degree to which we fetishize differences and discontinuities between ourselves and others and lose sight of what we share. Trust is only possible when one sees the other not only as different in features, manners, worldview, and language but also as oneself in other circumstances. What is realized in the other is recognized as a potentiality in oneself (and vice versa). Without this intersubjective trust, ventures into the public realm remain infinitely more perilous for the poor, for people of color, and for undocumented migrants than for those who claim exclusive rights to this realm and police it accordingly. In our contemporary world, the question of trust has also been made more urgent as electronic surveillance and the fetishization of data undermine traditional forms of face-to-face interaction, care, and conviviality.

Arendt's conception *of* "a trust in what is human in all people" is also basic to the project of ethnography, where one's relationships in the field carry a risk of mutual misunderstanding but also imply a willing suspension of disbelief, informed by the assumption that *as human beings* points of existential convergence and mutual understanding can always be found. These points are often predicated on shared phylogenetic traits like attachment or responses to separation and loss, as well as ontogenetic struggles to resolve sibling or Oedipal rivalries, reconcile our ties to things and our ties to persons, or strike a balance between competing existential strategies—agency and patiency, openness and closure, security and risk, self-realization and social constraint. It may come from wrestling with our vulnerability and mortality, or reflect "one of the major processes of our species, which has racked many, perhaps all, societies over thousands of years … the rise and fall of fervently held beliefs, as humans continually strive to understand how the world works and the reasons for their happiness or suffering—and to act on these."[5] To speak of the human condition, therefore, is to imply that existence not only is replete with contradictions, alternatives, and contrarieties but is also characterized by ongoing struggles to resolve, accept, or overcome them.

This broaches the question of the relation between thought and being and the extent to which the complexities of existence can be described by means of words and concepts. In drawing a distinction between the *vita contemplativa* and the *vita activa*, and by insisting that thought is grounded in the interactions and interests of everyday social life, Hannah Arendt repudiates the Cartesian prioritization of the res cogitans (mind) over the res extensa (body) and argues that thinking is never the passive ruminations of self-sufficient minds, a "soundless dialogue we carry on with ourselves,"[6] but a form of active engagement with those with whom we inhabit a common world. Like sharing stories, giving gifts, and exchanging greetings, thinking is not necessarily predicated on what we consciously know or believe beforehand. Much of what we habitually do in the course of a day is done without a moment's reflection. And it is this body of basic social and physical coping skills, this implicit knowledge that is shared with many others, that enables us to synchronize movements and achieve social attunement, sharing food, reciprocating favors, playing host, being a good guest, or helping someone in need without an explicit script to guide us. Meaning is thus praxeological (a matter of the way we engage purposefully with others in a shared habitus) before it is epistemological (a matter of our knowledge of the world).[7] And this is also something one learns in the course of fieldwork—that the most fruitful thinking is done in the course of interactions that are "this worldly" rather than "other worldly," situated rather than abstracted, practically oriented rather than theoretically framed.[8] When the discursive conventions of the academy, centered on reified coinages, arcane jargons, and fetishized categories work to widen the gap between us and those whose lifeworlds we purportedly seek to understand, we must confront the uncomfortable truth that we have allowed ourselves to participate in the neoliberal order that has ineluctably widened the gap between rich and poor. It is for this reason that the critique of identity thinking involves a suspension of one's political affiliation, either with the left or the right, the righteous or the wronged, since all human beings are susceptible to seeing the world at large solely from their own vantage point and reifying their particular perspective as if it were a universal truth. To militate against these tendencies, two strategies may prove useful. The first is to resist construing existential problems as reflections of one's own identity, or the identity of others, or a reflection of the identity of their relationships. Such a focus on who is in the right and who is in the wrong prevents everyone involved from seeing the problem itself. It is not simply their problem, but a human problem, and this changed perspective may enable them to approach it with greater clarity. It is not that no one is to blame, but rather that blaming others or oneself may be counterproductive in resolving the problem cooperatively.[9] The second strategy is to focus not on where we differ from others—in our ethnicity, language, gender, history, class, or faith—but on what we have in common.

In making the case for diapraxis over dialogue, Naveed Baig, Lissi Rasmussen, and Hans Raun Iversen recall an international class on interfaith dialogue at the University of Copenhagen in 2012 and the difficulties of finding common ground for a productive and peaceable encounter between Muslims and Christians, especially since two Nigerian students in the class had experienced the killing of a Christian neighbor's family in the furor following the Danish cartoon crisis in 2006. For these individuals, Muslims were evil.

> In the middle of the term, the class heard a guest lecture by Dr. Johnson Mbillah, at that time director of *Programme for Christian-Muslim Relations in Africa*, who came along with a friend of his, a Muslim sheikh. Having introduced his friend and himself as respectively Muslim and Christian and both of them Africans, Dr. Mbillah asked, "So, this friend of mine, is he first an African or is he first a Muslim? And I myself, am I first an African or am I a Christian?" You could hear a pin drop before Dr. Mbillah answered his own question: "No, my friends, we are first of all human beings, both of us!"[10]

While identity thinking binds us together in discrete groups or tribes, it also blinds us to what connects us across time and space, and how our sense of being-in-the-world is subject to continual fluctuation. While analytical models and explanatory concepts tend to foster the illusion of determinate subjects (neoliberal, transnational, racial, modern) and bounded societies, human beings have been transgressing borders from time immemorial, and lived experience suggests constant mutations in the degree and intensity of everything from cultural conformity and self-consciousness, to emotional states, interpersonal trust, and religious belief.[11]

When I reflect on my ethnographic sojourns in Aboriginal Australia and West Africa, and my experiences of traveling around the world, I do not recall incommensurable beliefs and insurmountable differences, but cultural variations on a recurring theme—our human tendency to think categorically and organize hierarchically, yet all the while blurring boundaries, crossing frontiers, and subverting hierarchies with empathic gestures toward equality and equity.

For thinkers like William James, Hannah Arendt, John Dewey, and Richard Rorty, the value of our speaking and writing is measured by the extent to which they help us cope with everyday life, carrying us into more fulfilling relationships with one another, and fostering coexistence. This same pragmatic spirit finds expression in Theodor W. Adorno's view that it is "delusional" to seek absolute truth or claim that "the real is rational" when what really matters is that Auschwitz does not happen again. "If philosophy is still necessary," he writes, "it is so only in the way it has been from time immemorial: as critique, as resistance to the expanding heteronomy."[12] Accordingly, it may be argued that humanity must not be contrasted with animality or materiality, and that humanism is best defined as a refusal to assign a higher value to abstract ideas than to particular living beings or regard ideas and numbers as having a more urgent claim on our attentions than the faces of real people.

At the heart of Adorno's negative dialectics is a call for modes of thinking and writing that go beyond concepts that allegedly correspond to reality or conform to rules of logical discourse. As he puts it, "objects do not go into their concepts without leaving a remainder ... the concept does not exhaust the thing conceived."[13] For Adorno, concepts are no more identical with objects than a brand name is a true description of a product, a social stereotype captures the essence of every individual, or a photograph is identical with its subject. Photos, writes Roland Barthes, are "a kind of primitive theater, a kind of *Tableau Vivant*, a figuration of the motionless and made-up face" beneath which lies all that has been lost, left behind, or could not be held.[14]

Elsewhere, I have merged Adorno's idea of negative dialectics with images of the limitrophe and the penumbral. The term limitrophe (from Latin *limit-, limes* boundary + Greek *trophos,* nourishing) suggests the life-giving potential of places, people, and powers that lie beyond the pale of our established lifeworlds, and emphasizes that existential vitality depends on transgressing what has been prescribed by custom, internalized as habit, or enshrined in received ideas of truth and reality.[15] The penumbral (from the Latin *paene,* almost + *umbra,* shadow) suggests a phenomenologically indeterminate zone "between regions of complete shadow and complete illumination," "an area in which something exists to a lesser or uncertain degree," and "an outlying or peripheral region."[16] For William James, the penumbral reminds us that "our fields of experience have no more definite boundaries than have our fields of view," while his notion of "the more"[17] conveys his conviction that neither the world within nor the world without can be completely captured or covered by conceptual thought. James is equally insistent that abstraction is not so much a rational means of mirroring the world but a magical defense against its refractory and incomprehensible aspects. Ian McEwan goes further, suggesting that our infatuation with abstract concepts and their endless interrelations implies a kind of fantasizing, in which the manipulation of ideas compensates us for our inability to manipulate the world.[18]

James's determination to "bring ideas and principles and beliefs down to the human level," "avoiding the violence [he] saw in abstractions," was his response to the horrors of the US Civil War.[19] In a similar vein, Adorno's critique of identity thinking was, in part, his response to Hitler's reduction of humanity to an ascending series of essentially incompatible racial types and national identities. In the aftermath of World War II, Adorno announced a new categorical imperative: that if thinking is not to entail hubris and harm, it must involve a continual, self-reflective "thinking against itself."[20] If we are not to become infatuated by the categories into which we place people for academic, conversational, or administrative convenience—male versus female, friend versus enemy, black versus white—we need the reality testing experience of direct engagement with real people in real situations. In this sense, negative dialectics is an attempt "to say what something is, while identitarian thinking says what something comes under, what it exemplifies or represents, and what, accordingly, it is not itself."[21]

Identity thinking[22] is typical of bureaucracies in which people and objects are numbered, classified, and categorized as if their idiosyncratic features were less significant than their superficial similarities. Consider, for instance, the term "refugee" and the discourse that identifies this figure with an undifferentiated mass, a crowd, a problem, a pathology, described as if there were no individuating stories to be told and no comparison to be made with those who identify refugees in these ways.[23] Identity thinking may be instrumental to the administration of the world, but it is inimical to expressing the complexities of life, and it is a precondition for violence.

In his account of how native forests are radically redesigned and planted to maximize the commercial exploitation of their timber, James Scott makes a similar point. A state's interest in commercial timber and revenue entails reducing the complex and variegated ecology of the forest to manageable dimensions. Quite simply, "The administrators' forest cannot be the naturalists' forest." In the same way, a "schematized process of abstraction and simplification" reduces complex patterns of social and community life to bureaucratic formulae. "State agents have no interest … in describing an entire social reality, any more than the scientific forester has an interest in describing the ecology of a forest in detail."[24]

Identity thinking risks degrading the very existence of whatever it subjects to ratiocination—a process that Niels Bohr called the "principle of destruction" (*Abtötungsprinzip*). As João Biehl observes, this process entails "bureaucratic procedures" that render "people invisible" and turn them into "absent things."[25] The Nazi stereotype of "The Jew" already presaged a genocide, since the faces, names, lives, sensibilities, and situations of actual individuals disappeared without a trace behind the grotesque façade of the reified term. In the same way *Das Man* occludes any engagement with the many individual beings who comprise the generalized "one." These racial, social, and utilitarian abstractions do not give us anyone to relate to as a person like ourselves; they actually prevent and absolve us from having any empathy or compassion for those who have been assimilated to those abstractions. Speaking of the difference between *I-Thou* and *I-It* relationships, Martin Buber observes that whenever I extract from a person "the color of his hair, or of his speech, or of his goodness," or identify him with a particular time or place, he "ceases to be Thou" and becomes an It.[26] Thus, with no firsthand knowledge of life in south Chicago, the president of the United States blames African-Americans (not their situations) for the murder rates in their neighborhoods and reduces their humanity to this statistic. Showing no compassion for the individual lives and stories of asylum-seekers, he orders the suspension of immigration from Iran, Iraq, Libya, Somalia, Sudan, Syria, and Yemen as if the persecuted citizens of these countries are tarred with the same brush as their persecutors. Every day, egregious examples of this exclusionary and isolationist policy make the news headlines. It may be too early to say whether mockery (Charlie Chaplin's *The Great Dictator* comes to mind) or widespread dissent (as during the Vietnam War) will prevent these policies from reaching their logical conclusion, but a comparison with the Nazi's anti-Jewish decrees of 1933 may prove apposite. In a Manichean worldview, nature is exploited for human gain, and certain categories of human beings are assimilated into nature and treated as means whereby those who determine the ends—the creation of wealth, the expansion of power, the racial purity of the nation, the civilizing of the heathen—can realize their vision. In promulgating a series of opposed terms—mind/body, subject/object, enlightened/primitive, culture/nature—in which the first is assigned a higher value than the second, identity thinking gives spurious legitimacy to social distinctions between higher and lower classes of people, while perpetuating a narcissistic belief in the omnipotence of one's own thought.

Our challenge is, however, to do more than condemn the identitarian thinking we find abhorrent—racism, sexism, ageism—by reflecting on the extent to which the generalizations we make in avowedly explaining or changing the world for the better actually lock us into similar discursive cages. In as much as liberal intellectuals frame their fields of study in categorical terms, they are hoisted by their own petard, for in their impassioned denunciations of racism and sexism, they paradoxically keep alive the discriminatory language they reject, while their invocations of humanism often reinforce their own parochial conceptions of human rights and diversity. All too often, the rich and powerful act as if they alone possessed humanity and were free to assign it to or withhold it from the powerless as they wished. It is also necessary to remember that while the West paid lip service to Enlightenment values of reason, democracy, and humanism, it belied those ideals in the violence of colonization, slavery, and the genocide of indigenous populations—often in the name of king, country, and God.[27] It is equally important to note that for many peoples, diversity and humanity are not based on physical appearance or cultural identity, but on how a person behaves. Thus, for the Kuranko of Sierra Leone and Guinea, personhood (*morgoye*) is a matter of how one comports oneself in relation to others—a question of social nous. While whiteness signifies magnanimity and transparency, and blackness is associated with enemies and the minatory powers of witches, Kuranko do not identify "white people" (*tubabunu*) as good, or think of themselves as "black," though enemies are referred to as *morgo fian* ("black people"). It is not that Kuranko are immune to stereotyping and scapegoating (see chapter 2), but not once during my many sojourns among them did people reduce my humanity to the color of my skin or the country I came from. Neither did they make blanket assertions about the intrinsic humanity or inhumanity of whites, but remarked how particular Europeans acted in relation to others, myself included.[28] Intelligence was a matter of social adroitness and practical know-how, and many Kuranko would readily concur with critical theory's recurring theme—that abstraction not only implies an estrangement of thought from life, but finds its apotheosis in the terrorist's appeal to God or the lynch mob's invocation of racial purity to justify murder.[29] Reflecting on National Socialism's xenophobic reduction of political life to a question of being for or against the state, Adorno observes that under such circumstances "freedom would be not to choose between black and white but to abjure such prescribed choices."[30]

World events in 2016–17—including the Brexit vote in the United Kingdom, the election of Donald Trump as president of the United States, the civil war in Syria, the migrant crisis in Europe, accelerating climate change, the rise of Isis, and the ever-widening gulf between haves and have-nots—have persuaded many people that we are again living in "dark times." As an intellectual, teacher, and writer, I asked myself how I might respond to these events. What kind of speech and action were called for in our beleaguered age? My initial impulse was to go back to some of the critical thinkers—notably Hannah Arendt, Theodor Adorno, Walter Benjamin, and Karl Jaspers—whose work was profoundly influenced by the catastrophes that overwhelmed the world in the middle of the last century. This prompted me to rethink the ethnographic method of "participant-observation" pioneered by Bronislaw Malinowski during his sojourn in the Trobriand Islands during World War I, not simply as a means of "doing anthropology" but as exemplifying the kind of practical humanism that Hans-Georg Gadamer defined as "keeping oneself open to what is other—to other, more universal points of view"[31] and not assuming that one's own worldview can be made a yardstick for measuring others.

What practical steps can we take to think and act without the conceptual railings and bridges that Friedrich Nietzsche cautioned us against clinging to?[32] This is more than a matter of applying the phenomenological epoché, invoking the naïve view that it is possible to "tear aside the web of concepts"[33] and experience life authentically and atheoretically; rather it demands moving outside our comfort zones and risking ourselves in situations where our mother language is not spoken, our customs not recognized, our expectations not confirmed, and our identities not recognized. This book is therefore a plea not to allow our craving for security and community to lead us to embrace the illusions of consolation, salvation, and omniscience that are offered by religion, politics, and science alike, but to perpetually make and remake ourselves in relation to others as if nothing were certain. It is also a reminder of the nuances, intricacies, and complexities that literature has always emphasized over generalizations and stereotypes. "Begin with a type," F. Scott Fitzgerald wrote, "and you find you have created nothing."[34] In a similar vein, Aminatta Forna dismisses "classifying [as] the very antithesis of literature. The way of literature is to seek universality. Writers try to reach beyond those things that divide us: culture, class, gender, race. Given the chance, we would resist classification. I have never met a writer who wishes to be described as a female writer, gay writer, black writer, Asian writer or African writer."[35] For Chimamanda Ngozi Adichie, our lives and lifeworlds comprise a multitude of overlapping stories, and it is the task of every writer worth her salt to avoid "the danger of a single story," such as the story of Africa as a synonym for poverty, catastrophe, and violence, a story in which "Africa" is assigned a single identity when, in reality, the term is a complete misnomer.[36]

1

MISTAKEN IDENTITIES
The Task of Thinking in Dark Times

> To be categorized is, simply, to be enslaved.
> —Gore Vidal, explaining why he refused to identify as "gay"

No longer doing fieldwork in far flung places, I have come to depend on riffling through old journals, talking with students, reading philosophy, and occasionally traveling abroad for my intellectual inspiration. Although these research methods are at once more adventitious and indirect than ethnography, they hopefully keep my thinking and writing grounded.

In the fall of 2016, I met with one of my students to discuss her current research. Born in China, Jiaying Ding came to the United States with her parents when she was seven. At school and at university, Jiaying became increasingly preoccupied with questions of identity. It was not that she sought a label that summed up who she was or that captured the experiences of the seniors with whom she was working in Boston and Beijing. Rather, Jiaying was struck by the impossibility of reducing persons to cultural, racial, sexual, or religious stereotypes. She found herself asking which of the problems faced by Chinese seniors reflected their ethnicity, which reflected their idiosyncratic experiences of aging and infirmity, and which could not be so easily pinned down. Turning to her own experience at Harvard, she mentioned "the hollow sense of one dimensionality" that sometimes overwhelmed her when she would give her one-minute "elevator introduction at a meeting or at the beginning of class" about who she was and what she was researching.

When I said "Chinese immigrants" it gave me an identity in a community that emphasized diversity, but it also felt alienating. I began to imagine my parents, sitting in puzzlement in the Old South Church, listening to a sermon. How can I reconcile my strong yearning for a place I can call home, of going back to China and seeking the resonances I feel I can only find there, with my growing conviction that people should not be treated one dimensionally, by their skin color, or by their status, or by other stereotypes?[1]

I suggested to Jiaying two ways out of this impasse. The first was to pursue a train of thought she had already discovered in Maxine Hong Kingston's memoir of growing up in Stockton, California. "Chinese Americans, when you try to understand what things in you are Chinese, how do you separate what is peculiar to childhood, to poverty, insanities, one family, your mother who marked your growing with stories, from what is Chinese? What is Chinese tradition and what is the movies?"[2] In other words, culture is best thought of not as delimiting one's identity but as a resource or fund on which one can draw creatively and variously, depending on the exigencies of the situation in which one finds oneself.

Like everything in life, the doctrine of diversity has its shadow side. In playing up difference and focusing on single traits such as skin color or nationality, we risk diminishing the significance of what we share. Furthermore, by reducing religious life to what is inscribed in religious texts (an error into which vociferous atheists and religious scholars often fall), or viewing happiness and unhappiness through clinical lens, or defending the rights of one group as if its moral claims on us were more compelling than the claims of others, our reified expressions of difference tend to blind us to the reasons we create such forms of distinction and division in the first place, as well as obscure the inherent dangers of these discursive forms.

Lila Abu-Lughod observes that life stories subvert "assumptions of homogeneity, coherence and timelessness ... by revealing the struggle, negotiation, and strategizing that lie at the heart of social life."[3] John Berger puts it even more forcefully: "In poor societies abstraction and tyranny go together; in rich societies it is indifference which usually goes with abstraction. Abstraction's capacity to ignore what is real (and the heart can abstract as well as the mind: unjustifiable jealousy, for example, is an abstraction) is undoubtedly where most evil begins."[4]

Although I argue for deconstructing the category terms we deploy in our efforts to make life intelligible and manageable, a case can be made for creating such constructs and even for compressing into them more rather than fewer associations. In the same way that the

God concept originates in kinship with images of paternal authority and maternal care, but accrues abstract ideas such as omnipotence, omniscience, infinity, and ineffability, identity terms tend to become condensation symbols that bring together images of ethnicity, kinship, history, and moral value, as in the Maori notion of *Maoritanga* explored in chapter 6 of this book.[5] One can, therefore, appreciate the appeal of identity thinking for minorities fighting for recognition. Cultural fundamentalism provides beleaguered people with a spiritually uplifting and politically powerful sense of shared identity.[6] Hannah Arendt's comments are edifying here. In a 1964 interview, she describes the "special warmth" that existed among Jewish people when they were dispersed and without a state, and argues that this "pariah status,"[7] "this standing outside of all social connections," "this sense of being an emigrant in one's own homeland,"[8] paradoxically generated an intellectual spirit of open-mindedness, "a trust in what is human in all people." But "this humanity," she goes on to say, "has never survived the hour of liberation by as much as five minutes." And so it was with the founding of the Jewish state. At the very moment of liberation, this "trust in what is human in all people" was broken. For Arendt, love is an emotion that arises between persons. One cannot love a people or a collectivity.[9]

When identity thinking passes from being a coping strategy to an entrenched dogma it effectively traps one in an oppositional way of thinking that perpetuates rather than bridges the gap between oneself and others. The Jews established a homeland in Israel only to treat Palestinians as second-class citizens. South Africa dismantled racial apartheid only to reinforce economic apartheid, dividing the country not by color but by class. And US neoliberalism turned a blind eye to working people, placing its trust in well-educated professionals who, it was believed, would solve the problem of growing inequality, even though this new class would exclude anyone who questioned its master narrative.[10] Perhaps this explains why marginalization is so often the necessary condition for recovering our humanity, and why an ethnographer living in a society where he or she is both marginal and powerless may momentarily achieve that state of open-mindedness that Arendt and Jaspers associate with *humanitas*.[11]

In any event, I told Jiaying that her comments resonated with those of Hannah Arendt and Maxine Hong Kingston—that there is more to a life than can be explained in terms of cultural background, social class, or ethnic identity, and the migrant may be more likely to know this than a person who has remained rooted in one place. This does not, however, preclude an individual playing up or playing down the

"Chinese" elements in her life depending on the situation in which she finds herself. Speaking of her aunt, who drowned herself and her newborn son after it was discovered that she had been unfaithful to her husband (who had migrated to the United States), Hong Kingston declares, "Unless I see her life branching into mine, she gives me no ancestral help."[12] Culture and ethnicity are not determinants of an identity one can do nothing about, but potentialities that may be drawn on in very different ways depending on the situation at hand.[13] Writer and academic, Sunil Badami writes of himself as a

> masala of multiculturalism … I'm different at different times, in different places and contexts, with different people. A man—but also a husband, a father, a son, a friend, a teacher, a writer. And more, including my Indian ethnicity *and* my Australian heritage.
>
> And despite all these different identities, they're all the same person: *me.* I'm just not only one identity, nor should I be defined by only one.[14]

Living in the United States, Sejal Patel confides that she needs the category word "Indian," because it "makes me feel that my otherness is shared" and "I don't have to attend to the world and its prejudices alone." At the same time, Sejal rejects the assumption that her Indian identity means that non-Indians cannot understand her or that her heritage prevents her from understanding them. Both as an individual and as a lawyer, Sejal emphasizes the power of "spending time face-to-face with others in order to see the humanity in them rather than the difference."[15]

Such "strategic essentialism"[16] may help one counter discrimination and disempowerment, as with the Black Lives Matter movement in the United States. What is compelling about such social movements is that they bring together ideas concerning a common cause or shared identity, and immediate, visceral experiences of moving and acting as a single body. Although such totalizations of identity have, historically, had revolutionary consequences and been liberating, sometimes, as in fascist states, they have been enslaving. What makes the difference is often the degree to which such mass mobilizations preserve or destroy people's rights to decide whether they will or will not go along with the crowd.

To be forced to identify as Black or Chinese, either because a powerful person insists that this is all you are or because your community considers this a matter of honor and solidarity, is to lose one's freedom to lead one's life in one's own terms. "Students of color" sometimes feel that they are recruited to a college on the basis of their outward appearance rather than their inner qualities—invited to be "on the table" rather than "at the table." Their struggle to decide the terms on which they will live their own life and choose their own identities, is exemplified by Zora Neale Hurston's declarations of independence— declarations that frequently put her at odds with the political agendas of black intellectuals and activists. "At certain times I have no race. I am *me* … I have no separate feeling about being an American citizen and colored. I am merely a fragment of the Great Soul that surges within boundaries."[17]

Sidra Ali's experience is relevant here. Sidra's parents migrated to the United States from Pakistan, and though she was born in the United States, Sidra confesses to "having spent much of my life explaining and defending my citizenship due to the color of my skin and the etymology of my name. I am routinely asked where I am from, and when my answer of 'Michigan' proves insufficient, I cite Jacksonville, Florida, my birthplace—much to the dissatisfaction of the questioner. The next question is always, 'Where are your parents from?' and when I answer 'Pakistan' the interrogator is relieved."[18]

Speaking of how irksome it is to be typecast as an immigrant when she is an American, Sidra cites the kinds of misidentifications she has to rebut or navigate in her everyday life.

> People assume I am Hindu and give me vegetarian meals. People assume I am unable to speak English and speak to me in slow, exaggerated, staccato sentences as if to preemptively help me to understand what they are saying. People assume I am a devout Muslim and refuse to shake my hand, even when I proffer it in a professional setting. People assume I am an Arab, and request family recipes for hummus and shawarma. People assume I am a suicide bomber and shift uncomfortably where they stand, or demand different seating arrangements on airplanes, or threaten to call airport security if I continue to insist that my small backpack can indeed fit into the overhead compartment. People assume that I have been oppressed and congratulate me on being a strong, "liberated" and "modern" woman. People assume it is my responsibility to speak on behalf of ISIS's frustrations, to understand the complex political climate of the Middle East, or apologize for actions undertaken by individuals who have tenuous ties to my nebulous identity as a "Muslim." People assume I am Latina and speak to me in Spanish; assume I am African American and ask me about my enslaved ancestors; assume I am white and deride me for my privilege; assume I am not attuned to the struggles of marginalized communities; assume that I am more than human. Such encounters leave me flayed—as if the curious party cannot accept my hope to sustain a conversation without identity markers.[19]

Sidra and Jiaying are not alone in their discomfort with the ways in which identity thinking influences the images of diversity with which universities now advertise themselves. Like me, they are troubled by the artifice of this window-dressing, in which a cherry-picked group of white, black, yellow, and brown men and women (rarely old or infirm) are captured smiling at the camera as though they had discovered in one another's company an oasis of peace and enlightenment. Too much is made of superficial differences, like skin color or dress. Although every individual sees the world differently and has a different story to tell, these utopian images inadvertently perpetuate the one-dimensional, reductive, and categorical ways of thinking that we associate with racism. For, despite appearances, the average genetic difference between any two human beings is greater than the average genetic difference between any two human populations (e.g., Europe and sub-Saharan Africa). As Alan Goodman notes, "There is no good scientific evidence beyond word length, convenience, and maintenance of the status quo (laziness in short), to continue to racialize human variation. Moreover, doing so may cause harm."[20]

Not only photographic images, but language itself can blind us to the nature of what is. Gadamer observes that "Greek philosophy more or less began with the insight that a word is only a name—i.e., that it does not represent true being."[21] By implication, true being is revealed less in our dialogues than in our actions, cooperating in building something, making music together, eating together, or sharing our tribulations. But such forms of interaction are precluded if not forbidden when our consciousness is clouded by notions of essential difference. In other words, diapraxis may be a better way of achieving *humanitas* than dialogue—doing things together rather than sharing worldviews. Indeed, theories, like prejudices, would seem to be one of the principal causes of misrecognition, since they tend to make the other an object whose only value is to confirm our suspicions or prove our point of view.

When James Baldwin left the United States for France, he wrote, "I wanted to prevent myself from becoming *merely* a Negro; or, even merely a Negro writer. I wanted to find out in what way the *specialness* of my experience could be made to connect me with other people instead of dividing me from them."[22] Though dependent on English literature—a literature of "white centuries"—Baldwin felt free to make that literature his own.[23] As for being seen solely as a Negro, he declared, "I don't like people who like me because I'm a Negro; neither do I like people who find in the same accident grounds for contempt."[24]

Edmund White's experience of moving to France resonated with Baldwin's. While Americans were trapped in "a politics of identity," foregrounding their particular affiliations and ethnicities, the French, according to White, extolled the virtues of centrism. "In France there is no Jewish novel, no black novel, no gay novel; Jews, blacks and gays, of course, write about their lives, but they would be offended if they were discussed with regard to their religion, ethnicity or gender."[25] Though White's remarks ironically deploy notions of national character, and seem idealistic in light of contemporary anti-immigration, anti-Muslim rhetoric, they reflect, like Baldwin's comments from an earlier generation, a deep distaste for the kind of cultural fundamentalism and racial profiling that reduces a complex human being to a caricature. By implication, the invocation of human rights, rather than LGBT rights, women's rights, or indigenous rights, may militate against the tendency to see one's own humanity as a special case and one's own suffering as worse than the suffering of others.

Theodor Adorno and Jean-Paul Sartre

Recent neuroscientific research on prejudice and stereotyping makes it clear that our tendency to think categorically has evolved as a basic aspect of neocortical functioning.[26] Although the hippocampal system, by contrast, "serves a different function in mental life in that it enables perceivers to form temporary representations of novel or surprising stimulus events … generally speaking, these episodic traces exert little impact on the status of generic knowledge, unless of course they are activated on a regular basis."[27] These different brain functions, which at once construct and deconstruct concepts or foreground and background stereotypes, imply a degree of ambiguity in the way we perceive others. And while the distinctions perceived between different things or persons may be morally neutral, we all too often learn to see them otherwise, regarding right as superior to left, light as better than dark, and the people we know as more trustworthy than those we do not.

When I went to the Congo in 1964 as a volunteer community development worker with the United Nations, some of my British friends were mystified by my interest in what they regarded as a heart of darkness, plagued by violence, poverty, and superstition. During my first disoriented days in Léopoldville (now Kinshasa), I experienced the Congolese as an undifferentiated mass, speaking a single unintelligible language. Though this reaction is perfectly understandable when one is overwhelmed by a foreign environment, it can easily lead one to withdraw, or make absurd generalizations about the natives as if it is magically possible to make them go away. Hence the racist comment, "they all look the same to me," or the irritation and contempt directed at almost everything "they" do, as if "their" *moeurs* have been carefully and cunningly devised with one end in mind—to make you feel uncomfortable or make your life a misery. Though I observed these traits in the whites I met in and around the UN Headquarters, my own culture shock took a different turn.

I was having lunch one day in a restaurant frequented by UN staff. For some reason, my focus shifted from the people at my table to the Congolese waiters in their white starched uniforms, unobtrusively coming and going, never exchanging any words with us, though taking our orders, refreshing our drinks, and serving our food. Suddenly, the waiters became visible to me and the expatriates with whom I had been exchanging small talk faded away. As this happened, one particular waiter came into focus. Handsome though he was, it was not his appearance that captivated me. Though he moved gracefully, it was not his comportment I admired. What struck me vividly, with the force of an epiphany, was that he was a person, an individual like me. And then I looked around, observing the other waiters, each one his own person, each with a life that was indelibly his own, and a story that was unlike any other. I realized that one does not live as a category, but as a person, despite our discursive habits of reducing people to their color, class, gender, or creed. At the same time, a deep sadness came over me as I realized that I was very likely perceived by most Congolese as *un blanc* and assimilated to the very class from which I now resolved to liberate myself.

The depth to which we absorb stereotypes may account for the incredulity expressed by individuals whose one-dimensional sense of their own identity is confounded when they receive the results of tests from such organizations as Ancestry DNA. That one carries genetic traces of forebears who belonged to nations or ethnic groups for which one has always felt a profound antipathy can be unsettling to say the least, though for some the disclosure of their genetically mixed make-up is liberating. As one man put it, "I'm a real man of the world. That's beautiful."[28]

"To think is to identify," declares Theodor Adorno, recognizing the impossibility of dispensing with concepts. "Necessity compels philosophy to operate with concepts, but this necessity must not be turned into the virtue of their priority—no more than, conversely, criticism of that virtue can be turned into a summary verdict against philosophy."[29] In other words, though our ways of thinking about the world entail concepts, we are also aware of the non-conceptual, the individual, the particular—of "things which ever since Plato used to be dismissed as transitory and insignificant."[30] And, hopefully, we are aware of the danger of turning concepts from means to ends, which is to say reifying them. For Walter Benjamin, dialectical thinking combines "a loyalty to ... individual items" and "a stubborn subversive protest against the typical, the classifiable."[31] It is focused on the interplay rather than the identity of things, and remains skeptical of all efforts to reduce the diversity of experience to timeless categories and enumerable theorems. It refuses to force life to be at the disposal of ideas.[32]

It is important to recognize, however, that our actions are not only preconditioned by entrenched ideas but may precipitate thinking that either confirms our prejudices or changes our minds. "Every thought is an afterthought," writes Hannah Arendt, "a reflection on some manner or event."[33] In a similar vein, John Dewey notes that thought never occurs in a vacuum as a kind of spontaneous combustion. There is always something specific that occasions and compels it, "some perplexity, confusion, or doubt."[34] This situated way of thinking about thinking brings me back to Karl Jaspers's notion of border situations. "We are always in situations," Jaspers writes.

> Situations change, opportunities arise. If they are missed they never return. I myself can work to change the situation. But there are situations which remain essentially the same, even if their momentary aspect changes and their shattering force is obscured: I must die, I must suffer, I must struggle, I am subject to chance, I involve myself inexorably in guilt. We call these fundamental situations of our existence ultimate situations (*Grenzsituationen*)."[35]

The notion of situation as developed by Karl Jaspers, Jean-Paul Sartre, and Simone de Beauvoir complements Adorno's conception of negative dialectics by reminding us that our freedom to repudiate identity thinking is often conditional on our circumstances in life—from having job security and a steady income to being a migrant or exile—and that an obsession with identity is often tied to economic insecurity and a sense of being marginal. Ironically, however, Adorno's undisguised antipathy for *Existenzphilosophie*, which he wrote off as a naïve subjectivism that blithely ignored the extent to which people were constituted by their objective circumstances, reflects his reading of Sartre's early writing on free choice and bad faith, and ignores Sartre's subsequent engagement with Marxism in which he acknowledged that we are at once shaped by circumstances beyond our control and respond to those circumstances in various ways.[36] There is, moreover, a compelling similarity between Adorno's insistence that "objects do not go into their concepts without leaving a remainder,"[37] and Sartre's view that lived experience contradicts and overflows the cognitive limits that we habitually imagine we can set upon it.[38] Both Adorno and Sartre are arguing against reductionism and reification. Not only is there always more to life than can be contained in concepts, but the illusion that a concept summarizes everything that is significant about a phenomenon or a person carries the risk that we will act toward the phenomenon or individual as though it were essentially and utterly different from any other. It is but a short step from speaking of "Africans" or "refugees" or "Muslims" to acting as if these categories were threats to the category in which we place ourselves, and therefore have to be separated from us or, worse, destroyed.

Gregory Bateson's notion of schismogenesis is relevant here—our cognitive habit of dividing the world into antithetical categories, such as black-white, us-them, male-female, then acting in relation to the designated "other" as if it were *by its very nature* inimical to oneself. In as much as each term begets its own negation, one becomes oblivious to what one has in common with the other. For Bateson, this ever-widening, mutually-confirming gulf generates distortions in our personalities, including, "a hostility in which each party resents the other as the cause of its own distortion," "an increasing inability to understand the emotional reactions of the other party," and a commensurate inability for each party "to see the other's point of view."[39] Though Bateson developed his notion of schismogenesis to explain mutual envy and antipathy between the sexes in Iatmul society, the concept is equally applicable to racial, national, and ethnic polarization.

Only by reversing this tendency through actively engaging with others can the destructiveness of oppositional thinking be avoided. This was the lesson Bateson drew from the Iatmul ritual of *naven*, which brings me back to ethnography as a form of radical empiricism—a term coined by William James to emphasize that experience includes transitive as well as substantive elements, conjunctions as well as disjunctions, and to encourage us to recover a sense of the immediate, active, ambiguous "plenum of existence" in which all ideas and intellectual constructions must be grounded.[40]

Radical empiricism is first and foremost "a philosophy of the experience of objects and actions *in which the subject itself is a participant*."[41] This implies that there is no constant, substantive self that can address constant, substantive others as objects of knowledge. We are continually being changed by as well as changing the experience of others. The self cannot, therefore, be treated as a thing among things; it is a function of our situations, and of our involvement with others in a world that is as diverse as it is ever-changing.

The importance of this view for anthropology is that it stresses the ethnographer's interactions with those he or she lives with as a student of life, while urging us to clarify the ways in which our understandings are shaped by our practical, personal, and participatory experience in the field as much as our detached observations. Unlike traditional empiricism, which draws a definite boundary between observer and observed, radical empiricism focuses on the interplay between them. As in quantum mechanics, one not only participates in the reality under investigation; one's methods alter and even constitute that reality. Accordingly, our knowledge is neither objective nor subjective, but intersubjective.

Given the arduous conditions of fieldwork, the difficulty of in-depth conversation in a foreign tongue, differences of temperament, age, and gender between ourselves and our interlocutors, and the changing theoretical fashions that impinge upon our consciousness, it is likely that "objectivity" serves more as a magical token for bolstering our sense of self in disorienting situations than as a scientific method for describing those situations as they "really are." Rather than claim that the systematic formulations and conceptual order we conjure in our writing mirror our lived experience, it may be more illuminating to explore the ways they provide defenses against the unsystematic, complex, and confusing experiences of living in an unfamiliar lifeworld. In demystifying the discourse of social science, George Devereux urged that our theoretical models be placed on a par with indigenous understandings, and our explanations seen in the light of theirs—as ways of alleviating anxieties over our inability to comprehend and control the world.[42]

A fetishist is a person who cannot relate to a whole partner, but only to a part—shoes, jewelry, scent. Something similar could be said of the racist. Not only is a single feature of the other's humanity magnified and made definitive; it is assigned a negative value in contrast to the value one assigns oneself, one's own race. An anthropologist is a fetishist too when relating solely to those elements that make the other ethnically, intellectually or ontologically different. It is ironic that anthropology once made fetishism a sign of primitivism, yet now treats ideas and objects as they were possessed of life, while treating living beings as simply the means whereby that other artificial life is produced.

Our endeavor to recover what James called the "plenum of existence"[43] may be as wishful as wanting to liberate Maori *taonga* (treasures) from the glass cases in European museums and return them to whence they came. The vital force (*hau*) that inheres in the objects may yearn for home, much as a prisoner yearns for release, but the lifeworld in which the objects were fashioned and exchanged is long gone, and there is no guarantee that they will be immune from processes of fetishization and commodification in their new abodes. Escaping the static categories of traditional empiricism and the identity politics of our contemporary world may be as impossible as recovering the social worlds where these objects once mediated vital relationships among the living. Our class upbringing commits us to classification, and the conventions of discourse trap us in dualisms and dichotomies. Even if we do throw off our conceptual chains, we fear the loss of professional identity and authority that might follow. To break away from the autarchy of the concept is like forfeiting classical harmonies and embracing Arnold Schönberg's atonality, a test of our ability to live "without the consolation that truth cannot be lost."[44] But unless anthropology continually tests itself in the real world, it risks becoming simply another intellectual defense against the complexities and contradictions of existence, another escape from the real.

2

Radical Empiricism and the Little Things of Life

> To arrive at a mode of writing that would allow a world to be disclosed,
> a world in which life pulsates with the beats of suffering and also with
> the small pleasures of everyday life, is a daunting challenge.
> —Veena Das, *Affliction*

One's consciousness is so conditioned nowadays by media-driven
generalities about terrorism, climate change, police brutality, social
inequality, racial divides, and genocidal war that even academics now
traffic in the rodomontade that was once the preserve of soapbox orators
and snake oil salesmen. Overwhelmed by categorical assertions,
sound bites, and discursive moralizing, some of us crave stories that
deliver no judgment, assign no blame, find no cause, and come to
no final conclusion—stories that begin a conversation rather than
foreclose it, re-humanizing a world that has become lost in thought.
Rather than illustrate some totalizing thesis, such stories bear witness
to the redemptive power of the particular, "the little things of life ...
in which the secret of reality lies hidden."[1] In these words, Hannah
Arendt echoes Hugo von Hofmannsthal's celebration of the homely,
fugitive, and minor experiences of life that "awaken in us again the
old fondness for the world."[2] In her introduction to Walter Benjamin's
Illuminations, Hannah Arendt celebrates her friend's "passion for
small, even minute things," and his desire to capture history in the
most insignificant moments, "its scraps, as it were." Benjamin was
particularly fascinated by two grains of wheat in the Jewish section
of the Musée Cluny "on which a kindred soul had inscribed the

complete Shema Israel," and he sought to achieve something similar on the printed page. From the beginning, Arendt notes, he was less attracted to theories and ideas than to particular phenomena. His central concern was for "directly, actually demonstrable concrete facts, with single events and occurrences whose 'significance was manifest'"[3]—the very phenomena that many academics would dismiss as contingent, ephemeral, and unenlightening. In the words of Theodor Adorno, Benjamin wanted to "break the bonds of a logic which covers the particular with the universal or merely abstracts the universal from the particular."[4]

Benjamin's vision entailed a particular style of writing, at once paratactic, aporetic, and literary. Perhaps Goethe's method of exact sensorial fantasy (*exacte sinnliche Phantasie*) comes close to capturing this kind of writing that juxtaposes discursive and narrative sections, contextualizes rather than abstracts, and switches between what cannot be grasped analytically and what may yet be shown descriptively, blurring the line between empirical method and intuitive perception (*Anschauung*).[5]

Understood existentially, storytelling and ritualization are strategies for transforming our experience of the world. Fantasy and ritual are supplements to real action, not substitutes for it—vital means of making life more thinkable and hence more manageable under trying conditions. When a Dinka knots a tuft of grass in order to constrict, delay, or tie up an enemy, or binds a stone with grass to restrict the movement of a prowling lion, he does not desist from practical action, for these devices, in Godfrey Lienhardt's words, are but "models of his desires and hopes, upon which to base renewed practical endeavor." "Symbolic actions," Lienhardt goes on to say, "recreate, and even dramatize, situations which they aim to control, and the experience of which they effectively modulate. If they do not change actual historical or physical events—as the Dinka in some cases believe them to do—*they do change and regulate the Dinka's experience of those events.*" Accordingly, religion and science provide alternative rather than competing courses of action, which is why Dinka "will accept medical aid at the same time as performing sacrifices for the recovery of the sick. Medicine is not an alternative to sacrifice and prayer, but may complement it."[6] This is where ethics departs from morality, for while morality knows what is best for us and for others and exhorts us to act accordingly, ethics is always uncertain about which strategy will bear fruit, is sensitive to the value of small things and small changes, and is always open to revision.

Big Thing and Small Thing

It was in a crowded, fetid room, lit by a single hurricane lantern, in the village of Kondembaia in the dry season of 1970 that I recorded Keti Ferenke Koroma's story about the value of small things. Like all Kuranko stories, the aim is not to impart knowledge but to inspire reflection, offering an audience a means of pondering life from a novel vantage point, and experiencing the world in a new way.

> Big Thing and Small Thing had a quarrel. Small Thing said that he was the elder. Big Thing said this was nonsense. "I am the elder. Haven't you heard people saying that I am big?" They went to the Big Men [the chief and his council of elders]. The Big Men told Small Thing not be so impudent. They said, "Everyone calls Big Thing 'big' and Small Thing 'small'. Small Thing repeated that he was the elder. The people said, "No, Big Thing is the elder. Have you forgotten the meaning of the word 'big'?"
>
> Small Thing asked Big Thing to accompany him on a journey around the chiefdom. Wherever they went they found people quarreling. Small Thing would say, "Let us sit down and listen." The Big Men would summon the people who had quarreled and ask them to explain themselves. When the explanations had been given, the Big Men would tell the troublemakers what a small thing it was that they had quarreled over. Small Thing would say to Big Thing, "Did you hear that?" And they would go on their way.
>
> They came to a village where people were making palaver about a man who had beaten his wife badly. Small Thing said, "Let us sit down and listen." They listened and heard the explanations from all sides. Again, people commented on how the quarrel had arisen over a small thing. Small Thing said to Big Thing, "Surely I am the elder, because people are always referring to me." Finally, Big Thing had to admit that Small Thing was indeed the elder.
>
> Therefore, everything begins with small things.[7]

In *The God of Small Things*, Arundhati Roy celebrates the "little events, ordinary things, smashed and reconstituted ... imbued with new meaning [that suddenly] become the bleached bones of a story."[8] But does one need to conjure a God of Small Things to celebrate the value of homely events, homely objects, homely words,[9] or resist the allure of grandiloquence? Perhaps all that is called for is the realization that not all phenomena can be named, and that rather than seeing the "big picture," we need to recover a sense of the countless little things that give us a measure of the real, reminding ourselves that what gives greatest meaning to life are those unremarked moments, minor events, moods, and emotions that may be compared with the soil and climate of a region that imparts to a vintage its terroir (distinctive regional character). By the same token, it is often a slight, a snub, a minor humiliation or loss of face that undermines us. To become fixated on the abstract and the absolute is to become estranged from the everyday imponderables that constitute life as lived—the small things in life that escape the clutches of the mind, that cannot be readily put into words, yet make or break us. "It's the little things that count" is undoubtedly one of the most tedious platitudes, since it is usually cited by those who have fallen short of greatness. But in the paradoxical, contingent, and fugitive character of small things lies the perennial discovery that life is worth living.

In a moving memoir, Caroline Heller renders an account of her father, Paul, a Czech doctor arrested by the SS in 1939 and imprisoned in a succession of concentration camps from which he was finally liberated in 1945. Recalling her childhood in Omaha, Nebraska, Caroline describes two heavily underlined copies of *War and Peace* and *Doctor Zhivago*—her father's favorite books. One passage in Boris Pasternak's novel, Paul Heller often read aloud to his children. When Yurii Zhivago rhetorically asks Anna Ivanovna what a person most needs in life, he answers that we need to overcome the past. But for Paul Heller, the past meant many things: guilt at having survived when so many had perished, regret for his lost youth, and a learned passivity and introversion that made it difficult for him to regain his "inner sovereignty" or a sense of belonging. This is why he set such store by Yurii Zhivago's answer to his question: *"What we need is something new,"*[10] though Paul Heller noted that this newness must also consist in novel ways of thinking that do not shy away from the contradictions and ambiguities at the heart of human existence. "I believe now that contradiction—sense and nonsense, lies and truths, moral and amoral, freedom and imprisonment, human will and causality, misfortune and fortune, sickness and health, birth and death, love and hate—are not as separable as we like to think, and must come together for a rendezvous in this dying world, rather than in an endless fight."[11]

The Wonder of Minor Experiences

It is to William James that we owe one of the most incisive critiques of the academic fetishization of substantives. His notion of radical empiricism brings our attention back to lived experience, and it reminds us that this experience is of connections as well as contrasts, changes as well as constants, relations as well as relata.[12] At the same time, James calls into question our attachment to abstract nouns, temporal framings, and categorical language, attuned as he is to the fact that transitional phenomena are not only ephemeral, but also profoundly intimate and affecting.

In Ted Hughes's first poem in *Birthday Letters*, entitled "Fulbright Scholars," Hughes recounts his first, half-remembered meeting with Sylvia Plath. But of only one detail can he be absolutely sure—that on that same day he bought the first fresh peach he ever tasted from a stall near Charing Cross Station. "At twenty-five," he writes, "I was dumfounded afresh / By my ignorance of the simplest things."[13]

At such moments there is no risk of becoming sealed off from the world; the danger, if any, lies in one's openness to it, with the possibility that one becomes the other or the object that has entered one's life. It is this absorption in the not-self that preoccupies Walter Benjamin in his essays on Baudelaire, for it is not that the poet thinks of Paris in the mid-nineteenth century as the site of a burgeoning form of commodity capitalism; rather that he lives the spirit of those times through his senses as he wanders crowded streets, explores mercantile galleries, and hangs out in cafés. Later, following in Baudelaire's footsteps, Benjamin will locate the spirit of that epoch in specific artifacts, in "little *métiers*," and in the miniaturized world of the arcades that he allows to affect him, to act upon him. Susceptibility, surrender, and a willingness to be shocked and surprised define both the method and madness of a poetic that makes present the character of the world. As Hofmannsthal notes, the arresting details of small things have a refreshing capacity to annul time, so that we are only aware of *"lived life and life that somehow continued to live on, because everything appeared to be the present."*[14]

What Jane Bennett calls the "wonder of minor experiences"[15] alludes not only to the small gestures that lift our spirits or bring enchantment to our lives; it speaks to the transitional moments in which identity is suspended and conceptual thought has no place, as when we open a door without thinking, are crushed by an unkind remark, or are moved to comfort a crying child.

Do we always need to explain our actions by reference to a conscious script we are following, a moral code we have internalized, or an ideology we espouse? Or do we only have recourse to notions of will and morality, or invoke class, cultural, gender, or ethnic identities when a door fails to open, a child cannot be comforted, or our passage through life is interrupted or blocked?

In the face of disaster (I am writing in the wake of Hurricanes Irma and Maria in the Caribbean, Puerto Rico, Florida, and Texas, and the mass shootings at a country music festival in Las Vegas, Nevada), commentators and survivors affirm life by celebrating "American resilience" and a determination to rebuild, as if endurance was dependent on conscious exertions of heroic will and expressions of moral courage. Despite devastating loss, however, human beings press on, not because they decide to do so but because life itself moves them. It is as if life itself surges up in the face of death—though in retrospect we tend to make endurance a virtue, and explain it by reference to our religious faith, moral fiber, or national character. But before God, morality, or social identity make their appearance in our thoughts, we are moved by a desire to live, which is why William James declared that the question as to whether God exists is irrelevant, since "Not God, but life, more life, a larger, richer, more satisfying life is, in the last analysis, the end of religion."[16]

That James's radical empiricism and pragmatism influenced the development of phenomenology in Europe[17] may be taken as a reminder that the new is always outstripping the old, promising a departure from received wisdom and entrenched habits. New directions in philosophical thought or novel ways of writing are reminiscent of the dreams of generations of European migrants who hoped to make a fresh start in the New World. They also affirm Michel Foucault's view that philosophical activity is the "critical work that thought brings to bear on itself ... the endeavor to know how and to what extent it might be possible to think differently, instead of legitimating what is already known."[18]

Wings of Desire

In an essay on existential phenomenology, Mark Wrathall writes that certain things "bear on us not by being available to thought, nor because we are expressly aware of them as such, but rather because they shape or influence our comportment with things."[19] Let us consider Wim Wenders's film *Wings of Desire* in light of this remark. The film begins with two angels discussing the minor calamities and joys that have marked the lives of Berliners during the course of the day. One angel suddenly confesses that he is weary of his ethereal life, of being privy only to what is spiritual in people's minds. "Sometimes I'm fed up with my spiritual existence," Damiel says.

> Instead of forever hovering above, I'd like to feel a weight grow in me, to end the infinity and to tie me to earth. I'd like, at each step, each gust of wind, to be able to say 'Now.' 'Now' and 'now' and no longer 'forever' and 'for eternity' ...

It would be nice, coming home after a long day, to feed the cat, like Philip Marlowe, to have a fever, and blackened fingers from the newspaper, to be excited not only by the mind but, at last, by a meal ... by the line of a neck, by an ear. To lie! Through one's teeth ... to feel what it is to take your shoes off under a table and to wiggle your toes barefoot.[20]

Damiel contemplates rebirth as a mere mortal. Instead of invisibly attending tragic events, he will once more be a part of a world where tragedy may, at any moment, befall him, but also where he may fall in love. The prospect of pain, uncertainty, and despair is offset by the possibility of again belonging to a world of simple pleasures.

His yearning is recognized by Peter Falk, an ex-angel who is aware of Damiel's presence and preoccupations. Outside a snack bar in a postwar wasteland, he reaches out to Damiel: "I wish I could just look into your eyes and tell you how good it is to be here, just to touch something that's cold ... to smoke, to have coffee, and if you do it together its fantastic, or to draw ... you know, you take a pencil and you make a dark line, then you make a light line, and together it's a good line. And when your hands are cold, you rub them together."[21]

Soon after this encounter, Damiel tells his fellow angel Cassiel that he is going "to enter the river."[22] He is going to know what no angel knows; he is going to give up eternity for life on earth.

Acting without Forethought

Although I am skeptical of the idea that there are experiences utterly bereft of any trace of conceptual thought, I have no doubt that the words and ideas at our disposal often fail to do justice to the evanescent particulars that make life worth living and endlessly fascinating. I am specifically interested in experiences that outstrip the concepts of morality and motivation on which we typically rely in explaining behavior.

In 1963, an Australian newspaperman, Douglas Lockwood, accompanied a patrol of members of the Welfare Branch of Australia's Northern Territory Administration into the Western Desert. The goal was to bring Pintupi people in from the Gibson Desert and relocate them on missions or government settlements to "save them from dying out altogether."[23]

The expedition leader, Jeremy Long, told Lockwood of an incident during a previous expedition in 1957, when an Aboriginal man with an amputated leg was brought in to the settlement at Yuendumu. Long discovered that this man, known as Peg-Leg Mick, had sustained a spear wound in a fight, and that his leg had become gangrenous. Because food and water were in short supply, the group was obliged to continue moving or perish. Normally, Mick would have been abandoned. But his potential father-in-law carried him for four months, sometimes covering thirty or forty miles a day. Although Japanangka, the "father-in-law," had a moral obligation to Jampijinpa, his "son-in-law," the exigencies of survival would have suspended that obligation had Japanangka chosen to give priority to the needs of the fittest members of the group, including himself.[24] In other words, Japanangka's actions support Jane Bennett's argument against reducing ethics to "a code to which one is obligated, a set of criteria to which one assents or subscribes," and the case she makes for seeing ethics as "responsive to the surprises that regularly punctuate life."[25] In arguing for the irreducibility of such moments when, to cite Hofmannsthal, "life flares up in us—the revealer of the unrevealed,"[26] we must assume that our humanity goes beyond our sociocultural identities and it is this "going beyond" that constitutes the ethical.[27]

Is it possible, however, that a proto-ethical sensibility attends our earliest experiences of life in a family, and explains the etymological connection between kinship and kindness? And is this disposition to care for our kith and kin, without any conscious moral calculation or expectation that we will be cared for in return, an expression of a universal and natural urge to bring life into the world and foster its growth—a process that phylogenetically exists before we invoke any moral code, make any conscious reckoning, or offer any rationale concerning it? Certainly kinship is often used as a metaphor for acts of kindness (brotherly love; hospital caregivers referred to as sisters; God as a loving father) but does kinship always explain kindness? Veena Das describes a little girl rushing into a crowd of screaming men about to throw a match on a house soaked with kerosene, and tugging at a man's shirt: "Uncle Ji, Uncle Ji, my baby brother is there," and the man turning at her angrily, "Why did you not say so earlier? Do you think we are the killers of children?" Sometimes, however, kin are not kind. Thus, Das describes a woman who discovered "that her brother, in a bargain to save his own life, had pointed a riotous crowd to the house in which her husband was hiding."[28]

Sometimes, too, those who are kind are not kin.[29] In *The Wherewithal of Life*, I recount the story of a Ugandan migrant's years of struggle to find permanent employment in Copenhagen and sustain a sense of self-worth in the face of rejection and prejudice. One summer, Emmanuel found temporary work ferrying tourists from their Princess cruise ship to Kastrup airport and happened to run into a Romanian woman who had been a fellow student at the Copenhagen Business School (CBS). Anna explained that she had taken on this summer employment to supplement her income from her regular job with the FLSmidth company, and she suggested to Emmanuel that he apply for a position that was presently being advertised there. She promised to help him submit his application and advise him on how to prepare for a job interview. When Emmanuel was offered the job, he could not believe his luck. Nor could he explain why Anna should have helped him unless it was because he was the only graduate from his year at CBS who had not found work. "I don't think those people in the municipal offices, the training courses we go to, which are supposed to help us penetrate the job market, know what our situation is like," Emmanuel told me. "They have our profiles, and they are supposed to help us, but they don't. And then I meet a girl with whom I have no relationship apart from the fact that we met once at the university, and everything falls into place … It was a miracle … That selflessness is not something you get in everybody." Anna's help changed the course of Emmanuel's life. When he ran into her at Kastrup airport he had been on the verge of going back to Uganda, even though this would mean leaving his wife and daughter in Denmark.

The change in Emmanuel's demeanor was as evident to me as it was to his wife. "Inside me," Emmanuel said, "it was as if someone had just opened me like this," and he made a gesture as if unzipping a jacket. "I had never felt like that before." I do not know whether some moral principle motivated Anna to help Emmanuel. But Emmanuel did not explain her magnanimity in such terms. It was a mystery, memorable for not being reducible to a sense of social obligation, or explicable in terms of a categorical imperative or moral code.

The paradigmatic example of the power of a simple or spontaneous act is the parable of the Good Samaritan (Luke 10:25–37). Here, an apparently unpremeditated act of neighborliness transcends what we often regard as the "big things" of life, namely our religious or social identity. In being asked, "Who is my neighbor?" Jesus does not preach a sermon (invoking a moral norm) but tells a story that provokes thought.

> A man was going down from Jerusalem to Jericho, when he was attacked by robbers. They stripped him of his clothes, beat him and went away, leaving him half dead. A priest happened to be going down the same road, and when he saw the man, he passed by on the other side. So too, a Levite, when he came to the place and saw him, passed by on the other side. But a Samaritan, as he traveled, came where the man was; and when he saw him, he took pity on him. He went to him and bandaged his wounds, pouring on oil and wine. Then he put the man on his own

donkey, brought him to an inn and took care of him. The next day he took out two denarii and gave them to the innkeeper. "Look after him," he said, "and when I return, I will reimburse you for any extra expense you may have."[30]

So unexpected and inexplicable are these acts of compassion, for both giver and receiver, they are often associated with the supernatural. Indeed, Emmanuel referred to his fortuitous encounter with Anna as "a heavenly intervention." Perhaps this is why the figures that exemplify such altruism are seldom earthly, instead they are imagined to be angelic, saintly, or extra-human. For Kuranko, the magnanimity that defines the moral ideal of personhood (*morgoye*) is symbolized by a totemic animal that once saved the life of one's clan ancestor when he was famished and parched in a wilderness. Guiding the ancestor to water or sacrificing a part of its own body as food, the animal becomes a totem (*tane*, lit. prohibited thing) to whom respect and protection are thenceforth accorded.

For the philosophical ethicist K. E. Løgstrup, this exemplifies what he calls "sovereign expressions of life"—spontaneous and unconditional acts of compassion toward another that eclipse any consideration of the cost to oneself. Such actions are both free and ethical, Løgstrup argues, because they are not wholly determined by moral rules. Nor can they be instrumentalized and generalized after the fact as moral norms.[31] Spur-of-the-moment acts of kindness, courage, selflessness, or mercy are all expressions, as it were, of an ethics before ethics. Such actions, Løgstrup argues, are not necessarily informed by moral principles, which is why those who spontaneously show courage or compassion often disavow such moral language on the grounds that they acted without a second thought, and not for a moment calculated the costs or consequences of their acts.[32] "The sovereign expression of life precedes the will," Løgstrup says, "its realization takes the will by surprise. It is one of those offerings in life which, to our good fortune, preempt us, and in whose absence we should be unable to carry on from one day to the next."[33]

To embrace Løgstrup's view that ethical action is not necessarily an enactment of a moral rule, nor open to ex post facto conversion into a categorical imperative, is to shed doubt on the possibility of gleaning moral lessons from any human life that might help us alleviate the suffering of others or prevent future tragedy. As I observed in my 1982 study of Kuranko storytelling,[34] the fervent discussion of ethical dilemmas that follows the recounting of any story may change the experience of a person's situation in life without, however, changing the social world in which that person is bound to live. Our attempts to wrest moral meanings out of a lifestory may be as misguided as our attempts to identify causes or allocate blame. To exhort us to remember Auschwitz lest it happen again may bolster our hope that we can improve our collective existence on earth, morally and materially, but history offers us no examples of how such gestures alter the future, even though they help us understand how we come to terms with the horrors of our past.

What I find compelling about the sovereign expressions of life is that they cannot be reduced to some moral principle or instinctual drive, and that such acts are timeless, as if they lay outside of history, outside of natural causation or cultural determination, and outside of any original intention or preexisting design. To act without forethought in aid of someone whose life is in peril may spring simply from the fact that one is in possession of life and the other is not. Emmanuel Levinas speaks of this as a sense of the precariousness of the other, and he reminds us of the shocking experience that an other, in whose presence I am, could, in suddenly becoming absent, render me incomplete, wanting, impoverished.[35] If, for a moment at least, one feels that both oneself and the other are in life together, then the other's peril is experienced as one's own. It is as if one acts, not in terms of one's own life or the life of the other that is at risk, but for life itself.

For Hubert Dreyfus and Sean Kelly, such moments "shine," and images of light, enlightenment, illumination, revelation, and clarification recur across cultures and throughout history. These moments are at once transcendent, since they appear to go beyond what custom requires or habit explains, and imminent, since they appear to disclose something that lies deep within us, but only become apparent in a moment of danger. Paradoxically, too, such moments exemplify freedom, when a person seems to act without reference to any social or moral conditioning, and necessity, for the action seems to be the result of some inner daemon or determinant that overrides one's conscious sense of duty, self-preservation, or even desire.

Between One's Own World and the World at Large

Many years ago, I worked as a volunteer for the United Nations Operation in the Congo (ONUC). I never settled to the work, partly because it was largely window dressing (creating the impression that hundreds of schools, market gardens, and cooperative enterprises were being created throughout the country), partly because civil war made travel outside the cities perilous. One day, I was summoned to a conference in Le Royal—the large apartment building that the UN had commandeered as a center of operations.[36] John Gifford, the newly appointed head of ONUC's Département des Affaires Sociales, was clearly irked by reports he had heard of my lackadaisical attitude to the aid and development projects to which I had been assigned. He gave me a choice between "buckling down and justifying your existence" or returning to the United Kingdom. In the preceding months, I had become increasingly disenchanted with the hidden agenda of the UN mission, regarding it as a continuation of colonial policies, but I had not mustered the courage to quit. Gifford's ultimatum relieved me of the burden of choice. Moreover, I could always blame him for throwing me out and absolve myself of my indifference to the humanitarian ideals to which my UN colleagues paid lip service.

I was surprised, therefore, to meet Mrs. Gifford at the airport, and learn that she too was on her way back to the United Kingdom. Her children were in a boarding school there, and she was going to visit them. I had met her briefly at a cocktail party when she and her husband first arrived in Léopoldville. She appeared to be sympathetic to my desire to live closer to Congolese people and not impose Western values on them, and she seemed to have a genuine, if maternal, interest in my welfare. Now, with a long wait for our Sabena flight to depart, we fell into conversation.

I was curious to know why her husband was not there to see her off but did not broach the matter. She was well aware of the circumstances that had led to my abrupt departure and apologized for her husband's insensitive handling of my situation.

"What will you do now?" she asked.

"I have no idea. I would like to return to Africa in some different capacity. Not go prying into places where I have no business of being."[37]

It was soon evident as we talked on that Mrs. Gifford shared my misgivings about the kind of work to which her husband had dedicated himself. My first thought was that Mrs. Gifford was, like me, skeptical about foreign interventions in the affairs of poor nations, or the manner in which Euro-American and Soviet interests had turned Africa into a Cold War zone. But her criticism was more personal, and I was taken aback that she should confide her disillusionment to a 24-year-old stranger.

Before their posting to the Congo, Mrs. Gifford explained, they had spent several years in Cyprus, also with the United Nations. During this time, their two older children were in a British boarding school. But the two younger children, aged four and six, had been with them in Cyprus.

"We are both Christians," she said. "In fact, we met at a church social. But I am afraid we differ in what our faith requires of us. For my husband, it demands unconditional devotion to the well-being of others, even to the extent of taking refugee children into our own home, regardless of the health risks to our own children. It may be that I have never fully understood Christ's call or example. But there is a limit, especially for a mother, to what she can give others without compromising her own children. Even sending our two daughters to boarding school was, for me, an act of abandonment. Our sensitive, vulnerable, seven- and eight-year-old girls, packed off to England filled me with such guilt. But my husband was, and remains, adamant. It will do them no harm. He left home at the same age. It toughened him. It prepared him for the work he now does for the greater glory of God. But tell me, Michael, is God's glory greater than the happiness of a child, or the bond between a mother and her daughters?"

I was too young for this moral burden. The questions were beyond me.

Mrs. Gifford saw my difficulty. "I am so sorry. What am I doing, offloading my tribulations onto you? You have enough to worry about. How selfish of me."

We were sitting on an upholstered bench. A dying aspidistra, an unswept parquet floor, and a slow-moving ceiling fan provided a tawdry backdrop to what then unfolded around us. Silent, unobtrusive, and shell-shocked, thirty or more nuns recently rescued by Belgian paratroopers from the rebel-held city of Stanleyville were patiently waiting to join our flight.

Mrs. Gifford looked at the refugees and felt ashamed.

"What *they* must have been through," she said.

I envied them. I had only glimpsed the war. And I too felt ashamed, that I was leaving the Congo unscathed; I had avoided my baptism of fire. *Et j'etais si mauvais poete | Que je ne savais pas aller jusqu'au bout.*[38]

I told Mrs. Gifford of my journeys to the interior. I cannot remember how she responded, though I think I know why I confided in her. My experiences echoed her own. It was my clumsy, makeshift way of telling her I understood her dilemma—torn between protecting those closest to her and offering succor to strangers with contagious diseases. Had I known at this time of Orwell's essay on Gandhi, I might have cited it.

For the seeker after goodness there must be no close friendships and no exclusive loves. Close friendships, Gandhi says, are dangerous, because "friends react on one another" and through loyalty to a friend one can be led into wrongdoing. This is unquestionably true. Moreover, if one is to love God or to love humanity as a whole, one cannot give one's preference to any individual person. This is also true, and it marks the point at which the humanistic and the religious attitude cease to be reconcilable.[39]

The tension between one's immediate everyday world, with its particular claims on us for hugs, greetings, smiles, support, solidarity, and the non-immediate world, with its large-scale demands to keep faith with our Gods, sacrifice to our ancestors, protest injustice, or secure greater equality for humankind, can never be fully resolved, though ideally a balance can be struck between them. At the heart of Mrs. Gifford's lament was that her husband gave more to the greater good than the good of his family. His *illusio* (or center of interest in life)[40] was a concern for humanity as a whole rather than his own particular family. Mrs. Gifford's dilemma was not unlike the dilemma that every migrant feels to a greater or lesser degree, torn between an attachment for a particular home place and a dream of making good in the wider world. If, as Pierre Bourdieu argues, the *illusio* implies an investment in a better life, how is one to distribute that investment between what one considers necessary for the betterment of the world and what one deems imperative for oneself or one's own kith and kin? For many Kuranko migrants, this ethical dilemma is presaged in traditional stories in which a person strikes a bargain with a djinn that will dramatically improve the person's lot but will require forfeiting the life of a child as the price for realizing this ambition. If, traditionally, the djinn gave objective definition to one's desire for something more than one presently possessed, education and migration now provide the means of changing one's fortunes. But when young Sierra Leoneans speak of education, migration, or religion, it is often with the exaggerated hope that these will produce magical transformations, bestowing on them the power to make their country great, to garner great wealth, to cure endemic diseases, to enjoy political power, or to be absolved of all their sins.

There is a discursive equivalence between these third-world imaginaries and the political agendas, economic projections, and intellectual generalizations that pervade the discourse of the first world. In as much as the intellectual struggles to strike a balance between the alienating language of the academy and the vernacular idioms of everyday life (the metaphors we live by, the stories we tell, the family histories we share), so the migrants from the global South struggle to strike a balance between the wider world into which they venture (symbolically equated by West African migrants with "the bush") and the familial world of the village or small community from which they set forth. This, then, is the space of ethics—the space betwixt and between the general and the particular, the homely and the worldly, the familial and the alien. We cross this space constantly, but seldom sustain a vital relationship between its contrary terms. We use the same language of microcosm and macrocosm in comparing nation-states to families or using metaphors from everyday life to describe the worlds of the gods or of the state, but the gap remains. Perhaps the ultimate answer is to escape from the contending imperatives, the competing demands, the Sturm und Drang of thinking our way through life. Perhaps we need the religious historian who, after listening to group of students fervently debating the rights and wrongs of Nixon's invasion of Cambodia in 1970, recounted the story of Jesus on the Waters (Matthew 8:23–27) and concluded "that what that story is trying to tell us is simply that in times of storm, we mustn't allow the storm to enter ourselves; rather we have to find peace inside ourselves and then breathe it out."[41] This is the peace that passes all understanding, and for Lawrence Weschler, who recounts this anecdote about the American religious historian's intervention in the student debate, this is the peace that Johannes Vermeer found in "a small room, an intimate vision" amid the turmoil of seventeenth-century religious wars, economic collapse, and social chaos.

3

THE WITCH AS A CATEGORY AND AS A PERSON

A witch deserves no respect. A witch is not a person.

—Morowa Marah

As the Ebola epidemic spread through Sierra Leone in 2014, people confronted a phenomenon unlike any they could recall. In the words of one woman, it was "like a sickness from another planet."[1] Confounded and overwhelmed, people fell prey to wild speculations, and rumor became as contagious as the disease itself.

There is nothing new in this reaction. In the 1980s, before HIV/AIDS was scientifically understood, it was rumored to be a disease of drug addicts or gays, introduced by African migrants, or seen as a divine punishment for immoral behavior. More recently, the influx of Syrian and Sudanese refugees in Europe has spawned similar stigmatizing stereotypes: the refugees are potential terrorists, will steal our jobs, rape our women, overtax our welfare services, or undermine our national identity. Thus, as Ebola spread, curfews and quarantines were imposed, schools, markets, and even hospitals were shut down, and rumors circulated as to who was to blame and what could be done to prevent further disaster. Many of these rumors involved the imagery of witchcraft.

In critical situations, identity thinking provides the consoling illusion that by organizing one's thoughts in a clear-cut way and putting definitive names to an indefinite phenomenon, reality can be rendered both comprehensible and controllable. This was as true of Sierra Leonean villagers as it was of the foreign experts arriving in Sierra Leone to manage the crisis. Though villagers identified witches or foreign agents as the cause of the epidemic, medical specialists saw it as virological rather than social in character. But in both cases, the same preoccupation with containment and cleansing was evident, and found expression in witch-hunting, ritual separations (quarantine), scapegoating, and state controls on human movement.

On 10 October 2014, Brigadier Stephen McMahon, Deputy Director of the UK Department of International Development's interagency task force in Sierra Leone, declared that international efforts to "eradicate" Ebola would "only be successful if Sierra Leoneans put aside tradition, culture and whatever family rites they have and do the right thing." McMahon went on to claim that "the reason for the spread [of Ebola] is these cultural practices that Sierra Leoneans don't want to put aside," and he concluded that "if the attitudes of Sierra Leoneans don't change, all the manpower and equipment [that the British] and other friends have brought will count for nothing because they will not be able to win the battle."[2]

To claim that Ebola was spread by local "cultural practices" was no more reasonable or helpful than claiming that it was caused by witches. In insisting on a categorical contrast between "rational" Western biomedicine and African "superstition," Brigadier McMahon appeared blind to the extent to which Sierra Leonean doctors and paramedics were risking their lives in the fight against Ebola, as well as the extent to which his thinking about social order was as permeated by images of purity and danger as the Sierra Leoneans whose customs he deplored. In fact, the importance of separating the living from the dead and imposing a quarantine on those associated with the dead is central to both traditional African mortuary practices and European medicine and, as it turned out, made it easy for Sierra Leoneans to learn and implement new forms of cleansing (with chlorine solutions) and quarantine.

My argument is that identifying the source of a contagion—whether a malevolent person like a witch or an impersonal agent like a virus—is possibly less important than recognizing the particular sufferer whose experience is eclipsed by the abstract terms that purport to explain it. It is this problematic relationship between particular experiences and categorical discourse that I now explore.

A Case of Witchcraft

Several years ago, an epidemic of insect-borne encephalitis swept through the village of Kamadugu Sukurela in northern Sierra Leone. There were many deaths, and the village was under a pall. Beset by fear, yet obliged to intervene, the village chief and his council of elders summoned a male witch-hunting cult known as *Gbangbane* from Farandugu, four miles away. At night, as we huddled indoors, the witch-hunters moved among the houses. Their ominous, muffled voices, the shuffle of feet in the darkness, and the staccato of their wooden clappers—*gban gban, gban gban*—infected us all with deep disquiet.

My field assistant, Noah Marah, and I spent several days in the village in the hope we might be of some use, but there was little we could do so we left. On our return two weeks later, we sought out a friend of Noah's, Morowa Marah, whom I had met on our initial visit. Sitting on the porch of Morowa's house and eating the rice and groundnut stew his wife had made for us, I asked Morowa to tell us what had happened in our absence. Morowa explained that the witch-hunters had diagnosed the cause of one man's illness as witchcraft and promised to deal with the witch before they returned to Farandugu. Apparently, *Gbangbane* had told the chief and elders that the offending witch would fall ill with chest, neck, and head pains and shit herself or himself before dying. The following day the sick man succumbed and died. Eight days later his sister fell gravely ill. In her pain and distress, she confessed she had killed her brother by witchcraft. "I was hunting him for a year," she said. "The first time I tried to kill him was when he went to clear his farm site, but I missed him. The branch only knocked out some of his teeth [such an accident had occurred]. But this year we [her coven] lay in wait for him on the path to his palm wine trees. We beat him up and injured him. Then he fell ill." The woman also explained her motive for wanting to kill her brother: she had once asked him for some rice and he had refused her. But why she had used witchcraft against her brother rather than cursing him, as is a sister's right, was not explained.

As the woman lay ill inside her house, *Gbangbane* came again and ordered that she be buried at once. Men bound her hands and feet and dragged her to the outskirts of the village. There they dug a shallow grave and buried her alive. Banana leaves and stones were thrown in on top of her. During this entire episode, all the women of the village remained indoors.

By the time that Morowa had finished his account I found it impossible not to accuse him of being accessory to a murder. My outrage astonished him, and he tried to help me understand. "If it had been my choice," he said grimly, "I would have had her thrown into the bush without burial. But we buried her in the grassland beyond the Mabumbuli [stream] so that when the grass is dry we can set fire to it and turn her face into hell. A witch deserves no respect. A witch is not a person."[3]

I was sensitive to the fact that Morawa and his wife had lost children, allegedly to witchcraft. I was also aware of the appalling tension in the community. But the image of a woman being buried alive poisoned my feelings toward Morawa and, for a time, toward those who shared his view. My only consolation came from Morowa's confession that shortly after the murder (for I could not think of it otherwise), the witch's shade or *pulan* invaded the village and Morawa had been the first to be haunted.[4] As he slept, it settled on his head. He opened his eyes but could not cry out. He lay in terror as though an immense weight were pressing down on him. Other men in Kamadugu Sukurela were also afflicted. The *pulan* terrorized the village. Finally, the chief and elders summoned a *pulan*-catcher (*pulan brale*) from Bambunkura, a village twelve miles away. This man, Musa, bagged the *pulan* in the form of a lizard in the deceased witch's house. However, her son, distressed by the tragic circumstances of his mother's death, refused to accept that the lizard was his mother's shade. Piqued, Musa went back to Bambunkura. But the *pulan*-haunting continued, and the deceased woman's son was now afflicted by it. Once more the *pulan*-catcher was summoned from Bambunkura, and the son was ordered by the chief and elders to pay the Le.8 (Sierra Leonean Leones) fee as well as apologize to Musa for doubting his skills. Musa then caught the *pulan* (again in the form of a lizard) and killed it.

These events introduce the ethical and epistemological issues I want to address in this chapter. The most obvious question is whether the Kuranko word *suwage* corresponds to the English word "witch" and whether there is any justification for calling Morowa's haunting "guilt" or "remorse" or the killing of the woman "murder." This is not just a matter of semantics and "accurate translation," for we have to work out whether it is possible to gain access to ideas and experiences designated *suwa'ye* (witchcraft) in Kuranko and understand them in terms of ideas and experiences familiar to us in our own culture. A critical issue here is elucidating the relationship between discursive notions of witchcraft and the lived experiences of women who actually confess to being witches—the question as to whether we can justifiably posit an identity relationship between episteme and experience.

These questions are as relevant to understanding Kuranko thought as they are to understanding the thought of anthropologists, for in both cases identity thinking all too often occludes any reference to real people or real situations. In ontologizing cultural representations of the nature of being, individual minds are subsumed under collective mindsets and individual consciousness reduced to unconscious processes or forms of *esprit collectif*. Thus, the pathology of conventional Kuranko thought, which denies personhood to a woman who in extreme distress confesses herself a "witch," is uncannily like the pathology of much anthropological discourse which buries the experience of the individual subject under the categories of totalizing explanation. However, as Jean-Paul Sartre puts it, "Being is irreducible to knowledge."[5]

The Stereotype of the Witch

To understand what Kuranko mean when they say a witch is not a person, it is necessary to clarify the indigenous concept of *morgoye* (personhood). *Morgoye* implies respect for and mindfulness of others, an abstract attitude in which personal purposes are consonant with collective goals. Ideally, a person is magnanimous, open, and straightforward in his or her dealings with others. A sociable person is "sweet" (*morgo di*); he or she likes the company of others. Or a person is "open" (*morgo gbe*; literally, person clear/white) and "straight" (*morgo telne*). An unsociable person is "bent" and "devious" (*morgo dugune*) like a crooked path. Or a person is "broken down" (*kore*), analogous to a dilapidated house (*bon kore*), a broken calabash, worn-out clothes, an abandoned farm, and similar "useless" things. Sometimes an antisocial person is referred to as a "bush person" (*fira morgo*) or an "unwell person" (*morgo kende ma*), *kende* meaning physically "healthy" as well as socially or morally "proper." Anyone who sets himself or herself apart from others is quite simply "not a person" (*morgo ma*).

The stereotype of a witch includes all these notions of deviance, resentment, wildness, and sickness; essentially, it is a dialectical negation of the moral concept of *morgoye*. As the Kuranko word *suwage* (literally, night owner) suggests, a witch acts surreptitiously, under cover of darkness, using powers that are invisible to ordinary eyes: witch weapons, witch medicines, witch gowns, witch animals, even witch airplanes. These are the things the witch-hunting cults attempt to track down, for *Gbangbane* cannot directly destroy a witch, only disarm her. Witchcraft (*suwa'ye*) is not inherited; it is an inborn proclivity, which is why, though witches are criminals, a witch's kin are never tainted by or held accountable for her actions. Witches have "bad *yugi*," something that cannot be resisted or explained away.

A witch's "life" (*nie*) supposedly leaves her sleeping body at night and moves around, often in the body of an animal familiar. As her "life goes out" (*a nie ara ta*), her body may be shaken by convulsions and her breathing cease. In this state of suspended animation, the body is vulnerable; if it is turned around, then the witch's *nie* will not be able to reenter it and she will die.[6] A witch will also perish if the dawn finds her out of her body. The animals most commonly associated with witches sum up the traits of witchcraft: predatory (leopard), scavenging (hyena, vulture), underground (snakes), nocturnal (bats, owls); indeed, the owl (*gbingbinyaga*) is sometimes called the "witch bird" because it is seldom seen and flies by night.

Witches are predatory and cannibalistic. But they do not attack a victim's "life" (*nie*) directly; they "consume" some vital organ (usually the liver, heart, or intestines) or drain away the victim's blood or break the victim's backbone by tapping him on the nape of the neck. It is said that witches work in covens and that the greatest threat of witchcraft lies within the extended family (*kebile*), i.e., "from those who share a common inheritance." As one man put it, "witchcraft is eating yourself" (meaning that a witch usually "eats" her own child, her co-wife's child, her grandchild, or her brother's child). Sorcery, by contrast, is "destroying others."

Witchcraft operates through blackmail and indebtedness. A witch will somehow "open the door" of her own house by nullifying the protective medicines that the household head has placed over the lintel. A witch from her coven then steals into the house and "eats" one of its occupants—usually a child, because children are less likely to be protected by personal medicines. The aggressor is obliged to discharge her debt at a later date by making it possible for her co-witch to claim a victim from her house. One informant told me that "only someone close to you could betray you to the witches by telling them where you sleep in the house and by opening the door to them." A Kuranko adage is often used in support of this reasoning: *sundan wa dugu koro worla bor duguranu de l sonti i ye* (if a stranger [guest] uncovers something hidden, someone living in that place [the host] must have told him where it was).

These popular stereotypes of witches and witchcraft are logically derived through a systematic inversion of what is regarded as an ideal balance between day and night, openness and closure, revealed (*kenema*) and hidden (*duworon*), village and bush, sociality and emotionality. That is what Kuranko men told me about witchcraft when I broached the subject with them. But directed interviews bring into relief only one dimension of a phenomenon, and many men were loath to discuss witchcraft with me in public lest their conversancy with the subject be taken as evidence that they were witches. It also became clear to me that conventional descriptions of the witch as a nefarious and self-seeking woman did not exhaust the semantic range of the term *suwa'ye*.

Thus, Kuranko acknowledge that the notoriously unstable and jealous relationship between brothers with the same father but different mothers (known as *fadenye*) is a potential source of witchcraft. It is also frequently pointed out that a farmer who produces a surplus above his subsistence needs, a man of wealth and position, and a child who excels at school or is well favored are all likely to be envied and resented— laying them open to accusations of witchcraft. The illicit use of destructive medicines to bring shame, adversity, or death to an enemy is also spoken of as witchcraft. So too is the use of poisons (*dabere*) that malevolent old women allegedly sprinkle in children's food or water. Nor are witches invariably women. Sometimes witchcraft is not associated with evil, but with any kind of extraordinary power. Thus, white men may be likened to witches because of their technological wizardry and remarkable mobility (in ships and aircraft), and legendary figures such as Mande Sundiata and Yilkanani are sometimes said to have been witches because their powers were beyond ordinary comprehension. Even more significant is the fact that *Gbangbane* (or *Gbangbe*), the witch-hunter, is spoken of as a witch. Here is how Saran Salia Sano of Firawa described *Gbangbe* to me:

> It is like the other *sumafannu* [secret things]. When you are a boy, you try to imagine what it is. You are told it kills people. You are afraid. But you also feel it is something extraordinary, and you want to see it. Then, when you are initiated, you see that it is a person—not an ordinary person, but a witch. Its witchcraft is greater than that of a host of people [*a suwa' ya morgo siyama n ko*]. *Gbangbe* is a *subingban* [ruler of the night]. He is immune to all evil and has the power to rob men of their shape-shifting abilities. *Gbangbe* forces people to confess. He seizes their possessions. The person cries out, "He's taken my things!" and the kinsmen plead with *Gbangbe* not to destroy them lest the person die.

I asked Saran Salia to clarify what he meant by "seizure" of a witch's "possessions," since the word *miran* can denote both material things and psychological "self-possession." Were people "seized" by terror when *Gbangbe* was abroad, or did *Gbangbe* actually take their property and physically force them to confess? To the Western mind, always keen to discriminate between "psychic" and "physical" realities, the question is crucial. To Saran Salia it seemed somewhat beside the point, but he gave me a specific example of what he meant.

The incident he described took place at Bandakarafaia six years earlier. It was night, and *Gbangbe* was out and about in the village. *Gbangbe* stopped outside a house:

> It seized this woman's headkerchief, shirt, and shoes. Inside the house, the woman started struggling and shouting, "*Gbangbe* has got me! *Gbangbe* has got me!" [*m'bi Gbangbe bolo,* "I am in Gbangbe's hands."]. Her kinsmen gave *Gbangbe* Le. 12, two mats, and ten kola nuts. *Gbangbe* said, "I have heard." He gave back the headkerchief and shirt, but not the shoes. The woman cried, "Give me the shoes." *Gbangbe* gave them to her. Then she shouted, "*Soburi* [hooray]! I've got them!" She became normal again.

"But were the clothes real?" I asked.

"They were like real ones, but they were witch's clothes."

Seeing my perplexity, Saran Salia recounted another case. It was the first I had ever heard in which a man had confessed to witchcraft. It happened in Firawa twelve years earlier. A man called Yimba Koroma became agitated and collapsed in his house one night while *Gbangbe* was out. On this occasion, *Gbangbe* seized the man in his witch's clothes and also seized his belongings (*suwa' ya mirannu*).

> The man's clothes tightened around his neck. He felt strangled. He cried out to *Gbangbe,* "Leave me alone, give me back my things!" He confessed to having eaten people's children. "I ate Yira, I ate Karifa and Yira. I ate them. Please give me back my things [*mirannu*]." *Gbangbe* told him to name his other victims. "No," he said, "I won't name anyone else." That is why he was not forgiven. He was a member of a night *kere.*

A *kere* is a labor cooperative; it epitomizes the spirit of fellowship and mutual aid in a community. So I asked whether witches in their night *kere* or coven were bound by the same ties of reciprocity that bound men in a farming *kere?*

"Yes," Saran Salia said, "except witches join forces to take life, not make it."

In the presence of women and children, men cultivate the fiction that *Gbangbane* is a bush spirit, not a person. But *Gbangbane* is a person, as Saran Salia observes, though not an ordinary person; he is a witch. Underlying this view is the notion that the same wild powers that can destroy people can also protect them. In short, *suwa'ye* is not just semantically ambiguous; it denotes an ethically indeterminate power or faculty. And though this power of *suwa'ye* is in essence "wild" or extra-social, whether it becomes good or bad depends entirely on how it is harnessed or used.

This pragmatist emphasis on practical ends rather than essential truths brings me to a consideration of the analysis by Barry Hallen and J. Olubi Sodipo of the Yoruba word *àjé*, commonly translated "witch." On the basis of detailed comparative research, they argue that it is impossible to define a universal category "witchcraft" that can cover without distortion all the phenomena commonly brought under this rubric.[7] Thus, while the Yoruba *àjé*, the Kuranko *suwage*, the Zande *mangu*, and the English *witch* all share some family resemblances, they also connote quite divergent phenomena and personality types. This point is vitally important. However, I do not agree with Hallen and Sodipo in construing this problem as basically semantic, a problem of accurate translation. True, the difference between Kuranko informants' stereotypes of witches and particular accounts (like those of Saran Salia) correspond to the distinction Quine makes between "standing sentences" and "observation sentences," the first being abstracted from immediate sensory experience, the second issuing from specific situations.[8] And it is imperative that we do not overlook the indeterminate relationship (the "empirical slack," the "evidential gap") between knowledge and event. But I do not see how we can overcome these discrepancies by defining our terms more precisely or seeking a complete fusion between thought and being. My own interpretive preference is to consider not what words mean in essence, but what they are made to mean in the contexts of everyday life. It is not words we want to compare when we try to understand the phenomenon we provisionally call "witchcraft," but the events and experiences that the words are brought to bear upon and purport to explain.

To this end, let us shift our focus to the level of event—to actual confessions to witchcraft and the situations of the women who make those confessions at a risk to their own lives.

The Compulsion to Confess

In sub-Saharan Africa, one can make a rough-and-ready distinction between accusation-oriented and confession-oriented societies, though in many cases accusation and confession are emphasized differently in different contexts. Of the Azande, E. E. Evans-Pritchard reported, "I have never known a Zande admit his witchcraft" and "I have only received cases of confession from one Zande ... perhaps the least reliable of my informants."[9] By contrast, other societies, notably in West Africa, are characterized by a rarity or absence of direct accusation and the presence of confession.[10] Yet other African societies are notable for the rarity of both direct accusation and confession.[11] And there are those, like the Korongo, that "have no witchcraft beliefs at all."[12]

Among the Kuranko, confession, not accusation, is the norm. But the rare and elusive character of these confessions, coupled with the fact that women usually confess during terminal illness or are killed on account of what they confess, makes it very difficult to gain direct knowledge of the experiences of the Kuranko women who own up to being witches. The ethnographer is obliged to rely on hearsay accounts of events that have often been half-forgotten, if not actively suppressed. Particularly problematic are the manifest prejudices of Kuranko men when speaking of women witches. Witchcraft epitomizes the worst in women, and men make witches the scapegoats for their anxieties about their own autonomy and strength. Indeed, their stereotypes of women as weak-willed, impulsive, and inclined toward hysteria are sadly similar to those still current in the discourse of many Western men.

To understand the witch as a subject, to rehabilitate her as a person in a society that reduces her to a negative category, is not unlike the task contemporary historians face in writing about the consciousness of the colonized and their "culture of silence."[13] Nevertheless, as Ranajit Guha shows in his groundbreaking study of peasant insurgency in colonial India, it is possible to glean from the distorted discourse of the oppressor fragmentary clues "to the antonymies which speak for a rival consciousness."[14] This is also my task.

Here, in summary form, are details of thirteen cases of witchcraft confession that give the relationship of the victim to the witch, as well as the background and confessed reason for the witchcraft:

1. No relationship. A man confessed to *Gbangbe* that he had "eaten" several children (all male). He died after confessing. (Case of Yimba Koroma of Firawa; informant: Saran Salia Sano, Firawa, 1979.)
2. No victim. Woman "succumbed" to *Gbangbe* but did not explicitly confess to being a witch. Her kinsmen "begged" and paid *Gbangbe;* the woman recovered her senses. (Case of woman from Bandakarafaia; informant: Saran Salia Sano, Firawa, 1979).
3. No relationship. A certain Fore Kande of Bandakarafaia tested his "witchcraft" against Saran Salia. Dying, he confessed, "I went abroad as a witch; I went and saw his Kome [a powerful bush spirit that Saran Salia was master of]; it killed me" (*m' bora suwa'ye ro; n' tara a ma felen n' ya l Komeye; wo le m' faga*). In other words, Saran Salia was immune to witchcraft attack, so the witchcraft boomeranged back on Fore, who died. He had never before shown animosity toward Saran Salia. (Informant: Saran Salia Sano, Firawa, 1979).

4. Brother's daughter's son. Informant's grandson died suddenly. A local woman was said to have confessed to killing him, but her family hushed up her confession. (Informant: Bunda Mansaray, Kamadugu Sukurela, 1972).

5. Brother. Eight days after her brother's sudden death, a woman fell ill and confessed she had once asked her brother for rice and he had refused her. After one unsuccessful attempt on his life, she and other witches beat him up and killed him. She was buried alive. (Informant: Morawa Marah, Kamadugu Sukurela, 1970).

6. Husband. Woman fell ill with chest and head pains; on her deathbed she confessed that her husband had never liked her. Indeed, her husband blamed her for the painful tropical ulcers on his foot. A diviner had told him "evil people" (*morgo yugunu*) were getting at him, and he had previously cursed the evildoer who, he suspected, was his own wife. Her first husband had divorced her because of her "bad behavior" (*son yugi*). There were no children by the second marriage (four years). After she died, her *pulan* came out and had to be caught and killed. (Informant: husband, Ali Koroma, Kamadugu Sukurela, 1972).

7. Husband; brother's son's wife. A child died suddenly. A few days later the child's paternal aunt fell seriously ill and confessed that she was responsible for the child's death. She owed her coven a child, but being childless, gave it the life of her brother's grandson. She said she had "got her destiny through that child," i.e., her sickness was a punishment for having killed him. When she entered her brother's house to get the child, the house was surrounded by fire from the anti-witchcraft fetish *sase*, and she had been badly burned when leaving. She also confessed that when, many years earlier, her husband had accompanied a white man into the Loma mountains to hunt elephants she had transformed herself into an elephant and tried to kill him. She had also prevented him from becoming chief. Finally, she told how, when *Gbangbe* was abroad, she would assume the form of a vulture or fly by plane and sit near the moon to evade detection. She would take her co-witches with her in a hamper on her back, but one night *Gbangbe* came unexpectedly and "seized" her hamper. Her co-witches, left stranded, cried out to her: "Mama Yeri, sole wara mintan de me tala minto?" (Grandmother Yeri, the hamper is burned, where are we going to go?) When her confession had been heard, she was taken from the house and left in the backyard to die. (Informant: woman's brother's grandson, Noah Marah, Kabala, 1970).

8. Husband. Woman confessed to feeling resentful when her husband gave more rice and meat from a sacrifice to her co-wives than to her. During her terminal illness, she confessed to trying to kill him by witchcraft, but his protective fetishes turned the witchcraft back against her. After her death, her *pulan* came out, turning food and water bad. (Informant: woman's co-wife's son, Steven Marah, Kabala, 1970).

9. Husband; co-wife's son. Woman confessed on her deathbed to killing her husband by witchcraft and eating her co-wife's son. My informant believed the confession to have been mistaken; the woman never showed animosity to anyone. (Informant: woman's co-wife's son, town chief at Fasewoia, 1970).

10. Husband. During severe illness, a woman confessed that her husband had refused to have sex with her during her pregnancy. Humiliated, she hired a night *kere* to beat him up; when the coven failed to find him, it fell on her instead. She delivered stillborn twins and died.

11. Not specified. A woman confessed on her deathbed that she was a witch and named four associates. *Gbangbane* brought the four women before the chief's court; they were ordered to demonstrate their powers and prove they were witches. They asked that some papaya and a lizard be brought; they were then locked in a room. When they were let out of the room they told the elders to cut open the papaya; they were seedless. They told the elders to examine the lizard; it was dead. Each woman was fined a cow. Two of the cows were sacrificed and a curse was put on the livers; the women were then obliged to eat the livers together with raw rice flour (*dege*) from the sacrifice. Within a few weeks three of the women died; the fourth, it was said, was not a real witch: "she wasn't guilty of actually eating anyone; she was a witch but did not practice witchcraft." (Informant: Keti Ferenke Koroma, Kondembaia, 1970).

12. Brother's son. When a small boy died suddenly, a diviner was consulted; witchcraft was diagnosed as the cause of death. The witch was cursed. Ten days later the boy's father's sister fell ill and confessed to having killed the child because her brother refused to give her rice. The woman was buried alive.

13. Co-wife's son's son. A woman quarreled with her co-wife's son's wife over the sharing of some locust seed cakes. Shortly afterward, her co-wife's son's son became ill and died. When the woman also fell ill she confessed to having killed the child to get even with his mother. She died after confessing.

What I find striking about most of these cases is that there are so few allusions to the stereotypical imagery of witchcraft. Covens and cannibalism are mentioned in only four cases (witches usually "kill" or "beat up" their victims); animal familiars and out-of-body travel in only one (case 7). Clearly, general beliefs about witchcraft and the particular experiences of self-confessed witches are seldom congruent. In other words, there is only a partial identity relationship between representation and reality. Writing about the Banyang, Ruel makes a similar point: "The relatively simple and unelaborated stereotypes of the witch as [an] anti-social, evil agent ... is for the Banyang quickly shattered into a great number of different 'images' or 'types' that a person's witchcraft potential ... can take."[15] Clearly, Banyang and Kuranko share with the Azande a tendency to "normally think of witchcraft quite impersonally and apart from any particular witch or witches."[16]

These observations are more than ethnographically interesting; they are theoretically important for anthropology, which, from its inception in the late nineteenth century to its recent debates about "the ontological turn," has never satisfactorily resolved the question as to how thought is related to being. All too often, direct extrapolations are made from collective representations to lived reality, as if conventional wisdom concerning how the world works mirrors, if not determines, individual experience.

This is not to say that worldviews do not reflect common concerns. But everyone has concerns that are unique to himself or herself, as well as ways of drawing on received ideas in working out viable solutions to personal dilemmas. Accordingly, human praxis both conserves a shared worldview and surpasses it. As Sartre puts it, "man is characterized above all by his going beyond a situation, and by what he succeeds in making of what he has been made—even if he never recognizes himself in his objectification."[17] Theodor Adorno's view of praxis is similar. It "is characterized above all by the fact that [something] qualitatively new appears in it ... it is a movement which does not run its course in pure identity, the pure reproduction of such as already was there."[18]

From Worldview to Lifeworld

The stereotype of the witch is a dialectic inversion of the stereotype of moral personhood. It encapsulates what Monica Wilson so aptly called "the standardized nightmares of the group."[19] For the Kuranko, collective anxieties center on self-containment and protection. But the deployment of various objects or medicines (*kandan li fannu*, enclosing/

protecting things), to magically seal off self, house, village, farm, and chiefdom reflects more than a traumatic history of military incursions; it is an index of a quotidian struggle to accommodate strangers who may be enemies, to negotiate relations with the nation-state without losing one's autonomy, to market one's agricultural products without being exploited by outside entrepreneurs, to open oneself up to the outside world without abandoning one's traditions, and to bring women into one's household as wives without disrupting established patterns of family life.

The notion of a witch as someone within the household yet in league with enemies without (her night *kere*) is grounded in the ambiguous social position of young married women, legally bound to their husbands yet emotionally attached to their natal families and lineage sisters. Something of this ambiguity is suggested by the phrases a man uses when giving his daughter in marriage to her husband's group: "Now we have come with your wife. She is your thief, your witch, your daughter, your all. We have brought her to you alive, but even in death she will remain your wife." One might also note that the animals most commonly associated with witches—palm-birds, lizards, toads, snakes, cats, vultures, owls—are also structurally ambiguous. Though they are "wild" they often enter and live within the village.

A woman is thus structurally ambiguous (situated between her natal family and the family into which she marries) and susceptible to competing emotions, especially in the first year of her marriage. Yet even when she becomes a mother and enjoys real control and influence over her children, whose destinies are said to be "in her hands," her husband "owns" the children, and should they suffer misfortune in life she is likely to be blamed. As a sister, she enjoys some degree of control over her brothers, because they marry with bridewealth received from her marriage, but her requests for support from her brothers are not always met. While many women find fulfillment in marriage, others are neglected or abused by their husbands, persecuted by their senior wives, and ignored by their brothers. In four of the cases cited above, unjust apportionment of food was the cause of resentment; in two others, it was conjugal neglect. And the target of witchcraft attack was either a husband (five cases) or brother (one case) or a surrogate for the person the "witch" wished to harm: a co-wife's child (one case) or grandchild (one case) or a brother's child (one case) or grandchild (two cases).

Although witchcraft fantasies may be explained in terms of insufferable personal situations, one might ask why these women did not seek more mundane ways of redressing injustices, such as asking the Leader of the Women (the *dimusukuntigi*) to represent their cases in the chief's court, or enlisting the help of the women's cult, *segere*, or, in the case of a brother's negligence, using the sister's power to curse?

To answer these questions, references to kinship stress and women's subservience are not enough. Such factors condition women's experience but do not wholly explain it. It is therefore necessary to consider the psychology of witchcraft confession in more depth.

Kuranko people endure the tribulations of life with a fortitude that many Westerners, conditioned to expect medical science to guarantee them long lives without excessive suffering, might find unsettling. In the course of my fieldwork, I helped sick people as much as my medical knowledge and supplies permitted. At first, however, it was usually I who sought people out, giving electrolyte solution to infants with dysentery and chloromycetin to people suffering from conjunctivitis, and supervising courses of antibiotics. Even when distressed by the deteriorating condition of a child, parents showed little interest in my medical resources. Afflicted by painful and debilitating diseases such as elephantiasis, encephalitis, malaria, and leprosy, men and women assented to my help rather than sought it. As for their attitude toward sick kinsmen or friends, it was often, to my mind, apathetic and perfunctory. *In toro* (you suffer), they would say in commiseration, then turn away, as if taciturnity and neutrality in speech gave a magical mastery over pain.

Such stoic self-mastery is nowhere more assiduously cultivated than in the rites of initiation. Initiation involves a battery of ordeals calculated to test the mettle of neophytes. To stay awake in a smoke-filled room, lashed with switches, upbraided and bullied by elders; to be tormented by tales of bush spirits and lethal medicines; to have one's genitals cut and not wince or cry out; and to undergo traumatic separation from one's parents are regarded as ways of learning the sternest and most important lesson in life: to endure pain, show forbearance, and be masterful in the face of every adversity. "To resist is hard [not sweet]," the saying goes, "but freedom [from trouble] comes of it" (*in sa ro, a fo ma di, koni lafere hayi la*). Despite men's view that women control their feelings and withstand hardship less well than they do, this theme pervades both men's and women's initiations.

It is therefore understandable why Kuranko were indifferent to my medical interventions. To place themselves in a stranger's hands meant cutting themselves off from kin and from the tried and tested world of their own medicines, most of which, it must be remembered, have a protective and insulating function. It would entail forfeiting their autonomy. A Kuranko adage sums up the dilemma: *Morgo ben ta nyenne bolo komo ko* (Better to be in the hands of a *nyenne* than in the hands of *Kome*). Both *nyenne* and *Kome* are bush spirits, but *Kome* is especially awesome and capricious. Thus, the known is always preferable to the unknown, the familiar to the foreign. Better the devil you know than the devil you don't.

It is not only Kuranko who adopt this view. One encounters it often in our own society when a seriously ill individual prefers to decide his or her own treatment rather than submit to impersonal and disempowering medical regimes. Sometimes the risk of death is preferred over the sacrifice of one's autonomy and dignity.

The seemingly fatalistic attitude of Kuranko in the face of misfortune reflects not a blind acceptance of suffering but an active recognition that it is an inevitable part of life. Pain and sickness are not seen as aberrations from which one might be saved. The insane and sick are never sequestered. Death is not denied. Nor do people react to suffering with the outrage and impatience so familiar in our own society—the tormented sense that one has been hard done by, that one deserves better, that permanent health, unalloyed happiness, even immortality, might one day be guaranteed as a civil right. In my experience, Kuranko people show little interest in an afterlife where one might escape the tribulations of this world yet retain one's worldly identity. To die alone, to be refused decent burial, to have one's lineage die out: such things are terrible, not one's own extinction.

The focus, then, is on the field of relationships of which one is a part, not one's self per se. Accordingly, illness is seen as a disturbance in the field of social relationships (which include ancestors, God, bush spirits, and witches), not a result of disease entities such as germs or viruses. Thus, if you behave badly or even harbor ill will toward another person who is innocent or protected by medicines, then the malice will react against you and make you ill. It will be said that the other person's *hake* has "got out" on you (*a hake ara bo*) or that his *hake* "goes against you" (*a hake si bo i ro*). To "set things straight" or "clear things up" (the Kuranko images are the same as ours), you must beg forgiveness (*ka madiyale ke*) of the person you have wronged or confess (*ka porondo*) your ill will.

So pervasive is this notion of agentless, retributive justice (*hake*) that diviners commonly advise confession as a way of making things right or "cool," of clearing or straightening the path between people. Indeed, people often spontaneously confess animosity to neighbors and friends in everyday life, speaking of the "pain" (*koe dime*) oppressing them. Or women wishing to forestall possible punishment for adultery sometimes sit down with their husbands and unburden themselves with such words as *"M'buin, ma be Fore lon; i hake ka na n'to"* (My husband, we and Fore are [having an affair]; may your *hake* not get out on me).

But why is the onus usually on women to confess? Why, when illness strikes and diviners are consulted, are women blamed? And why, when *Gbangbane* is abroad, do women fall prey to secret fears far more than men? The answer to these questions lies in the contrast between the sequestered life of women and the public life of men.

For the Kuranko, the physical contrast between house (*bon*) and backyard (*sundu kunye ma*) implies a symbolic contrast between the courtyard (*luiye*) that opens onto the village, the domain of men, and the back of the house, which is the domain of women. It is said that women are encompassed by men as the house is encompassed by *luiye*. As a consequence, men go out, women turn in upon themselves. While men seek the causes of discord in the world around them, women search for the causes within. Men apportion blame, women take the blame; men accuse, women confess.

But the pressures that bring a woman to find the cause of a child's death, a husband's bad luck, barrenness, or family discord *in her own thoughts and deeds* are not only social. Certainly, the advice of a diviner, the carping of a husband or senior co-wife, kinship stress, village gossip, and the terrifying sound of *Gbangbane* moving about in the night all work to erode the confidence of an already vulnerable woman. But the precipitating cause of confession to witchcraft in over half the cases I collected was severe illness, illness seen as punishment for unconfessed sins.

"The Last Freedom"

It may appear that Kuranko women are so conditioned to bear responsibility for the misfortunes around them that they readily assent, when pressure is put upon them, to serve as men's scapegoats. The self-confessed witch would seem to embody this self-abnegation to an extreme degree: a victim of a world that denies her any legitimate outlet for her frustrations and grievances. But such a conclusion only recapitulates the prejudices of those Kuranko men who see women solely as a category—for "witch," "scapegoat," and "victim" are all category words, and negative ones at that.

For this reason, it is important to recognize that witchcraft confession is also a desperate stratagem for reclaiming autonomy in a hopeless situation. This is borne out by the allusions to witch possessions (*suwa'ya mirannu*) in several cases (*miran* also means self-possession), and in other cases (7, 11), by the defiant attitudes of the women in the face of death. But even when such defiance is not evident, witchcraft confession can still be seen as a powerful form of self-expression in which words and images substitute for acts.[20] Confession to witchcraft exemplifies what Victor Frankl calls "the last freedom"—that which remains to us when external circumstances rob us of the power to act: the choice of determining how we will construe our plight, the freedom to live as though it were our will. It is the freedom Jean Genet discovered as a child when accused of being a thief. Reduced to an object for others, a projection of their fears, a scapegoat for their anxieties, his escape was into neither suicide nor insanity, but took the form of a decision to become his fate, to live it as though he himself had conceived it: "I decided to be what the crime had made of me—a thief"(J'ai decidé d'être ce que le crime à fait de moi—un voleur).[21]

Thus, the self-confessed witch does more than passively submit to the succession of misfortunes that have overwhelmed her. Nor does she blindly recapitulate the stereotypes men promulgate; rather, she actively uses them to give voice to long-suppressed grievances and to cope with her suffering by declaring herself the author of it.[22] She determines how she will play out the role that circumstance has thrust upon her. She dies deciding her own identity, sealing her own fate.

It is not enough for us to decide whether witchcraft is a social pathology or the individual witch a victim of some delusional psychosis, for our task is to throw light on the lived experience that lies behind the masks and facades of category words—even those used by the self-confessed witch herself. Such an approach demands to know not whether a witch's death is "suicide" or "murder" but how that death is lived. It seeks not to know whether *hake* is best translated as "guilt" or "shame" or whether *suwage* is semantically equivalent to "wiltch," but what experiences find expression in these words and how we might recover them. It is for this reason that I have no sympathy with those anthropologists and philosophers who endlessly debate the rationality or irrationality of witchcraft beliefs. Beliefs have no reality apart from the people who make use of them, and to try to see how beliefs correspond to some allegedly "objective" reality or how they cohere as a so-called "system" seems to me far less edifying than trying to see what people do with beliefs in coping with the exigencies of life. At this level, the bizarre appearance of Kuranko witchcraft images is less significant than the realities of human distress that find expression through them—realities with which we can readily identify.[23]

4

THE NEW MATERIALISMS

> The subject enters into the object altogether differently from the way the
> object enters into the subject. An object can be conceived only by a subject
> but always remains something other than the subject, whereas a subject by
> its very nature is from the outset an object as well ... To be an object also is
> part of the meaning of subjectivity; but it is not equally part of the meaning
> of objectivity to be a subject.
> —Theodor Adorno, *Negative Dialectics*

Although scholars have often invoked animism, fetishism, totemism,
and anthropomorphism as signs of primitivism and flawed reasoning,
many contemporary anthropologists have embraced these category
words to signify not simply modes of thought but modes of being—
alleged evidence of the radical alterity of certain cultures and of the
essential multiplicity of the human condition. Indeed, so pervasive is
this new exoticism that some writers now speak of a "post-human" turn
in which the lines between persons and animals, or persons and things,
are not only contested but deemed to have no ontological foundation.[1]

Rather than ask whether the new materialism fulfills a wish to re-
enchant a world that has become globally uniform and intellectually
flat (an effort to reinvent the primitive) or is simply another example
of an all too human tendency to confuse forms of thought with forms
of being, I want to explore the existential conditions under which
things appear, by turns, inert or vital, objects or subjects. This requires
bracketing out questions as to the nature or essence of persons and
things in order to understand the different effects and appearances
that emerge in the course of their interactions. It is in this emphasis
on relations over relata, the transitive over the intransitive, that I

depart from the "prevailing ethos of new materialist ontology" and its assumptions that materiality is intrinsically vital, agentive, self-creative, and productive.[2]

Melquíades's Magnets

In the opening pages of *One Hundred Years of Solitude*, Gabriel García Marquez describes the dramatic impact of ice and magnets on the inhabitants of Macondo. As the gypsy Melquíades carries his metal ingots from house to house, pots, pans, tongs, and braziers tumble "in turbulent confusion" from their proper places and follow him down the street, like the enthralled children of Hamelin in the wake of the Pied Piper. "Things have a life of their own," Marquez writes, "it's just a matter of waking up their souls."

That ironware can spring to life, or water shape-shift from liquid to solid to gas, appears to be a potentiality of the things themselves, and even an expression of their intentionality and will. But the "life" of these things depends on the presence of a magnet in the first case, and on whether the water is cooled or heated in the second. These effects do not necessarily require a human agent and may occur naturally or accidentally. But they are always the outcome of a relationship between one thing and another—an object and its environment, or matter and mind. Moreover, these relationships are never enduring. When José Arcadio Buendía offers a mule and a pair of goats in exchange for Melquíades's magnets, he is convinced that he will be able to use them to attract gold from the ground and thereby become rich. When the magnets fail to fulfill their promise he exchanges them, together with three colonial coins, for a magnifying glass whose power to eliminate distance and generate fire has persuaded José Arcadio Buendía that he has now acquired a formidable weapon of war.

It is difficult to distinguish subject and object here. While the subject of the story is José Arcadio Buendía, one might also argue that the subject is the magnetized ingots or the magnifying glass, or their "magical" effects. Though these "things" are mere objects when not in use, they seem, when taken up and put to use, as if they were subjects, revealing their potentialities to attract things to them or transmute one thing into another. But as Heidegger observed, the thingness of a jug "does not lie at all in the material of which it consists," but rather "in its being *qua* vessel," able to be filled and emptied, or hold a liquid.[3] This potentiality of things to attract, magnify, fill or fulfill, is a function not of a thing-in-itself but of a relationship between a thing and a person. Just as Melquíades's magnets participate in the gypsy's subjectivity when taken up and deployed by him, so José Arcadio Buendía appears, at least in the eyes of his long-suffering wife, to be in thrall to the magnet's powers, and reduced to the status of a hapless object.

We are, by turns, creators of the world and creatures of it, and it would be as spurious to claim that human beings are always and necessarily subjects as it would be foolish to claim that the extra-human world is always and necessarily inert. But there is a risk that in describing the appearance of a person or a thing in a particular context we will conclude that our description reveals the "real" essence of the person or thing, leading us to confuse causation with agency. Why Melquíades's magnets induce ironware to move may be explained in terms of material cause (the phenomenon of magnetism) or of efficient cause (Melquíades's deliberate deployment of the magnets), but it would be a mistake to confuse movements that occur without consciousness and will with movements that are a result of intentionality and purpose.[4] There is a world of difference between "being subject to change" and "being a subject that brings about change."

Clearly, the words "subject" and "object" are epistemologically ambiguous. The word "subject" may refer to a particular person (José Arcadio Buendía) as well as an abstract construct ("magnetism" or "magic"). Although idealist thought posits the subject as a transcendent category ("the human") that is intrinsically different from other categories, including animals, material objects and divinities, the human cannot be conceived without reference to what it allegedly is not. Phenomenologically as well as dialectically a "subject" always implicates an "object," whether that object is a goal, a thing, or another person. An object can never be an object in itself; it is only an object in the consciousness of persons.[5] In brief, it is the dynamic relationship between what we tend to reify as subjects and objects that is interesting, not the intrinsic properties of the terms as such.

Object Relations Theory

In object relations theory, subject and object connote a felt distinction between experiences that appear to originate or belong within us ("inner" or "subjective") and experiences that appear to originate from outside us ("exterior" or "objective"). Two important conclusions follow from this. First, "who" we are always implicates "what" we have, whether this is a natural ability, an item we own, a language we speak, a belief we espouse, a trade we practice, or a place we live. That is to say, being and having are mutually entailed. Second, at any moment, to varying degrees, we are both actors and acted upon. In Hannah Arendt's words, every person is at once a "who" and a "what"—a subject who actively participates in the making or unmaking of his or her world, and a subject that suffers and is subjected to the actions of others, as well as forces that lie largely beyond his or her control. This oscillation between being an actor and being acted on is felt in every human encounter, and intersubjective life involves an ongoing struggle to negotiate, reconcile, balance, or mediate these antithetical possibilities, such that no one person, group or entity ever arrogates agency so completely and permanently to itself that others are reduced to the status of mere things, objects, ciphers, or contingent predicates.

This interplay between one's experience of being an actor and being acted upon is a constant in every human life, and it would be a serious mistake to define any individual, society, or period of history as being characterized by either agency or patiency, freewill or fatalism. Nevertheless, Westerners have conjured an extraordinary range of vocabularies to describe essential differences between themselves and others, based on the assumption that "we" and "they" construe the relationship between subjects and objects, persons and things, in essentially different ways. While "we" make "rational" distinctions between animate and inanimate, human and non-human, or words and things, "they" are supposedly immersed in a pre-rational, vitalist, and anthropomorphic mode of being that Lucien Lévy-Bruhl called "mystical participation," in which the world of objects is typically experienced as animate and therefore capable of responding to human spells, incantations, and special forms of ritual address such as sacrifice and prayer.

While I am inclined to bracket out such terms as "rational," "irrational," "mystical," and "prelogical," it is important to recognize that people in all societies oscillate between different modes of thinking, speaking, and acting depending on the situations in which they find themselves. Bereaved individuals everywhere are prone to hear voices and see ghosts, and in all societies, people imagine that abstract ideals and precious objects are as worth dying for as significant others. Moreover, not only are material objects and imaginary figures endowed with human attributes such as consciousness and will; human beings whose beliefs are abhorred and whose behavior is condemned will be treated as mere objects, deplorables, or trash. Rather than interpret these phenomena epistemologically as true or false, or morally as good or bad, or historically as signs of barbarity or civilization, I prefer to explore them psychologically and pragmatically, as means whereby human beings grasp and process their immediate experience through things external to themselves, such as the language and customs they share with others, the animals, plants, and landscapes that surround them, the material objects they make and use, and the invisible agents (viruses, bacteria, divinities, and heavenly bodies) that lie beyond their ken.

Being and Having

Because we think through things, it is only natural that we should think of things as vital to our existence, thereby transplanting into them the thoughts and feelings we recognize in ourselves.[6] In apprehending our humanity through the extra-human, and in processing subjective experience through material objects, we tend to lose sight of the difference between persons and things, humanity and divinity, humanity and animality. We readily assume, for instance, that the principle of reciprocity operates not only between human beings but potentially between persons and animals, persons and things. Though Jean Piaget argued that anthropomorphic thought is characteristic of an early stage in child development (and, by implication, an early stage in human cultural evolution),[7] it is clear that this manner of thinking is present in people of all ages and in all societies. It reveals itself in the imaginings of laboratory researchers working closely with great apes.[8] It finds expression in popular speculations about the conceptual and spiritual lives of animals. And it explains our fetishistic attitude toward prized possessions, such that the loss of our valuables will precipitate the same bereavement reaction as the loss of a beloved person. Being is in all societies invested in and distributed among the things that people use and call their own. Having is not only a metaphor for being; it is actually experienced as a mode of being, such that the bonds we form with persons through "object cathexis" are phenomenologically continuous with the bonds we form with objects and ideas.

Consider the ontological metaphor of container-contained—a metaphor that is as central to object-relations theory as it is common to cultures throughout the world.

The model of container-contained was central to the psychoanalytic work of Wilfred Bion who postulated that we can only process, comprehend and accept overwhelming life experiences ("Beta elements") by working them through with a caring other—someone who can contain or safely hold us and on whom we can rely in constructing life-affirming rather than life-negating responses to unbearable experiences.[9] But we can also feel contained and safe within our dwellings and neighborhoods, with our language, our treasured mementos, and our cultural values. This mutual substitutability of caregivers, abstract ideas, home places, and sacred objects is predicated on our human capacity for playing with reality.

In the recent work of Peter Fonagy and Mary Target,[10] play typically oscillates between a subjunctive or "pretend mode," in which images and ideas are allowed to take on a life of their own, and a mode of "psychic equivalence" in which ideas are made to stand for some external reality. For Bion as well as Fonagy and Target, concepts are equated with any thing that helps a child objectify and vicariously control its relationship with the world, such as mother's milk, food, toys, blocks, paints, and found objects. Conceptual thought, in this view, is a means whereby one manages one's life in relation with others, a way in which we contain and control life experiences that threaten to engulf, undermine, or nullify us.

In *From Anxiety to Method in the Behavioral Sciences*, George Devereux argues that we share with all living organisms a deep-seated need to be recognized and responded to. "Denial of response" can be so traumatic that in most societies cultural strategies exist for alleviating people's panicked reactions to the unresponsiveness of matter. Most notably, physical occurrences are interpreted animistically and human meanings are projected onto the extra-human world.[11] Thus, a thunderstorm will be said to embody the malicious intentions of outsiders, and a "natural" disaster such as a flood, mudslide, or earthquake will be construed as a manifestation of ancestral displeasure. Devereux's thesis applies equally to our tendency to use objects or graven images as surrogate persons, so that faced with an unresponsive person or someone who is beyond our reach or control, we substitute for that person a doll, mascot, figurine, or icon, and act on it, speaking to it, nurturing it, harming it, as the case may be, as though it were, in effect, the absent person. Is it possible that the "new materialism" is a manifestation of Devereux's "trauma of the unresponsiveness of matter," a defense against external forces over which we seem to have little control (global warming, epidemic diseases, economic collapse) that involves thinking and acting as if these forces were not only open to the human mind but were "actants"[12] or "quasi agents" with "trajectories, propensities, or tendencies of their own."[13] Before reaching any conclusions on this matter, let us continue to explore in an empirical vein the ways in which objects are subject to thought and subjects think about themselves through objects.

Container and Contained

The model of container-contained is as central to Kuranko thought as it is to object relations theory—a reminder that analogical reason in both Western and non-Western traditions tends to deploy identical ontological metaphors and reflect similar existential dilemmas. In Kuranko, *miran* refers to any material possession, particularly if it contains, encloses, and protects, such as a house, clothing, a water vessel or cooking pot, and to any personal attribute that gives one a sense of presence and substantiality of being, such as forceful speech, technical skillfulness, and social adroitness. But *miran*, in both senses of the term—material possession and self-possession—is never a fixed property or attribute. In practice, a person's *miran* may be bolstered by fetishes that symbolically enclose, contain, and protect the vital spaces that define his or her being—body, house, village, chiefdom—in exactly the same way that in a consumer society material possessions bolster and define a person's sense of substantiality and standing. For Kuranko, the notion of a full container is a common metaphor for anyone who is in command of himself and doing his utmost to do what is socially expected of him. But self-possession and morale may be undermined, sapped, or lost. In this respect, *miran* bears a family resemblance to the Latin American notion of *susto* and the Polynesian notion of *mana*, the loss of which leads to physiological weakening, psychological disequilibrium, and social death. Just as a person's property can be stolen, a pot broken, and a house fall into disrepair, so a person can lose self-possession and confidence when his or her *miran* is "taken away" by more powerful others (such as autocratic parents, forceful public speakers, and powerful bush spirits) whose voice and power "press down" with great weight, diminishing the *miran* of those in their presence.[14] Then it is said that "the container has tipped over and its contents spilled out"—a metaphor for loss of self-control or for a state of indolence or despair when one has "let oneself go" (*nyere bila*). Ideally, a balance is struck in which everyone's voice, presence, and property is accorded due recognition in relation to his or her role, age, and gender. But some people assert themselves beyond their due station—as in the case of a Big Man who exploits his position to take advantage of an inferior, a senior co-wife who abuses her junior partners, a man whose jealousy overrules his better judgment, or a woman whose emotions are not held in check. A kind of intersubjective logic then comes into play, based on the principle of reciprocity, according to which one has the right to counter in kind any action that has the effect of directly nullifying, diminishing, belittling or erasing one's own being, or indirectly doing so by taking away properties that one regards as essential to one's being. The Kuranko phrase *ke manni a nyorgo manni* (something happened, its counterpart then happened) reveals the kinship between the social logic of partnership and the abstract calculus of retaliation.

Since *miran* blurs any hard and fast distinction between having and being, it can be augmented by taking the wherewithal of life from others—through theft, witchcraft, abuse, and humiliation—or by giving such things as respect, food, help, and protection that will be returned in equal measure at some later date. At the same time "real," symbolic, and fantastic calculations enter into people's notions of what constitutes their due, and Kuranko folktales, like folktales throughout the world, with their magical agencies, supernatural intercessories, and miraculous transformations, attest to the vital role played by wishful thinking in making everyday life endurable.

Consider Janet Hoskins's fascinating examples of magical thinking in her ethnography of the Kodi of Sumba (Eastern Indonesia). When Kodi talk about their life experiences they seldom do so directly by telling life stories. When people spoke to Hoskins about their personal possessions, they did so in stories that were in effect life stories, and subjects that were not publicly spoken of in Kodi—such as sexual politics—would find oblique expression in accounts people gave of objects.

> A young girl I knew well never confessed her feelings of romantic long-ing and later disappointment to me directly, but she was fascinated by the story of a magic spindle that flew through the air to snare a beloved. When later her own romantic hopes were dashed, she sent a message to her lost lover through the secret gift of the object ... A famous singer and healer who also wanted a female companion composed long ballads to his drum, introducing each ritual session with a history of efforts to cover the drum properly so it could be pierced by a male voice and travel up to the heavens ... Another man, famed as a storyteller and bard, said he received his "gift of words" in the simple, woven betel bag he carried with him at all times.[15]

That objects are surrogates for people, metaphors for social relationships, and serve as objective correlatives of subjective moods and states, may, Hoskins suggests, have a lot to do with the fact that in Kodi ritual life, objects often substitute for persons. Thus, in life-crisis rituals, a knife can substitute for a man, a cotton board or gold pendant can take the place of a woman, a betel bag can be buried in lieu of a person. Interestingly enough, Hoskins points out that the objects that stand for persons are very often containers: a betel pouch, a hollow drum, a porcelain vessel, a funeral shroud.[16]

Acting and Being Acted Upon

In the foregoing accounts of how subjective attributes find expression in material objects, we discern how the intrapsychic struggle to lift one's spirits, bolster one's confidence, and increase one's sense of presence is mediated by the manipulation of things. While some would see this affective labor as "magical"[17] or "libidinal"[18] by comparison with the "real" work of making a living or finding fulfillment, I am less interested in defining the essence of an action than in exploring its repercussions in people's lives. This pragmatic approach brackets out epistemological and ontological questions as to whether an action is rational or irrational, scientific or religious, real or fantastic, in order to explore the degree to which it enables a person to satisfy his or her existential needs for security and shelter, love and honor, well-being and recognition. I now turn to another ontological metaphor that, as with the image of container-contained, posits a crucial intersubjective relationship between persons and things, in this instance string, cords, bindings, lashings, and weavings.

In his seminal study of transitional objects and transitional phenomena, the psychoanalyst D. W. Winnicott describes the actions of a troubled seven-year-old boy whose parents sought his professional help. The boy's mother suffered from depression, and during her absences in hospital, he had stayed with his maternal aunt. Increasingly, however, his parents had become concerned by his behavior—a compulsion to lick things and people, a habit of making compulsive throat noises, threats to cut his little sister into pieces, over-controlling or losing control of his bowel movements. In Winnicott's first interview, the boy revealed an intense preoccupation with string, and subsequently his parents told the psychologist that this "obsession" worried them because their son had gotten into the habit of tying up tables and chairs and had recently tied a piece of string around his elder sister's throat. Winnicott suggested to the mother that her son was dealing with his fear of separation and using the string in an attempt to deny it, much "as one would deny separation from a friend by using the telephone."[19]

With this insight, the mother talked to her son about the times she had gone away from him and about his fear of losing touch with her. Six months after the first interview, the mother told Winnicott that her son had stopped playing obsessively with string and joining objects in the way he had—though the string play subsequently and temporarily reappeared, once when the mother had to return to hospital and another time when she again suffered a bout of depression.

Winnicott's analysis provides invaluable insights into ritualization, for it succinctly demonstrates that the manipulation of objects, abstract ideas and personae in our external, social environment is analogous to, but possibly more significant than, the intrapsychic manipulation of images of these things (symbolic disguise, displacement, repression, projection, reversal, rationalization, scotomization) in enabling human beings to come to terms with distressing situations. Both fantasizing and ritualizing are predicated on the logic of intersubjectivity. By this I mean that all human beings tend to equate, or draw analogies between, their relationships with other persons, their relationships with their own thoughts and emotions, and their relationships with things, ideas, and words. As a corollary, human beings tend to act in critical situations as if one of these modalities of relationship could be effectively substituted for the other. In Winnicott's view, these are all "object-relations." "Transitional objects," such as pieces of string, teddy bears, or toys enable children to manage their difficult but inevitable separation from parents or caregivers, as well as laying the foundations for adult responses to traumatic change, separation, and loss.

Yet, objects can sometimes not only replace persons but occlude them, leading to pathological forms of dissociation. In a compelling case study, Bruno Bettelheim describes a traumatized boy called Joey who so distrusted people that he converted himself into a machine. Secure in this mechanized image of himself, he functioned as if by remote control. Indeed, Joey's machinelike behavior was so convincing that even his therapists found it difficult to respond to him as a human being. Joey lived the mechanistic image as a literal and embodied truth:

> During Joey's first weeks with us we would watch absorbedly as this at once fragile–looking and imperious nine-year-old went about his mechanical existence. Entering the dining room, for example, he would string an imaginary wire from his "energy source"—an imaginary electric outlet—to the table. There he "insulated" himself with paper napkins and finally plugged himself in. Only then could Joey eat, for he firmly believed that the "current" ran his ingestive apparatus. So skillful was the pantomime that one had to look twice to be sure there was neither wire nor outlet nor plug. Children and members of our staff spontaneously avoided stepping on the "wires" for fear of interrupting what seemed to be the source of his very life.[20]

Winnicott's and Bettelheim's clinical examples help us understand that thinking does not occur in a vacuum, abstracted from lived situations, arising from natural curiosity or wonderment, or reflecting internalized cultural patterns. In the case of Joey, it is crucial that we take into account the crises this child suffered in his early life. According to Bettelheim, Joey was rejected by his parents even before he was born. "I never knew I was pregnant," his mother said. Joey's birth "did not make any difference ... I did not want to see or nurse him ... I had no feeling of actual dislike—I simply didn't want to take care of him."[21]

Although the new materialism "calls for a detailed phenomenology of diverse lives as they are actually lived—often in ways that are at odds with normative theories or official ideologies,"[22] it often presents itself as an inversion of old binaries, showing that the mundane is exotic, appearances are realities, objects are subjects, and causation is agentive. Though one may doubt the epistemological validity of this reasoning, it inadvertently reveals one of the phenomenologically most compelling aspects of human relations with the non-human, namely a chiastic tendency to essentialize and polarize key terms, then reverse the relationship between them, speaking as if "our" perspective was actually "theirs." Thus, when we experience strong emotions when watching a beautiful sunset, we readily say that the sunset "moves" us as though it has agency. In giving primacy to the object, the subject masks the part it plays in constituting the experience of being moved.

To construe experience relationally brings us to consider the ways in which subjectivity is objectively constituted and, reciprocally, how objectivity is subjectively perceived. Appearances are explained neither as functions of the mind nor of external reality but seen as emerging from the space between an experiencing subject and the objects of his or her experience.

In this view, we achieve our sense of being subjects through the objects and others with which we interact, just as those objects achieve the appearance of subjectivity or value through us. Keith Basso refers to this process as inter-animation and shows that it is our interactions with a landscape or place, moving, working, and living in it, that generate a sense of the landscape as actually imbued or impregnated with subjectivity.[23] As Sartre puts it, "When knowledge and feeling are oriented toward something real, actually perceived, the thing, like a reflector, returns the light it has received from it. As a result of this continual interaction, meaning is continually enriched at the same time as the object soaks up affective qualities."[24]

It is important to remind ourselves that in traditional societies "work" includes a range of actions that we in the West would designate as ritual, magical, or even social action[25] as though these were secondary or surplus to the supposedly primary activities of gardening, herding, farming, hunting, or gathering. The phenomenology of labor that I have outlined here suggests that identical elements appear in all intersubjective action. Among the Warlpiri of Central Australia, the "ceremony" associated with sacred sites involves the collaborative effort of patrilineal "owners" (*kirda*) and their uterine kin (*kurdungurlu*) who supervise or "police" the body painting and decoration of those who will perform the ancestral dances that are said to draw out, reawaken, or bring back into embodied presence the primordial forms of life (*kuruwarri*) that reside in the earth at that site and along the ancestral songlines that connect the site with others. In ceremonial labor, then, one reproduces a social past whose reappearance is linked to the burgeoning of desert plants and the increase of game animals after rain or the raising of a child in one's care, as well as metaphorically likened to the action of waking from sleep, or dawn breaking after a long night. In short, Warlpiri notions of labor as a form of begetting or procreation echo Marx and Engel's view[26] since at the same time that one "increases" animal and plant life, one reproduces the social relations most crucial to one's identity—with patrikin, matrikin, and affiliated countrymen (*warlalja*) and affines (*jurdalja*). Moreover, one also reproduces one's own sense of kinship with the site that, depending on one's relationship with it, will be called father (*kirda*), father's father (*warringiyi*), mother's brother (*ngamirni*), mother's father (*jamirdi*), etc.

Dancing vigorously on the land may be likened to carving an ancestral mask, giving birth or making a farm. In common parlance, one puts one's sweat and blood into the task at hand.[27] The intense labor of the dancer, carver, mother, or farmer is felt to flow into the object or other, which becomes endowed with subjectivity. It then appears to speak to the human subject in response to the human subject's action on it. The distinctive stomping of Aboriginal men's dance sends vibrations into the ground that are taken as evidence of the stirring into life of the ancestral essences (*kuruwarri*) that steep the earth underfoot. Among the Bamana of Mali, the "energy of action"[28] is reified as *nyama*—a vibrant force that animates all living things and whose strength is correlated with the stress or intensity of the effort put into a vital activity. Thus, the "arduous labor," skill, concentration, and effort involved in ironworking entails the "release" of *nyama*, as does the work of formal speech, hunting, and circumcision. Indeed, so overwhelming is the *nyama* released from such practices that an unskilled worker may be blinded or killed by the force.[29] This notion that inept labor may create a negative force in the object worked upon is similar to the Maori notion that the vital force (*hau*) that is carried by every fabricated object may be "turned aside" (*whitia*) and cause illness and misfortune if the object received in exchange is not passed on or reciprocated.[30]

Insofar as labor transfers vitality and spirituality from the laboring subject to the object worked upon, labor creates an intersubjective relationship between people and things. This is why artists in many societies experience themselves as channels through which divine inspiration flows into the object. Gola mask carvers in Liberia believe they are inspired by djinn who appear to them in dreams.[31] Throughout Africa the notion that some inner force finds expression in the object carved leads to elaborate precautions being taken to ensure that the carver is in the right frame of mind when sculpting a figurine or mask or in a good relationship with his spirit allies. Among the Anang of southeast Nigeria, the carver relinquishes other commitments, avoids working to the point of exhaustion or in the heat of the day, and abstains from sexual intercourse lest he create an imperfect work or risk injury to himself in the course of the carving.[32] Yoruba carvers are equally sensitive to the ways in which an art object may imitate its creator's personality. One master carver, Owoeye Oluwuro, told William Bascom "that a traditional Èfòn sculptor, before he initiated any important commission involving the carving of human eyes, mouth, and nose, had to make a sacrifice of sugarcane, dried maize with red palm oil, and pigeons to prevent the entrance of ugliness into his carving." These sweetening, smoothing, and uplifting images help guarantee that no clumsy adzing will despoil the carved face or create ugly features that might then be transmitted to the face of the sculptor's next child.[33]

Explaining how he transforms logs into art, the Tanzanian woodcarver Lugwani observes, "I do not impose my own ideas on the wood—it tells me what to do; it helps me to think creatively." And in commenting on the carving of one particular abstract sculpture, Lugwani noted that at first the log seemed resistant, but after two weeks work he was able to say, "I am no longer fighting the wood; it has revealed itself to me and we are working together."[34] Similar reflections may be found in Henry Glassie's study of Turkish traditional art and artisans. "In things they do not see things, but people," he writes; "the artist's gift suffuses an object with spirit."[35]

Clearly, then, the labor expended on an object is gradually felt to inhere in the object itself, investing it with social value. When, as among the Warlpiri, ritual labor demands the collaboration of many different people, the actual place where the ceremonial work is carried out accumulates a value that affirms the intersubjective bonds between both owners and ancestors and *kirda* and *kurdungurlu*. That the process of working on an object comes to be experienced as an inherent property of the object itself also helps us understand why religious ideas are so often entailed by labor action. Sustained, intensive, and collective labor not only creates a binding intersubjective relationship or covenant between self and other, or subject and object; it produces a sense of value that is felt to inhere in the site where that labor takes place. Thus, landscapes become storied or sacred, as though the earth itself contained the narratives and scripts that human beings have created as moral constraints and guidelines for their lives.

We may now ask under what conditions does the reverse process occur? How does a valued object, embodying the vitality of those who have worked to produce or reproduce it, come to lose value and die? Is this loss of value also a function of the kind of relationship obtained between a human subject and the thing that is the object of his or her labor?

In West Africa, masks can sicken and die when not worn in ceremony or when out of circulation and may even be mourned and given burial rites like a deceased person. In Aotearoa (New Zealand), there is a Maori saying that for as long as a person lives on the land or returns regularly to it, a fire burns there (*ahi ka*). But if one goes away and does not return, the fire goes out (*ahi mataotao*). And in Aboriginal Australia, a sacred site unvisited for several generations—like grassland left unburned or kinsmen who have gone away for a long time—is figuratively dead, and as such may be mourned, and felt to be haunted by dangerous spirits. But in Warlpiri thought, death and life are functions of relationship rather than absolute and final states. A neglected site, a forgotten ancestor, a primordial event may all be, so to speak, out of sight and out of mind, but none is necessarily lost to the world; it may be brought back into being whenever the living return to it, remember it, dream of it, or perform ceremony that gives it presence. Any landscape is filled with marks, signs, and vestiges of The Dreaming that people notice and discuss as they walk around. But such attention is strictly speaking not a form of remembering, a bringing of the past back to mind; it is an interaction that actually discloses the incipient vitality in the place, quickening it into life and making it present. *Walku* is thus best translated not as death, but as loss,[36] absence, or potentiality, and its opposite, *palka*, not as life, but as embodied presence.

Death is thus a form of temporary estrangement rather than a permanent state of nonbeing. It occurs whenever any object, place, or person whose being depends on a vital relationship with other beings loses that life-sustaining link. The link may be borne in mind, to be sure, but a mere memory or disembodied conception of a person or place is artificial. It is map, not territory.

Estrangement may also be deliberately created as a way of expressing power. Paradoxically, it is only when one masks the context in which an object is produced that it attains a reified form that cannot be subject to questioning, and therefore imposes itself on our consciousness, as it were, not through any memory of the work that went into it or the lives that were sacrificed to create it, but simply from its presence as sheer facticity.

We might conclude, then, that identity thinking is redeemed when language is returned to life—by our descriptions of its effects in the real world, our focus on relations rather than relata, and our refusal to endow any of the terms involved in the processes of thinking and living with a constant value.

Closing Remarks

For Aristotle, agency is very different from causality, though this difference may be more apparent than real. A person may appear to be exercising free will but in reality is acting under duress. A piece of iron may move under the influence of a magnet, yet if the magnet is hidden, the iron may appear to be alive and ensouled. The question is not whether objects, like bodies, "evince certain capacities for agency" or that "the difference between humans and animals, or even between sentient and nonsentient matter, is a question of degree more than of kind."[37] Rather the question is: under what conditions do objects appear to be subjects. This question demands that we consider interactions between subject and object, and the contexts in which these interactions occur. It is undeniably true that under certain circumstances objects appear to have agency (if only because of their forceful presence, impact, and effects), just as under certain conditions humans behave as if they were things, and animals appear to be human. In different circumstances, objects appear to be inert, and animals seem to lack humanity. A. Irving Hallowell's Ojibwa ethnography makes this contextual specificity of meaning very clear. In the Ojibwa language, there is an implicit category distinction between animate and inanimate. Although stone, thunder, and objects such as kettles and pipes are grammatically animate and Ojibwa sometimes speak of stones as if they were persons, this does not mean that Ojibwa are animists "in the sense that they dogmatically attribute living souls to inanimate objects such as stone"; rather they recognize "potentialities for animation in certain classes of objects under certain circumstances. The Ojibwa do not perceive stones, in general, as animate, any more than we do."[38] Among the Kuranko, it is axiomatic that will and consciousness are not limited to human beings, but distributed beyond the world of persons, and potentially present in totemic animals, fetishes, and even plants. The attributes of moral personhood (*morgoye*) may, indeed, be exemplified in the behavior of totemic animals, divinities, and the dead, while antisocial people may lose their personhood entirely, becoming like broken vessels or ruined houses. In other words, being is not necessarily limited to human being.[39] But this is a human understanding, born of the experience of exchanging the roles of actor and acted upon, of subject and object, in one's interactions with others.

Crucial to understanding the ways in which we understand ourselves in relation to others and to objects is the phenomenon of re-cognition—a word I hyphenate in order to emphasize that cognition is always reflexive and mediated. Re-cognition is an expression of our dependency on things external to ourselves, including our language, in order to process, grasp, and articulate what is going on within us. Interiority can only be apprehended through exteriority. Accordingly, all thought is analogical. It involves drawing comparisons between something felt to lie within our immediate sensory experience and something that is felt to exist outside it. Hence such metaphors as "my thoughts are muddy" (like a stream after rain), "my feelings are running high" (like a river in flood), "his expression was stony." It is this unceasing passage of inner experience into the exterior space of the world and back again that is the essence of re-cognition. But in this process, the external objects that have enabled thought to occur tend to be seen as participating in the thought process itself. Because they are vital to our conscious life, objects through which we become self-conscious are seen as sharing in that vitality, and even possessing consciousness themselves.

Though we may agree with Jane Bennett, that "we need to cultivate a bit of anthropomorphism ... to counter the narcissism of humans in charge of the world," to "chasten ... fantasies of human mastery," and to develop greater respect for the environment,[40] such political and ethical assertions do little to explain the psychology and persistence of anthropomorphic thought. That the new materialism, like the ontological turn, is idealist in character cannot be doubted, for in both cases the constitutive terms of idealism—subjectivity, mind, thought, will, intentionality— are extended into the world at large. Instead of seeing divinity everywhere, vitality is discerned in all things. Yet both views preserve the notion of mind against a world that is increasingly felt to render our intellectual mastery of it ineffectual. The new materialism is not so much a revelation that matter is ensouled, vibrant, or mindful than a defense against the sheer obduracy and otherness of the material world. Whether it is the degradation of the environment, climate change, or the extinction of species, we react to the unthinkable by deploying the age-old strategy of imagining that the material world is, like the social world, open to negotiation. In their zeal to impute vitality and agency to objects, the new materialists are not so much creating a new paradigm as unwittingly registering the cognitive consequences of thinking through things, as well as our all-too-human tendency to reduce anxieties about our limited capacity to control or comprehend the external world by imagining that it obeys the same rules that govern our intrapsychic and intersubjective existence. But objects obdurately remain objects, regardless of the ways in which we subject them to our thinking; we, as thinking subjects, are so deeply influenced by the world of which we are a part that we too are, to a degree, objects.

That human beings resist the notion that the extra-human is not only beyond their comprehension and control, but only appears to participate in subjectivity, may be understood as a defense against the unresponsiveness of matter in an age when our waning powers to sustain life on earth make this issue more vexed than it has ever been.

5

WORDS AND DEEDS

The word *fire* can't burn down a house.

—Kuranko adage

I begin with the paradox that although we writers and academics set great store by words, many of those whose lives we write about are far less concerned with presenting their experience in the form of either personal stories or explanatory treatises. Just-so stories will be preferred to long-winded accounts of the whys and wherefores of life events, and for those who are more entertained by make-believe stories, the highest value is placed on those that are action-packed and bear no direct resemblance to one's immediate life. The question of our responsiveness to the people whose social worlds we are so curious and concerned about—how we do justice to their ways of life and their priorities when they are so very different from ours—has troubled anthropologists since the early twentieth century when Bronislaw Malinowski asked what kind of "ethnographic magic" can enable an anthropologist "to evoke the real spirit of the natives, the true picture of tribal life."[1] For is it not true that our academic tropes, our key concepts, and our ways with words often function rather like Trobriand spells, which Malinowski was astute enough to see as means of inducing effects, not on barren ground, stormy seas, or an unresponsive neighbor, but on the consciousness of the spell casters, a means of bolstering confidence in what they were doing, focusing their minds, raising their hopes, and encouraging self-restraint in consumption?

Malinowski's emphasis on language as "a mode of action rather than as a countersign of thought"[2] presages Ludwig Wittgenstein's proposition that "one cannot guess how a word functions. One has to *look at* its use and learn from that."[3] If, as Wittgenstein argued, "the deed, the activity, is primary, and does not receive its rationale or justification from any theory we may have of it,"[4] then the gap we sometimes perceive between words and deeds, episteme and techne, or expressive and instrumental functions, is often illusory. As speech act theory shows us,[5] language does things other than describe reality; it changes our experience of reality. So too does silence.

In the following pages, I share some vignettes from my fieldwork that illustrate some of the practical entailments of avoiding speech. In some of these situations, and for some of these people, a culturally learned preference for economy in speaking is clearly present. In other situations, the reasons for not speaking, or for speaking in riddles, are biographical or historical or strategic, though these multiple perspectives are present to different degrees in any given social situation, which is why interpretation in anthropology is never a matter of applying a single model but of exercising choices as to which model among the many available to us is most edifying. Not all anthropologists succumb to the obscurantist tendencies of academic culture, or do so all the time, and, as I hope to show, though a person may choose silence over speech in one setting, he or she may be irrepressibly talkative in another.

Bearing in mind the importance of what Malinowski called "context of situation, let me begin with E. E. Evans-Pritchard's famously frank introduction to the Nuer, where he describes, not without humor, his frustrations in getting his informants to answer his questions.

"Who are you?"

"A man."

"What is your name?"

"Do you want to know my *name*?"

"Yes."

"You want to know *my* name?"

"Yes, you have come to visit me in my tent and I would like to know who you are."

"All right. I am Cuol. What is your name?"

"My name is Pritchard."

"What is your father's name?"

"My father's name is also Pritchard."

"No, that cannot be true. You cannot have the same name as your father."[6]

The *dialogue des sourds* continues until Cuol grows weary of fending off the anthropologist's questions and demands some tobacco.

Evans-Pritchard writes that even the most patient ethnographer would not be able to make headway against this kind of opposition. "One is just driven crazy by it. Indeed, after a few weeks of associating solely with Nuer one displays, if the pun be allowed, the most evident symptoms of 'Nuerosis.'"[7] Nonetheless, a clue to Cuol's uncooperativeness is to be found two pages earlier, when Evans-Pritchard notes that it would probably have been difficult to do fieldwork among the Nuer at any time, but "at the period of my visit they were unusually hostile, for their recent defeat by Government forces and the measures taken to ensure their final submission had occasioned deep resentment."[8] In fact, between 1920 and 1930 the Royal Air Force regularly dropped incendiary bombs to spark bush fires and flush out Nuer warriors, and machine-gunned both Nuer and their cattle from the air.[9]

Cuol's responses to Evans-Pritchard's questions remind us that speech is a form of action, as J. L. Austin argued in *How to Do Things with Words*, and that avoiding speech also has performative power, particularly when loose talk risks placing oneself, and significant others in a vulnerable or perilous position. In the closing chapters of Franz Fanon's *The Wretched of the Earth*, the famous Afro-Caribbean psychiatrist and revolutionary recounts a European policeman's experience of torturing prisoners during the French-Algerian war for independence in the 1950s—an experience that had proved so traumatic that the policeman needed psychiatric care. After expressing mystification as to why prisoners would endure hours of beating, waterboarding, and electrocution rather than talk, the policeman expresses the opinion that this intractability was not fair to the torturers. "You might as well talk to a wall," he complains—a comment that recalls George Devereux's observation that human beings find it difficult to accept that the material world, and sometimes other people, are unresponsive to their overtures. The policeman is less outraged by the brutal consequences of his actions than by the uncooperative and recalcitrant attitude of his victims. If they behave like objects, he seems to be saying, they deserve to be kicked around. But the prisoner is a person, who screams in pain, and dies—and this torments the tormenter, despite the political justifications he gives himself for "just doing his job."

> To all the questions we asked they'd only say "I don't know." Even when we asked them what their name was. If we asked them where they lived, they'd say "I don't know." So of course, we have to go through with it. But they scream too much. At the beginning that made me laugh. But afterward I was a bit shaken ... But above all it's after the electricity that

it becomes really too much … Mind you, we'd like to avoid that. But they don't make things easy for us. Now I've come so as I hear their screams even when I'm at home.[10]

Muteness is sometimes a weapon of the weak. I discovered this quite early on in the year my wife and I lived with an Aboriginal family in the rainforest of Southeast Cape York, Australia. Like Evans-Pritchard, my questions were met with averted eyes, stony silence, or the curt response, "I dunno." Whether asking our hosts how we could improve our fishing skills (since we were largely living off the land), where we should pitch our tent, or why a man had to avoid his mother-in-law, the response was generally evasive. If a view was expressed, it was always conditional. "Might be a good idea not to camp under those bloodwoods." "I don't know if I talk right way or wrong way. If I talk wrong way, well might have to think different way." To some extent this taciturnity and prevarication reflected people's traumatic history of relations with whites. Why open yourself up to the people who had stolen your land, reviled your beliefs, and could not be trusted? Yet this circumspective style of talking was just as evident within the camps, and it quickly became apparent to me that not voicing an opinion was a tactic for avoiding blame if your advice had disastrous consequences. And so we would sit for hours, waiting for someone to suggest we go fishing, or set off on a visit to another camp, as if it was better to do nothing than do something for which you could later be blamed. I should add, however, that the avoidance of talk is prescribed among in-laws, possibly because affines are at once strangers and potential allies. But here again, the repression of speech is a strategy for avoiding ambiguity and misunderstanding in fraught social relationships.

When I began my fieldwork among the Kuranko in 1969 I quickly discovered the value people placed on parsimonious speech. Taming the tongue was a primary metaphor for self-mastery—comparable to enduring pain and controlling one's emotions. Old men would show me their tongues, blistered by the many times they had bitten them rather than blurt out some inappropriate or potentially incendiary remark. Adages I had heard as a child—"silence is golden," "least said, soonest mended"—resonated with the Kuranko view that untamed speech sows dissent while silence repairs relationships and reintegrates the world.[11] It took me many months to learn that when neighbors called on me, talk was not required. Kola nut or a cup of tea might be offered before you sat together in amicable silence. Not only were people uninterested in speculation for its own sake; they were extremely wary of any attempt to second guess a person's inner thoughts or feelings. Sociality demanded circumspection in speech, not uncontrolled self-expression. Whenever I tried to ascertain what a person thought about a particular event, or another person, my interlocutors would declare, "I am not inside them" (*n'de sa bu ro*) or "I do not know what is inside" (*n'de ma konto lon*), thereby reminding me that social opacity was as much of a phenomenological issue for them as it is for us. But despite a preoccupation with the hidden intentions of others, and the ever-present danger of malice and witchcraft in everyday life, Kuranko probably spend less time trying to penetrate the interior recesses of other people's minds than we do, preferring to judge people in terms of how they act toward others, irrespective of what is on their minds or in their hearts. Even an inveterate tattletale can learn to button his lip. Just because you think something, or feel something strongly, you should weigh your words well and be ever mindful of the social repercussions of letting the world know what you are thinking or feeling.[12]

Let me try to capture this attitude in a single anecdote. During fieldwork in 2007–8, I accompanied Sewa Magba Koroma on a visit to the grave of his best friend, cousin, and namesake (*togema*), who had died a year before, not long after graduating from Milton Margai Teacher's College. Sewa Balansama had been in a motorcycle accident and died of complications from internal injuries.

That afternoon, Sewa told me what this friendship had meant to him. "We were the same age. We bore the same name. We went to the same school and were in the same class. We came from ruling houses and had the same code of conduct. When we came to Kabala for high school we were always together. Every evening, strolling up and down the street in Yogomaia. Even our girlfriends were sisters."

Sewa hesitated, as if struggling to find the right word. "He was the quiet one," Sewa said at last. "Intelligent. Perfect in every way."

Sewa was suffering from a swollen throat. His eyes were sore. Perhaps from the Harmattan. Did I have any medicine that might help?

"There is no medicine for grief," I said.

"I have not been so tearful since my son died," Sewa said, alluding to the summer in London when his wife gave birth prematurely. The baby survived only a few hours before his lungs failed.

It was not only these tragedies that oppressed Sewa. That morning he had learned that a Canadian NGO was planning to build its headquarters on the site where his friend was buried. No one had told the Canadians that the place was a graveyard, and they had not bothered to find out. Sewa Balansama's grave was located under the great granite wall of Albitaiya, and we later strolled past the house where he used to live and see his name still painted on the closed wooden shutter of his room.

How hard, I wondered, would it be for me to go back to the house at One-Mile where my first wife and I lived thirty-eight years ago, and find it gone? And would I be able to control my emotions, as Sewa had tried to control his, pretending that his tears had been caused by a viral infection or dust in his eyes?

Over the last few years, my research focus has moved from Sierra Leone to African immigrants in Europe, and my experience of getting to know some of these individuals has brought me back, time and time again, to the contrast between societies characterized by an economical attitude to speech, consumption, and emotional expression, and societies like ours in which loquacity, excess, and extravagance are tolerated, if not approved.

Emmanuel Mulamila grew up in eastern Uganda where his Rwandan father had taken refuge in 1962, together with thousands of other Tutsi fleeing the Hutu revolution. When Idi Amin came to power in 1971, the eastern region resisted, and harbored rebels against his regime. Although Emmanuel's father was apolitical, he was detained by Amin's secret police and murdered in 1979 when Emmanuel was eight. Rather than remain in eastern Uganda and suffer prejudice and persecution, Emmanuel's mother migrated with her children to her natal village in western Uganda, only to discover that they were not wanted there either. This was partly because a woman is supposed to be looked after by her husband's people even if her husband dies, and she has no strong claim on support from her patrikin. But it was also because the refugees were regarded as strangers and a burden on a family already suffering from the effects of a drought in the region. So Emmanuel found himself persona non grata in a place where he did not speak the language and, though he was sent to school, he could not understand what people were saying. His plight was made worse by having to work in the fields before and after school and survive the school day by eating banana peels and sweet potato parings scavenged from the homes of his teachers.

Though a victim of constant verbal abuse and bullying, Emmanuel gradually learned to turn the tables on his persecutors, first by buying them off—giving them items of cutlery and clothing that the family had brought with them from eastern Uganda—and then by distracting them by acting the clown and entertaining them with comical stories. Emmanuel referred to these stratagems as "tricks" and as "building smoke." "I learned to make people laugh," he told me. "That is how

I could survive most of the bullying. Whenever you make fun and people laugh, they'll share bites to eat."

Emmanuel's story of surviving a harrowing childhood is a compelling example of what one can do with words, and it reminds us that our emergence as a species depended on a capacity for what George Steiner calls "counterfactuality"—a performative skill with words and actions that enable us to create and escape into alternative realities. "The uses of language for 'alternity,'" Steiner notes, "for misconstruction, for illusion and play, are the greatest of man's tools by far." For our hominid ancestors, "fiction was disguise: from those seeking out the same water-hole, the same sparse quarry, or meagre sexual chance. To misinform, to utter less than the truth was to gain a vital edge of space or subsistence."[13]

In 2002, Emmanuel immigrated to Denmark to marry a Danish woman he had met in Uganda. His arrival coincided with the adoption, by the recently elected Liberal-Conservative government, of immigration legislation that made it difficult for foreigners, as well as Danish citizens with immigrant backgrounds, to obtain family reunification with non-European spouses. It was against this background of xenophobia that Emmanuel experienced his first inklings of what it would mean to live in Denmark married to a Dane.

Despite being a graduate of a Ugandan university, acquiring fluency in Danish, and completing a second degree at the Copenhagen Business School, all Emmanuel's attempts to find work came to nothing. His resourcefulness, sense of humor, and skill at building smoke were unavailing. When he dropped his Ugandan surname and adopted his wife's name as a ruse to get a job interview, matters became even more complicated. The interviewers had expected a Danish woman—Emma Olsen—not an African man. Despite Emmanuel's attempts to explain the foreshortened version of his first name and the adoption of his wife's surname, he was accused of false pretenses and angrily dismissed.

In 2014, after twelve fruitless years of looking for a job commensurate with his qualifications, Emmanuel decided to study for an International Truck Driver's License. When I visited Copenhagen on that visit, I took my wife to meet Emmanuel, his wife Nanna, and their daughter Alice Maria in their Copenhagen apartment.

After Emmanuel had prepared a dinner of salmon and salad, we sat at the kitchen table, drank to one another's health and listened as Emmanuel told us about his life since I had seen him a year ago. Largely for Francine's sake, Emmanuel related some of the grueling childhood experiences he had once shared with me: harshly caned by teachers, bullied by older students, ostracized by his maternal kin. As a child, Emmanuel had learned to take beatings without flinching, to put on a brave face, to suffer in silence. He acquired the knack of turning himself to stone, dissociating himself from his pain. As a migrant he had also learned what to show and what to hide, how to feign and not give offence, his feelings hidden, his thoughts kept to himself.[14] To criticize such coping strategies in terms of a bourgeois code of sincerity, transparency, and honesty would be absurd, since, for people without power, the skills of stealth, cunning, dissociation, two-facedness, and even trickery become the means of survival—techniques of "building smoke" as Emmanuel put it, of "provocative impotence" to use Sartre's phrase, or "weapons of the weak" as James Scott has it.[15] These are not symptomatic of moral collapse or of a failure to "get a life," since the powerless know only too well that those in power are masters of speaking with forked tongues.

Though Emmanuel knew the risks of being open to strangers, he had nonetheless remained alert to every opportunity that came his way, though carefully assessing each one lest it prove to be another trap, another dead end, another humiliation. When I asked Emmanuel how far he had come with acquiring an international truck driver's license, he said he had passed the Danish exams, and would take the EU exam in a few days. He enjoyed being in command of a powerful truck, seated high above the traffic, a master of his domain. And now that Alice Maria was growing up, it would not be a hardship if he was away from home for several days and nights at a time. There was one obstacle, however, that he was still struggling to get around. A psychologist who worked for his driving school had become curious about him. Sensing that he was far better educated than any of the other trainee drivers, and fluent in Danish despite being a foreigner, she accompanied him on test drives, "prying" into his life and repeatedly asking him questions to which he was prepared to give only minimal answers. Given his experience of doors closed in his face when it was discovered he was African, or "overqualified for the job," or educated at an Islamic university, Emmanuel also feared that if the psychologist learned details of his childhood she would diagnose him as suffering PTSD (post-traumatic stress disorder) or suspect him of planning a terrorist attack. "I kept asking myself, what relevance did her questions have for driving a truck. Did she think I would load it up with explosives and destroy the Danish Parliament? Or was it simply a friendly interest?"

Emmanuel's suspicion of the psychologist's inordinate interest in his personal life echoed the preoccupations of other migrants I had come to know well in the course of my fieldwork in Europe. Like Emmanuel, Ibrahim Ouédraogo had endured extraordinary hardships as a child. He had grown up in a remote Mossi village in the Sahel (Burkina Faso) where his father was chief. Drought made it increasingly difficult to grow crops or feed livestock, and for nine months of the year villagers were surviving on baobab leaves. Many people migrated south, but Ibrahim's father felt obliged to remain in the village that his ancestors had ruled for hundreds of years. Though many of Ibrahim's age mates died of hunger, and death was a constant presence in his life, he was able to get some basic schooling in a nearby village and dreamed of furthering his education and exploring the wider world. As a young man, working in an Ouagadougou hotel, Ibrahim met a Dutch woman touring Burkina Faso and fell in love. And so he came to the Netherlands where he found work delivering mail and, at the time I met him, washing dishes in the Royal Open House.

In 2011, I was staying with Ibrahim and Evelien in their Amsterdam apartment and learning to see Europe through Ibrahim's eyes. One thing that struck me time and time again was his quiet outrage not only at how little most Europeans knew about village life in West Africa but how rarely they reflected on the source of their own wealth and power.

> I would like people here to appreciate and be proud of what they have, but also to be aware of the difficulties of being poor and of getting an education in countries like mine. I think people in Europe should be more satisfied with what they have, and not always thinking how they can be better or get more. They waste too much. It is a consumer society. People consume, consume, consume. Instead of repairing things they throw them away.

That morning, we had breakfasted on brioches and *pain au chocolat* that Ibrahim had brought home from the Royal Opera House. The food items had passed their use-by date and though they were still edible they would ordinarily have been thrown away. There was no way we could eat everything Ibrahim brought home, even though he could not bear to let it go to waste, and the back stairwell of the apartment was piled high with salvaged foodstuffs. This obsessive economizing did not surprise me, for my father was a child of the Great Depression, and as a small boy I had become all too familiar with his habits of eating the leftovers from dinner; hoarding paper bags, pieces of string, jam jars, and tin cans in the belief that "you never know when they might come in handy"; not to mention his do-it-yourself philosophy, realized in his ability to single-handedly build crystal sets, repair radios, make wooden toys and furniture, create compost for his garden, and renovate our house.

My conversations with Ibrahim helped me appreciate the connection between economizing on food, economizing on words, keeping one's feelings under control, and social viability. To eat more than one's fill, hog the conversation, or express one's emotions without inhibition were inimical to the ethos of reciprocity and sharing that lay at the heart of social life. Economizing was not simply a response to scarcity; it was a way of protecting one's social world from the divisive effects of unbridled passions and dissenting views. And while Ibrahim envied Europeans their freedom of speech, their independence of mind, and the value they placed on education, he missed the bonds of family and community that were central to the life he had known in Burkina Faso. In our conversations he kept returning to his critique of Europeans as unable to curb their emotions, endure discomfort, or hold their tongues. Although I was critical of Ibrahim's glib stereotypes of Africans and Europeans and his tendency to universalize his personal experiences, I appreciated the illocutionary force of what he was saying.

One evening, Evelien and Ibrahim took me to a Surinamese restaurant where they had arranged to meet several friends. Over dinner, Ibrahim confided to me that it had taken him a long time to get used to eating out. He could still see no point in accompanying Evelien to a coffee bar and spending six euros on a cup of coffee when they could have coffee at home. I told Ibrahim that Sierra Leonean friends in London often admitted the same misgivings, preferring to spend money on food they could prepare at home rather than pay exorbitant restaurant prices for food that was prepared behind the scenes by strangers. Ibrahim explained that he and Evelien had an allotment outside the city where they grew vegetables in the summer. "I don't trust the food you buy. It doesn't taste like fresh food should."

"There must have been many things you found difficult to get used to when you came to Amsterdam," I said.

Ibrahim was only too happy to provide examples. "I could not understand why Dutch people were always talking," he said. "Talking on the phone, gossiping, talking about themselves, all the time. In Dutch they call it 'having your heart on your tongue.'"

"And here I am, talking too much and making it impossible for you to eat!"

Ibrahim smiled.

"In Burkina it's not good to be too direct," Evelien interjected from across the table. "For example, when Ibrahim and I decided to get married we wanted to avoid any difficulties with the immigration authorities, so instead of filing for a civil marriage we explored the possibilities of a religious marriage. Ibrahim went to the imam of his mosque, and said, 'I know of an African guy who is thinking of marrying a Dutch woman.' And when Ibrahim visits my sister [Evelien's sister had recently been seriously ill in hospital], he sits with her, holding her hand. He doesn't get emotional with her and say everything that's on his mind."

"It is the same in Sierra Leone," I said, thinking of how long it took me to adjust to a form of sociality that required sitting with someone in silence rather than busily baring one's soul, making small talk, or engaging in detailed conversations about abstract matters.

Evelien said, "Ibrahim will ask my friends, 'Are you well? How is your family?' and be amazed at all the personal details they give in response."

"People are always prying into your life," Ibrahim said. "Always asking me what jobs I am doing, whether I like them, how much I earn. It is too much, really."

Feeling somewhat embarrassed by my own barrage of questions, I fell silent, allowing the conversation to follow its own course and giving Ibrahim a chance to feed his daughter Karfo who was sitting in a high chair to his right.

Later, however, as we were eating dessert, Ibrahim returned to the theme of excess. "That is the problem with your society," he said. "You want things straight away. You can't wait. You don't know the meaning of patience. You are like children. You expect endless pleasure and abundance. You do not know how to live with hardship."

"We Europeans cannot defer gratification," one of Evelien's friends said in English.

"And the waste!" Ibrahim said. "The things people throw out. There is enough old furniture thrown out on the street to furnish a small village." Ibrahim paused for a moment, as if silenced by despair. "There are many people who risk their lives to come here," he said. "It is horrible, because when they are in Africa that think of Europe as El Dorado. But it's not. One of my first jobs in Amsterdam was at a restaurant like this. I was surprised to see people ordering food then leaving half of it uneaten on their plates. There were things they did not even touch and were thrown away. It was really, really difficult for me to see this. The first time I saw it, I could not believe my eyes. I wanted to cry, because I knew how it was in my country. Many employees in the restaurants are migrants, like me. They know that if they serve too much food, much of it will be left on the plate. So they serve the minimum. They economize."

"What about the job you have now?"

"It's the same problem. If the expiration date is today, you have to throw that food away. We are not even allowed to give it to the people who work there. Evelien suggested I ask my boss if it would be possible to donate this food to homeless people, but then we realized this might not be a good idea because, in the past, there had been problems with contaminated food. Honestly, it breaks my heart to see this waste. So, without saying anything to my boss, I decided to take the food that had not been touched, and bring it home—the sugar, tea, coffee, pastries that haven't been used, all this saves a lot of money, and gives us things to eat."

"It's not just food," Evelien said. "Ibrahim is intrigued by how quickly people divorce in Holland. He's shocked by how much people expect from a relationship, how little patience people have. Rather than solve their problems together, they'll abandon the relationship."

Everyone was quiet, even contrite, but Ibrahim had not finished.

"People might be well educated," he said, "but they don't use their heads to make life more efficient, to make the most of what they have."

As our conversation continued, I felt increasing uncomfortable with the way in which we had so easily slipped into making the kind of categorical assertions I was so critical of in academe, and I found it difficult to both appreciate the rhetorical function of Ibrahim's sweeping generalizations about Europeans and preserve my view that all identity thinking places us in danger of taking our personal opinions to be faithful representations of a universal reality.

I experienced the same ambivalence when Sewa Koroma shared his experiences of struggling to make ends meet in London. What sustained Sewa were thoughts of home, as if evoking memories of his late father, his natal village, and his happy childhood could compensate for the state of eclipse that made it sometimes impossible for him to see any way ahead in London. He once cited a Kuranko adage: if you move a chicken in the evening from one place to another, it will be agitated all night and only become settled when the new day dawns. After three years in London, Sewa confided, "I am still not settled. So it must still be night."

"What unsettles you?" I asked.

"When I worked in a restaurant," Sewa said, "I hated to see so much food left uneaten and thrown away. I hated to see people stuffing food into their mouths and talking with their mouths full. At home we eat in silence, out of respect for the food, which is always scarce and to be savored."

He mentioned a friend of his from Mali. Some English women asked if he had ever experienced a famine in Mali. Sewa's friend could not answer. He was in tears. Only when he had dried his eyes could he tell them that he had not known what it was to have a full belly until he was twenty. And he described a famine so devastating that he sometimes had to drink cow urine and eat leaves or wet clay to stave off hunger. In London, he found it difficult to watch the garbage trucks picking up furniture and clothing that would be dumped and never used. "In England," Sewa said, "life is a choice between cellphones, what we will wear to work today, which shoes, which shirt. At home we sometimes did not even have a choice between rice and cassava, meat or fish, only between eating enough today or going without tomorrow."

What lessons might we draw from these vignettes for how we write anthropology? Clearly there is a cultural difference between societies of scarcity and societies of abundance. As Herbert Marcuse observed, the rise of mercantile capitalism in Europe produced a bourgeois culture focused on the conspicuous consumption of things and words, coupled with "an idealist cult of inwardness" that generated a discourse disengaged from social life and practical matters, which were seen as definitive of the lower orders.[16] Moreover, the emphasis on accumulating capital, whether in the form of material wealth, renown, or knowledge, diminished the value traditionally accorded labor—the everyday work of making a living and creating a viable society.

Whether we reference Claude Lévi-Strauss's fascination with the unconscious structures of the human mind, Michel Foucault's emphasis on discursive formations, or Eduardo Vivieros de Castro's conflation of thought with being, we see how anthropology echoes bourgeois idealism in its assumption that conceptual thought can not only encompass but transcend lived experience. In this logocentric view, loquacity becomes a sign of sophistication and authority while silence becomes a mark of shame. I hope to have shown not only that economy in speech and explanation may be more compatible with sociality than verbosity and volubility, but also that silence may, as the Kuranko worldview suggests, be often more therapeutic than talk. If, to quote Ishmael in Herman Melville's *Moby Dick*, traditional societies tend not to place "the conceit of attainable felicity" in "the intellect or the fancy, but in the wife, the heart, the bed, the table, the saddle, the fire-side, the country," then it is because the greatest fulfillment in life emerges from one's relations with others rather than oneself alone.[17] Excessive verbalizing is symptomatic of a Western preoccupation with plumbing the depths of one's soul, expressing one's thoughts, and talking things through,[18] whether to appear authentic, protest an injustice, achieve a psychoanalytic cure, or resolve political conflict through dialogue.

In the aftermath of the civil war in Sierra Leone, a very different view was widely held. The UN Special Court, set up to try those responsible for atrocities during the country's decade-long conflict, was seen by many to be a response to Anglo-American demands and a capitulation to Eurocentric notions of justice. But even more compelling was the reluctance of people to talk in public about what they had been through. There were two aspects to this attitude, the first practical, the second psychological and social.

In the refugee and amputee camps, people spoke of washing their hands of the past, not because they could ever forget its horrors, but because they saw less profit in raking over dead coals than in turning their attention to the practical tasks of rebuilding their lives—money to replace a lost license, seed rice to start a farm, fees for schooling, materials to build a house. Besides, they were realists. People were not going to confess to crimes they committed during the war lest they get marked for revenge or arrested and prosecuted.

People's stoicism also reflected their powerlessness to take revenge, their conviction that only an attitude of live and let live would enable them to accept the reality of having ex-rebels in their midst, and a wariness of the consequences of rehearsing in their thoughts or conversations the suffering they had experienced. One old friend put it bluntly:

> Reconciliation, forgiveness, forgetting … these are all relative terms. In Sierra Leone right now, we are letting sleeping dogs lie. You understand? We are fed up with the war. Fed up with atrocities. We simply do not want it to happen again. I have no way of taking revenge on the rebels who took away my livelihood, but at least I can rid myself of them. I can shut them out of my mind. I can expel them from my life.

I was reminded of a passage in Hannah Arendt's *The Human Condition*.[19] Forgiveness implies neither loving those that hate you, nor absolving them of their crime, nor even understanding them ("they know not what they do"). Rather, it is a form of redemption, in which one reclaims one's own life, tearing it free from the oppressor's grasp, and releases oneself from thoughts of revenge and memories of one's loss that might keep one in thrall to one's persecutor forever.

Violence is a form of excess, writes E. Valentine Daniel.[20] But loquacity is a form of excess too that risks doing violence to the very experiences it wants to make sense of. This is why our language must be measured and tempered, rather than used to fill silences, or speak that which the sufferer cannot speak. And this is why we should be as mindful of what words express as what they do, or cannot do, and perhaps take a leaf out of the unwritten book of the people with whom

I have worked in West Africa, for whom dialogue is less important than diapraxis—creating conviviality by eating, working, dancing, and making music together, or simply acknowledging the experience of another human being with a simple gesture, a single word.

𝒥 6

CRITIQUE OF CULTURAL FUNDAMENTALISM

> When the state or quasi-state ... and the self-contained subject ... become coeval models of each other, xenophobic nationalism—which is but human subjectivity totalized—is the result.
> —E. Valentine Daniel, *Suffering Nation and Alienation*

Perhaps at no other time in recent history have the concepts of culture and nationality been so fervently fetishized. Though Benedict Anderson notes that "nation-ness is the most universally legitimate value in the political life of our time,"[1] the same could be said of culture, or of race—a word that "culture" or "ethnicity" simply euphemizes. In emphasizing bounded belonging and safety in numbers, such concepts are, of course, linked to widespread anxieties among marginalized peoples about their ability to grasp and influence the global forces overwhelming their lifeworlds. While globalization has become an empowering myth of the affluent West—where the celebration of market rationalism, information superhighways, and the retributive justice of smart weaponry now complements imperialist myths of manifest destiny and white supremacy—cultural and ethnic identity have become the catchwords for many of those disadvantaged by colonial and postcolonial inequalities in the distribution of power. In emergent notions of cultural identity and national sovereignty, powerless, dispersed, and disparaged peoples imagine that they recapture something of the integrity and authenticity they feel that they have personally lost. "There is no salvation without culture," observed Maina Karanja, a former Mau Mau fighter and now spiritual leader of the Kikuyu Nine Clans (Kenda Muiyuru) sect in Kenya. "If we truly want to be saved we must … go back to our traditional ways."[2] In his poignant ethnographic account of radical social change among the Sora of Southern Orissa, Piers Vitebsky describes how an elderly shaman he had known for forty years, Monosi, expressed the hope that the anthropologist's notes and tapes could be packaged and protected for future generations. Monosi called this data "culture" (using the newly known Oriya word *Sanskruti*).[3]

For Maina Karanja and Monosi, culture promises both personal and collective survival, if not salvation. This point is crucial. Although concepts of culture, race, and nation denote abstract, imagined, and collective subjectivities, their meaning is inextricably connected to the experiences of individual subjects. This does not mean that nationality is "essentially a belief—a deep sense of conviction concerning one's personal identity,"[4] but rather that the national imaginary operates with both "we" and "I" forms.[5] Thus, notions of nationhood draw on images of intimate home life and parental protection, or hold out the promise of personal salvation, significance, and continuity, while simultaneously evoking ideas of belonging that transcend individual subjectivities. This fetishization of the nation may be understood as a totalization of human subjectivity, a process that may lead to empowerment or violence. By fusing the personal and the social, the biographical and the historical, alienated individuals may gain a satisfying sense of solidarity with others. But, as E. Valentine Daniel points out, "the same discursive strategy can produce xenophobic nationalism and racial violence."[6]

Underlying all quests for solidarity and belonging lies an assumption that each person's individual being not only is but must be embedded in collective fields of being that outrun it in both space and time, such that the actions, words, and energies of everyone are consummated in his or her relations with the many. This desire to embed one's own being within some transpersonal matrix of Being helps us understand the functional necessity of such category terms as cosmos, culture, society, world, and genealogy in human thought, as well as the need to know one's origins and one's fate. The search for roots or ancestry, and for ends and afterlives, is less a search for determinate moments when the ego emerges from nothingness or disappears into the void— moments that have no before or after—and more a search for extensions or beginnings in a time and place *before one's own*, and for continuity in a time and place that *outlives and outlasts one's own singular existence*. Stories that link microcosm and macrocosm provide these crossings between the singular and the trans-subjective.

In what follows I focus on the way that identity thinking works out a rough synthesis of individual and iconic subjectivities, such that self comes to be identified with and experienced as coterminous with one's culture, history, race, or nation. My critical aim is, however, twofold. First, I examine the conditions under which such thought becomes destructive. My focus here is on reification—the ways in which general knowledge claims are made on the basis of specific events, and the process of thinking becomes eclipsed by the product it yields—a moral point, an irrefutable argument, a doctrinal conclusion. Bruce Kapferer's observation is pertinent: "Nationalism makes culture into an object and a thing of worship. Culture is made the servant of power."[7] My second aim is to examine the opposite tendency, in which thinking remains a particular and private matter, unable to bridge the gap between the I and the we or negotiate general understandings on the basis of individual experience.

Culture in the Discourse of the Other

Much has been written about the ways in which the culture concept has been substantialized and territorialized within anthropology.[8] My concern here is with the ways in which iconic terms such as culture, race, and nation are deployed among the people with whom anthropologists have customarily worked. Though culture may be said in both cases to sanctify sweeping generalizations based on spurious notions of primordiality, homogeneity, coherence, and timelessness, these modes of identifying and othering tend to differ subtly in academic and indigenous discourse.

At its inception as a science in the late nineteenth century, anthropology borrowed the bourgeois concept of culture from German romanticism, and the history of our discipline during the twentieth century may be seen as a succession of critical revisions in which empirical findings and polemical repositionings have led us to purge our discourse of the idealist connotations of the culture concept. Nowadays, we accept without question that culture is invented as well as inherited, contested as well as received, textual as well as contextual, territorialized as well as deterritorialized, material as well as mental, practical as well as discursive, embodied as well as idealized, high as well as low, local as well as global, and that the difference between tribal societies and modern societies cannot be reduced to a distinction between superstition and science or irrationality and reason, and that knowledge is always tied to historical, ethical, political, and practical imperatives.

It is ironic, however, that as these deconstructions of the culture concept were taking place within anthropology, there was a substantive conceptual shift among political conservatives toward a xenophobic rhetoric of cultural fundamentalism that excludes immigrants and foreigners from the European nation-state, while at the same time many of the people among whom anthropologists traditionally worked embraced the idea of culture and begun using it, also in an essentialistic, exclusionary sense, for their own counter-hegemonic ends. As anthropologists repudiated place-based notions of culture and explored "post-culturalist" positions,[9] many indigenous peoples became "deeply involved in constructing cultural contexts which bear many resemblances to such cultural entities."[10]

In Australia, Aboriginal activists have adopted the culture concept to denote a venerable and unique "spiritual" heritage, tied to land, language, and collective identity, and encapsulated in the notion of the Dreaming. In Aotearoa (New Zealand), many Maori speak of their culture in a similar vein as *taonga* (treasure)—a sacred heritage that has survived the brutality of conquest and colonial rule. And throughout Melanesia and Micronesia, culture—in the symbolic form of *kastom*— has become central to the counter-colonial discourse of identity. In all these cases, we are dealing with abstract and ambiguous terms— Aboriginality, Maoritanga, *kastom*—whose appeal lies less in their correspondence to any objective reality than in their strategic value for mediating private and public realms. The culture concept thus functions like a ceremonial mask, bringing together idiosyncratic and abstract features in a single gestalt.

One sees this clearly in many of the stories submitted to the National Inquiry into the Separation of Aboriginal and Torres Strait Islander Children from Their Families. In some instances, the story of losing one's mother and one's birthright is experienced as a "wound that will not heal" or a hole that cannot be filled—"something missing" that makes a person "an empty shell."[11] As one witness noted: "I wish I was blacker. I wish I had a language. I wish I had a culture."[12] In other stories, however, reunion with one's lost birth mother presages the recovery of a general sense of cultural belonging.[13] As one person put it, "For the first time I actually felt like I had roots that went down into the ground. But not only into the ground—that went through generations."[14] Another observed, "I started taking interest in Koori stuff. I decided at least to learn the culture."[15] After meeting her mother and family for the first time, Jeanette Sinclair said she found it easier to identify as an Aboriginal.

I had somewhere I belonged. That was really great and it was like that hole you walked around with had been totally filled. The first time I went back, that's what it was like although I realise now it can never be really filled in. Ninety per cent of the hole can be filled in but I think you are always missing that ten per cent. That's just my personal opinion. You can never get the ten per cent back because you missed out on the bonding, the fondling and the cuddling. Also you've missed out on building relationships over a period of time; you can't create a relationship out of thin air.[16]

Such comments reflect wishful thinking as well as a sober sense of reality. The romantic yearnings indicate the magical power of cultural fundamentalism to bolster the hope of *communitas* in a fragmented world. But not only do these stories document the ways in which childhood flight from the culture of one's adoption—expressed in unassuageable longings to be with one's original family, in fantasies of family reunion and of rescue, and in running away from home— they presage a political repudiation of the dominant culture. Indeed, it may be that because the National Inquiry was nationally publicized that stories of personal grief occasionally took on this kind of ethnic and political edge, the logic being that in negating the culture that negated you, you magically affirmed your true birthright, your original being.

What is interesting about this mode of affirmation is its subtle shift of emphasis from a specific biographical situation to the situation of Aboriginal people in general.

I think compensation for me would be something like a good land acquisition where I could call my own and start the cycle of building good strong foundations for Aboriginal families.[17]

I've learned skills in my life but I have never lost sight of the fact that I'm an Aborigine first and foremost. That is why I am working in the Aboriginal Medical Service. I've finished my training, I'm very proud of that. I've achieved something. I wanted my poor old mother to be so proud of me ... I wanted her to know and to understand why I'm working with my people.[18]

It is in this generalizing of subjectivity from self to society, this shift from personal story to shared history, that a political discourse begins to emerge—a progression that Ghassan Hage speaks of as one from "homely" to "sovereign" belonging.[19] Indeed, when one compares the stolen children stories published by Coral Edwards and Peter Read in 1989 with the testimonies and stories told before the National Inquiry in 1997 there is a noticeable increase in the degree to which Aboriginal people frame personal experiences in political terms—a reflection both of the way in which the issue of the stolen generation entered public and national consciousness in the intervening years and of the extent to which many of the "stolen generation" moved from addressing their own separation and loss to helping others deal with theirs.[20] But generally speaking, the stories told to the National Inquiry are stories that remain collapsed in privacy—a function, partly, of the Inquiry itself, which needed tragic stories to make its case for social justice, and partly of the marginality of Aboriginal people in Australia, where land rights, recognition, and sovereign belonging are still to be achieved. As one witness put it, "all we've got is sort of ourselves."[21]

Us and Them

In order to explore the culture concept in its most iconic and essentialized form, consider the following story from Aotearoa (New Zealand). Drawn from a popular magazine, the story concerns a young Maori couple who, like many other young Maori, have revived traditional Maori facial tattoo (*moko*) as a way of affirming their cultural identity.

Most married couples show their commitment to each other by wearing wedding bands but Bay of Plenty husband and wife Chris and Taukiri Natana have more obvious symbols of their love. The pair, from Ruatoki, have *moko* on their faces. They say that, as well as empowering them in their fight for Maori sovereignty and strengthening their link with family and ancestors, the *moko* signifies their unity as a couple.

"To me, the *moko* is showing who you are; what culture you are; what you believe in," says Chris. "Just as other cultures wear a ring around their finger to represent their unity, this represents our unity, our oneness, on our faces. It's been drilled there to stay."[22]

Chris Natana's comments help us understand that as a cultural icon, *moko* implies a nesting set of identifications, encompassing personal and transpersonal frames of reference. At one extreme *moko* symbolizes a set of unities—of the couple, of the family, of the *iwi*, and of Maori—at the other extreme, it symbolizes a distinction between Anglo-Celtic and Maori culture. In fact, it was this implication that most concerned the parents of the young Maori couple, who argued that it would be seen as "confrontational and threatening."

However, the question I want to broach is less concerned with these symbolic strategies for achieving unity despite difference (the exchange of rings and *moko* that weld, as with the classical *symbolon*, two halves or hearts into one) and more concerned with the potentially divisive and reified polarities that these strategies make use of. While the aim of invoking cultural identity may be to transform old hierarchies of dominance and subordination into new egalitarian social alignments, this is seldom all that occurs. Just as European bourgeois notions of culture tend to imply what Roy Wagner calls an "opera-house"[23] conception of civilized sensibilities that stand in contrast with and bring into relief a notion of plebian taste or "popular" culture, so current uses of the term "culture" in Australia, Melanesia, and the Pacific tend to iconicize tradition as superior to modernity. The result of invoking culture is not therefore an ironing out of difference in the name of some notion of common humanity, but the radical inversion of existing inequalities. As Frantz Fanon pointed out, decolonization inevitably entails a "complete and absolute substitution"—a radical reordering of the world in which the last become the first and the first become the last.[24] Thus, in Australia, many Aboriginal activists use quantitative European chronology rather than indigenous mythology to emphasize the length of time that Aboriginal people have inhabited the continent. The image of 40,000+ years of continuous settlement then underwrites ideologies about the depth of people's spiritual relationship with the country, the antiquity of art and ritual, and the primordial power of Aboriginal values. In Aotearoa (New Zealand), many Maori also use firstness as a powerful rhetorical figure—an expression of what Liisa Malkki calls "romantic autochthonization."[25] Maori are *tangata whenua*, people of the land, having settled the country one thousand years before pakeha—non-Maori people—arrived. The primordial, venerable character of indigenous culture then gives force to the essentializing argument that Maori people are wiser than pakeha, more eco-sensitive, more caring in their family lives, more attuned to community than to self. As Maori activist Kathie Irwin puts it: "Pakeha culture, derived as it is from Western civilization, is primarily concerned with the rights of the individual. Maori society is primarily concerned with the rights of the group, which provide the context within which the rights of the individual are considered."[26]

Hearing such polarizing generalizations, liberal pakeha sometimes accuse Maori of "reversed racism," which it is not, at least as long as the discourse is not at the service of power elites but remains a rhetoric of the powerless struggling to regain some sense of *turangawaeawe*, autonomy and self-determination, in a country where historically they have been made second-class citizens. The word "racism," like the term "rape," refers to violently asymmetrical situations in which the strong dominate the weak; the terms simply do not apply in reverse. Still, I want to ask whether this kind of iconic othering and cultural fundamentalism—"strategic essentialism"[27] as Naomi Schor and Elizabeth Weed call it—is in fact compatible with reconciliation and pluralism.

My feeling is that any kind of identity thinking is insidious because, like all reification, it reduces the world to simplistic, generalized category oppositions such as Us versus Them that become an obstacle to interactions based on common human concerns. Always defensive and idealistic—as is all magical thought—it resists empirical testing, fearing that the complexity of lived experience will confound its premises. This is why I want to propose that when popular thought promulgates naturalized and localized definitions of identity, anthropologists must place this essentializing strategy in historical perspective and social context and guard against adopting it themselves. Before elaborating further on anthropology's role in "denaturalizing identity,"[28] let me critically review a second case of identity thinking in contemporary Aotearoa (New Zealand).

In an article on immigration policies in New Zealand, published in 1995, Ranginui Walker observes that according to the second clause of the Treaty of Waitangi, the Crown guaranteed the "sovereign rights" of chiefs over "their lands, homes and treasured possessions."[29] On this basis, the High Court of New Zealand found in October 1987 that the government's Fisheries Management System breached customary Maori fishing rights under the Treaty. Subsequent negotiations between the treaty partners—Maori and the Crown—ended in settlement. Ignoring the division and dissent that actually plagued this case, Walker argues that this kind of negotiation between equal partners should be seen in "all fields of human endeavour" in Aotearoa.[30] But it has conspicuously not been applied in the field of immigration policy, where the Crown has decided unilaterally to admit 25,000 immigrants a year from ninety-seven countries around the world. Although under Article 1 of the Treaty, immigrant intakes are a Crown responsibility and do not require consultation with Maori in every case, Walker argues that the "original charter for immigration into New Zealand is in the Preamble of the Treaty"[31] and limits immigration to the countries of Europe, Australia, and the United Kingdom. Any deviation from this agreement requires consultation with Maori—a stricture reinforced by the Human Rights Commission. It is biculturalism, not multiculturalism, that New Zealand needs.[32] However, Walker says, there appears to be collusion between corporate business interests and the Crown to use immigration to counter "the Maori claim to first-nation status as *tangata whenua* (people of the land)."[33] As *tangata whenua*, Walker argues, Maori have "prior right of discovery and millennial occupation of the land" and are not therefore immigrants in the same sense that non-Maori are and should not be compared (as they are, incidentally, in recent books by two pakeha academics— Anne Salmond and James Bellich) with the Europeans who colonized the country under force of arms in the mid-nineteenth century or the Pacific Rim migrants of the postwar period. Moreover, as *tangata whenua*, Maori have the right to reject migrants from any culture or nation that is not specified in the Treaty they signed with the British Crown in 1840. Specifically, this means Asian-born migrants, whose number almost doubled in size from 6.6 percent in 2001 to 11.8 percent in 2013. Particularly abhorrent to Walker is the way in which New Zealand citizenship has been commoditized and Asians welcomed to New Zealand simply because they bring capital into the country. The effect of this policy will be to marginalize poor and unskilled Maoris, to increase Maori unemployment, and to produce a neocolonial situation in which the country's assets, resources, and land are sold— like citizenship—to foreigners.[34]

I concede that Walker's intention is not, like Pauline Hanson's in Australia, to demonize wealthy Asians, though the designation itself is inaccurate and pejorative. Nonetheless, everything about Ranginui Walker's article conspires to reinforce non-negotiable distinctions based on culture, history, wealth, and ethnicity. While the distinctions purport to be ways of protecting Maori interests and our Treaty partnership, they leave little room for revising our views as to who and what are foreign and antithetical to New Zealand. Though Walker's avowed concern is with "wealthy Asians," his Treaty-based argument for deciding who can and cannot be admitted to New Zealand effectively excludes a vast proportion of global humanity, including poor Asians from Vietnam, Laos and Cambodia, as well as recently arrived refugees from such troubled countries as Iraq, Somalia, and Afghanistan. Indeed, Walker uses the Treaty in bad faith—as a historically sacrosanct charter for deciding which potential migrants to New Zealand are compatible with Maori cultural interests, and which are inimical—since he admits that the Treaty has already undergone "deconstruction" and hermeneutic renegotiation as a result of Waitangi Tribunal hearings, and has now clarified the meaning of Maori sovereignty *not as it was understood by the Crown in 1840* but as it is necessary for New Zealanders building a bicultural partnership in the late twentieth century.[35]

Using culture ethnocentrically and essentialistically is always problematic; it always entails demarcation, denial, division, and exclusion, and as such, visits the danger of inhumanity and intolerance upon us. Multiculturalism may redraw the line to include more people than were hitherto included—as Te Papa, the national museum of New Zealand, shows with its displays that incorporate Pakeha, Pacific Island, Chinese, Maori, and European peoples as part and parcel of "our place"—but as long as culture is invoked as the discursive means of drawing and redrawing boundaries, vast areas of human experience and reality are going to be suppressed, abolished, and ostracized. And always one will be haunted, for good historical reasons, by the possibility that culture will extend itself logically, through a "horripilation," as E. Valentine Daniel calls it, born of its perennial insecurity and fright, into an ideology of nationhood built around notions of true belonging and true believing that demand as a condition of these truths that those who do not belong, those who do not believe, those who are outside the truth, be exterminated as threats to the nation's integrity.

Thinking Ourselves beyond the Nation

Let me now pursue this pragmatist critique of culture by exploring some recent anthropological research on social suffering in which the language of cultural essence and national identity is annulled.[36] As Hannah Arendt observes, people who have endured extreme pain, speak of its particularity, its unsharability, and its resistance to language.[37] Pain reduces a person to his or her visceral bodiliness. One's whole being is subtracted from one's ordinary personality, identity, and routines, even from the family and friends that defined one's intersubjective world. One becomes merely a vulnerable body-self that either functions or does not, that either lives or dies, depending on forces outside one's control, and despite one's worth, wealth, or cultural identity. Pain makes questions of identity trivial, as Maja Povrzanovic notes of the Yugoslavian war. While the "grammar" of nationalism figured significantly in the discourse of international commentators and national leaders, the "forgotten majority" of civilians were struggling "to defend not primarily their 'national territory' but the right to continue their lives in terms of gender, occupation, class, or place of residence *and not be reduced to their national identities.*"[38] One is reminded of E. Valentine Daniel's observation about torture victims: "At this level of experiencing pain it appears that one is unlikely to find any significant effect of culture."[39]

Ranginui Walker privileges the politics of cultural identity over all other ways of thinking about human imperatives, experiences, and rights. This is not because he is hard-hearted or indifferent to the personal plight of immigrants and refugees; it is because he shares the conservative view—albeit for non-right-wing reasons—that a discourse built around solidary, centralizing notions such as culture, nationhood, and identity better serves political ends than a discourse focused on personal pain, confusion, and rootlessness. While the former promotes collective transcendence, the latter lapses into subjectivity, and too easily individuates and psychologizes the phenomenon of loss. But there is evidence that diaspora and social suffering may indeed provide the critical environment in which new and vital forms of pluralism emerge. Thus, it is interesting that many urban Maori—children of the urban migrations of the 1950s and 1960s: "people of the four winds" (*nga hau e wha*)—have repudiated *iwi*-centered notions of identity, solely constructed around the icons of land, genealogy, and language.[40] Disempowered and disaffected though they may be, many young Maori refuse to see Maoritanga as their salvation; indeed, they regard such "cultural" trappings as abstract, artificial, antiquated, and irrelevant.[41] What they seek is not an identity but a life.

Some of the most compelling evidence for the *dépassement* of nation and culture comes from studies of refugees. Consider the case of recent Tamil refugees in the United Kingdom. Before the civil war in Sri Lanka, Tamil immigrants and expatriates in Britain set great store by their cultural heritage, their national history, and their language. For the last wave of migrants, however—mainly refugees and asylum-seekers—the contrary is true. These people are "nation-averse"; they have "opted out of the project of the nation."[42] While previous generations of Tamil immigrants emphasized a "land-bound" notion of nationhood, the last wave have given up on solid boundaries and claims to territory, either at home or in the United Kingdom; the future, for them, is fluid—a matter of strategic opportunism and constant movement. "You ask me about Tamil nationalism," one refugee said to E. Valentine Daniel. "There is only Tamil internationalism"—by which he meant moving about the globe, seizing whatever opportunities arose, taking whatever initiatives one could to survive. There is no going back. "The only past they knew or cared about—and did not want to be caught in—was the recent past of war, rape, torture, and death that they had just escaped."[43] Daniel speaks of a "disaggregation of identity," a "diaspora of the spirit," an indifference to the very idea of the nation-state, reflective of the way Tamils now participate in a world of shared suffering rather than cultivate a belief in a common homeland or history. Daniel's findings may be compared to those of Ann-Belinda Steen Preis, who has made an intensive study of the videotapes in circulation among Sri Lankan Tamil refugees in the West. Struck by the fact that these videos do not project any unified, standard image of Tamil culture,

Steen Preis makes use of Daniel Sibony's argument that "in the current malaise of identity, both subjective and collective, where boundaries vacillate and identity sometimes collapses, sometimes condenses, the idea of difference is no longer satisfactory to account for this stir; it is too simple and too congealed." Empirically, one confronts "globally unfolding 'mutations' of identity" or a "myriad of bolting identities" in which territorialized notions of culture, having become untenable, are replaced by open-ended questions of belonging, broached through seemingly contradictory images of dispersal and reunion, continuity and discontinuity, attachment and loss.[44] These studies suggest that the marginalization of "culture" in migration literature as irrelevant or ideological may thus reflect a marginalization of the concept in migrant experience itself.

"There's no such thing as 'England' anymore," declared a young white reggae fan in "the ethnically chaotic neighbourhood of Balsall Heath in Birmingham."

> This is the Caribbean! ... Nigeria! ... There is no England, man. This is what is coming. Balsall Heath is the center of the melting pot, 'cos all I ever see when I go out is half-Arab, half-Pakistani, half-Jamaican, half-Scottish, half-Irish. I know 'cos I am [half Scottish/half Irish] ... who am I? ... Tell me who I belong to? They criticize me, the good old England. Alright, where do I belong? You know, I was brought up with blacks, Pakistanis, Africans, Asians, everything, you name it ... who do I belong to? ... I'm just a broad person. The earth is mine.[45]

I now turn to two Central African examples of what Barbara Myerhoff has called "accidental communitas."[46] In her research among Hutu refugees in rural Western Tanzania, Liisa Malkki draws a contrast between refugees in the camps and those who dispersed and settled in and around the township of Kigoma on Lake Tanganyika. While the camp refugees defined themselves as a nation in exile, recollecting "traces and afterlives"[47] in order to nurture their dream of returning to a homeland where they truly belonged, the "town refugees" sought ways "of assimilating and manipulating multiple identities—identities derived or 'borrowed' from the social context of the township." This engendered a cosmopolitan, creolized sense of self that celebrated its adaptiveness and "impurity." Concludes Malkki, "deterritorialization and identity are intimately linked.[48] But equally critical to this link is social suffering and the struggle to survive.

Consider the multiplex and opportunistic world of the modern African city. Academic or ideological antinomies of tradition and modernity, or of synthesis or syncretism, fail to cover the empirical complexity of life in such lifeworlds. In Kinshasa, for example, strategies of adaptation and the ethos of community reflect the quotidian struggle against poverty and crime, and cannot be understood in terms of external concepts such as Europeanization, Zaireization (through the state-sponsored *Recours à l'authenticité* [Recourse to Authenticity]), Traditionalism, or even a combination of these terms. If there is any symbol that unites the disparate domains of household, market, street, church, and politics, it is maternal[49]—an icon that immediately recalls the symbolic centrality of the Madonna among poor Italian migrants to the New World. As Robert Orsi notes in his seminal work on the everyday religious life of Italian migrants in East Harlem, domus and neighborhood were "the source of meaning and morals." Indeed, "These people could not understand the proud italianità of Italian Harlem's middle-class immigrant professionals who had managed to find some identification with the Italian nation. *The immigrants did not know an Italian nation—they only knew the domus of their paesi.*"[50]

What is at play in these multiethnic contexts are the exigencies of survival, not ideology. Quotidian life involves a kind of perpetual bricolage in which whatever is at hand is taken up, tried out, rejected, or put to use in order to cope, and in order to endure. As with people in crisis anywhere, life is ad hoc, addressed anew each day, pieced together painfully, with few consoling illusions. To get through the day, or through the night until morning, little or no thought is given to what is true, meaningful, or correct in any logical or ideological sense; one's focus is on what works, on what is of use, on what helps one survive. Under such circumstances, cultural and national identity, imagined or imminent, are, as Orsi notes above, luxuries the poor cannot afford.

I do not want to make a case for cosmopolitanism over nationalism; both may be effective, if magical, strategies for coping with powerlessness. Neither do I want to argue that a people's degree of suffering or dispersal may always explain why they abandon territorialized notions of identity. But though we cannot confidently pin down the determinants of alternative refugee responses to loss we can evaluate their consequences.

I have argued that cultural fundamentalism, whether nostalgic or utopian, risks setting groups off one from the other on the basis of differential rights that reflect different origins, essences, and aspirations. The result may be that refugees—the last-arrived, the least-powerful, and most lost—are made victims of secondary colonialism. In Aotearoa (New Zealand), for example, so absorbed have Maori and the Crown become in creating the apparatus and protocols of a bicultural State, that habits of radical othering, disempowerment, disparagement, and prejudice—once directed toward indigenous people—are fast becoming projected onto new migrants, whose voices of protest and claims for cultural recognition and respect often go unheeded and heard. "Why do you wear your national costume in public places?" an Anglo neighbor recently asked a Somali migrant. "For the same reason you do," the Somali replied. "But we don't," retorted the neighbor. But of course we do, and it is only our blindness to the way in which cultural symbols are caught up in discriminatory power relations that permits such a question to be asked. Like clothes, cuisine, speech, and belief, skin color frequently focuses this unspoken sense of refractory difference. Radhika Mohanram, a Tamil-New Zealander, states it powerfully: "The black immigrant disturbs the biracial Maori-Pakeha body by revealing the hierarchy of bodies. In this hierarchy, Pakeha come first, Maori second, and the black immigrant a distant third."[51] In secondary colonialism, the denigrated third becomes a scapegoat for both the erstwhile subaltern (the Maori) and the erstwhile elite (pakeha).

It is, however, the experience of the least powerful and of the most marginal—people like refugees—who may define the very grounds on which a pluralistic (rather than a multicultural) society can be created and provide our most trenchant criticism of the language of cultural and national identity.

In contemporary Britain, people of "mixed race" (the very term is a pleonasm) are fast becoming the rule rather than the exception. Sebastian Naidoo, whose father is South African Indian and whose mother is white and British, is not untypical of this exasperated generation. Presented with questionnaires that require one to specify one's ethnic identity, Sebastian sometimes checks "Indian," sometimes "Other," but once "I just scrawled 'human' over the whole lot. I wanted to make fun of their questions and show them how arbitrary their racial categories were."[52] The same problem of identity thinking arises in cross-cultural marriages. Of one such marriage—between a Romanian-born Jew and a Hindu—the Indian wife commented, "I don't see cultural differences; I can only see him." Another British-born woman married to an Australian-born Chinese husband spoke in a similar vein: "In day-to-day life we tend to think that 'my perspective is my perspective,' it has nothing to do with race or culture. I hope our children will be interested in both cultures and get the best of both worlds."[53]

The problem with identity terms and collective nouns such as culture, nation, race, or tribe is the same problem that inheres in any discursive strategy that seeks to convert subjects of experience into objects of knowledge. Such strategies are inevitably reductive. In transmuting the open-endedness and ambiguity of lived experiences into hermetic and determinate items of knowledge, persons tend to become epiphenomenal instances, examples, or expressions of reified categories. The truth is, however, that it is the phenomenal interplay between persons and such categories—between the confusion and flux of immediate experience on the one hand, and finite forms and fixed ideas on the other—that constitutes the empirical reality of human life and should constitute the object of anthropological inquiry. This is why I insist that culture be seen as an idiom or vehicle of intersubjective life, but not its foundation or final cause. Though this view echoes the conclusions of writers like Arjun Appadurai, who see the task of contemporary ethnography as the "unraveling of a conundrum: what is the nature of locality as a lived experience in a globalized, deterritorialized world?"[54] I do not think the resolution of this conundrum can come from simply demonstrating the ways in which the cultural imaginary is conditioned by global forms of electronic media and mass migration unless they are seen, like culture itself, as specific instances of an intersubjective dialectic that has, from time immemorial and in countless societies, reflected the human struggle to strike a balance between autonomy and anonymity, so that no one person or class ever arrogates agency so completely to itself that others are reduced to the status of mere things, or creatures of circumstance. Every person demands, as a condition of being human, that he or she have some say over his or her own existence, some place in the world where his or her actions count. Despite the impinging or competing demands of others, and the overwhelming force of that which simply happens to us without our cognizance or choice, each of us expects to call some of the shots, to resist being merely a piano key moved by the will of others or the inscrutable workings of fate, and move as an equal among equals, in a world that is felt to be as much one's own as it is beyond oneself.

✵ 7

EXISTENTIAL SCARCITY AND ETHICAL SENSIBILITY

> If we really want to understand the moral grounds of economic life and,
> by extension, human life [we must start with] the very small things; the
> everyday details of social existence, the way we treat our friends, enemies,
> and children—often with gestures so tiny (passing the salt, bumming a
> cigarette) that we ordinarily never stop to think about them at all.
> —David Graeber, *Debt: The First 5,000 Years*

In the summer of 1966, having completed my master's coursework
at the Department of Anthropology at the University of Auckland,
I was eking out a living as a cleaner and gardener but hoping for
a junior teaching position that would give me access to a university
library and enable me to begin research on my MA dissertation. I
had already decided on my topic. Inspired by Marshall McLuhan's
Gutenberg Galaxy and his argument that new technologies of
communication generate new mindsets and sensibilities that have
radical repercussions for human social life, I planned to research
the impact of literacy in early nineteenth-century New Zealand in
order to better understand the Maori fascination with literacy in the
decade between 1830 and 1840 and the radical disenchantment with
reading and writing that followed colonization. Theoretically, I did
not know how this project would connect with my passion for French
structuralism, which dated from 1964 when I stumbled upon Claude
Lévi-Strauss's *Elementary Structures of Kinship* while working with the
United Nations in the Congo and decided to return to university to

study anthropology through fieldwork in Africa. Having witnessed firsthand the violent effects of the Cold War in Central Africa, I had become skeptical of the ideology of aid and development, and instead of working to change indigenous peoples, I wanted to undergo a change in my own thinking by immersing myself in their lifeworlds on their terms. This notion of disengaging or distancing oneself from one's own lifeworld in order to engage directly with another is, of course, the essence of the ethnographic method. For Emmanuel Levinas, it involves a journey and an awakening (*l'éveil*) in which one does not so much discover the core of oneself within but is carried beyond oneself and reborn in union with another.[1]

The assumption here is that trading places and switching roles is not only potentially edifying, it reflects an intrinsic human capacity that we might regard as proto-ethical. Whether expressed as empathy, mimicry, or reciprocity, the proto-ethical arises from intersubjectivity and "dyadic consciousness"[2]—the sense of ourselves that is shaped by our responsiveness to the other,[3] the other's reciprocal responsiveness to us, and our ceaseless comparing of our own situation with the situation of others that leads us to ask why there are such profound differences not only between the appearances and customs of human beings but between their fortunes, fates, and qualities of life. If these inequalities are neither natural, nor divinely preordained, then one might ask why some should flourish and others suffer; whether, despite cultural and personal differences, it behooves us as members of the same species to redistribute the wherewithal of life in ways that alleviate the suffering of the have-nots even if this means the enforced redistribution of the possessions of those that have. There are times when we exaggerate our differences from others, calling them cockroaches, vermin, animals, or mere things while retaining for ourselves alone the designation "human." At other times, we recoil from the idea that we are more deserving than others, and we assume ethical responsibility for their welfare as though they were ourselves in other circumstances. This quandary is spelled out in *Genesis*, where Cain is a tiller of the ground, and Abel a keeper of sheep. Cain offers a portion of his harvest to God; Abel offers the firstlings of his flock and the fat thereof. God accepts Abel's sacrifice but ignores Cain's. In a fit of jealousy, Cain kills his brother. To God's question, "Where is thy brother Abel?" Cain responds, "Am I my brother's keeper?" thereby broaching one of humanity's first existential dilemmas: do we have a responsibility to care for and protect others? And where, if anywhere, do we draw the line between those we are obliged to look after and those we are not?

Let me quickly return to the summer of 1966 when, having passed my MA exams with flying colors, I found myself passed over for the teaching positions on offer, all of which went to others in my cohort. As I scraped grease from the stainless steel surfaces of a fast food kitchen or pulled weeds in a Remuera garden, I felt that Dame Fortuna had deserted me. But not long before Christmas I got wind of a Department of Anthropology that had been established at Victoria University of Wellington, headed by a Dutch anthropologist called Jan Pouwer who had done fieldwork in Papua New Guinea and was an ardent structuralist. I phoned Professor Pouwer immediately, explaining my background and plans, and asking if there were any teaching positions open in his department. Unfortunately, Professor Pouwer had already hired a junior lecturer, but he invited me to come see him if I was ever in Wellington, which I did that January on my way to visit my girlfriend in the South Island. That Jan and I hit it off had a lot to do with our shared enthusiasm for structural analysis, but I was also charmed by his ebullience, uninhibited by his deafness and awkwardness with English, and when I went on my way he expressed regret that he was not able to offer me work. Three weeks later everything changed. The husband of the woman that Jan had hired as a junior lecturer committed suicide. He happened to have been in the same geography master's program as my brother-in-law, and so I heard at firsthand how he had walked out of a class and leaped to his death from the top floor of the Easterfield Building on Kelburn Parade. His distraught widow immediately resigned her teaching position in the Department of Anthropology and returned home to Australia, leaving Jan Pouwer to find a replacement at short notice. I unexpectedly became the beneficiary of this woman's tragedy. Her loss had become my gain. In a curious way my fate was now connected to hers, despite the fact that we would never meet and I would never know her name. Yet in the years that followed, I would often be brought to ponder the ethical questions that arise from this kind of accidental changing of places or reversals of fortunes.

These questions are often inchoate, rather than fully articulated. They are felt rather than spelled out. In as much as they are concerned with right and wrong, they are ethical feelings, but because they do not necessarily lead one to act on them and because they cannot be readily reduced to moral or legal codifications, it is difficult to know how imperative they are. Clearly, moral and legal codes do not cover every human situation, and there are circumstances when one will be forgiven for "getting around" the law or "taking the law into one's own hands." In other words, what we know full well to be a moral imperative (thou shalt not kill; one should treat others as ends, not means) or to be illegal (invading the territory of another sovereign state or crossing an international border without a valid visa) may, under certain circumstances, be felt to be justified. Whence does this feeling of rightness or justice come from if not from the moral and legal codes that one internalizes in the course of socialization in a particular culture or faith? Slavery was once legal, and convention found no moral fault in buying, selling, and working to death people who were assumed to be mere beasts or chattels. Yet there were exceptions to the norm—people who not only felt slavery to be abominable but acted to ban it. Although colonialism was predicated on a similarly benighted view that so-called primitive people had no rights to the lands they inhabited and could be dispossessed or murdered without moral qualms or legal impediment, the history of colonialism includes the names of men and women who felt these assumptions were wrong. There is often, it would seem, a split or tension between abstract moral and legal systems and an intuitive, unsystematic, emotional sense of right and wrong that derives from a consciousness of our common humanity. The Danish ethicist K. E. Løgstrup's calls these spontaneous, unconditional, and non-conformist expressions of compassion toward another "sovereign expressions of life." Not only do they eclipse any consideration of the cost to oneself, they derive neither from espoused moral principles nor can they be instrumentalized and generalized after the fact as moral norms or categorical imperatives. Such actions are both free and ethical, Løgstrup argues, because they are not wholly determined by moral rules.[4] Such spur-of-the-moment acts of courage, kindness, selflessness, or mercy are all expressions, so to speak, of an ethics before ethics. "The sovereign expression of life precedes the will," Løgstrup writes. "Its realization takes the will by surprise. It is one of those offerings in life which, to our good fortune, preempt us."[5]

This view has proved edifying in my research among migrants who cross international borders illegally and whose recourse to deception, cunning, and disguise in defying police and border guards is justified on the grounds that these transgressions reflect a quest for life against death—a quest that transcends considerations of the moral and legal codes of particular nation-states. Deprived of the possibility of life in their countries of origin—either through civil war, political persecution, or dire poverty—the migrant feels ethically justified in searching for the wherewithal of life somewhere else, regardless of the laws that define that place as exclusively the home of its legitimate citizens.[6]

Natural Justice

Even before I embarked on research among migrants, my fieldwork in northern Sierra Leone and my fascination with storytelling as a form of ethical conversation, led me to questions of natural justice—the often inchoate sense we have of right and wrong that finds expression in a small child's sense of fairness,[7] an athlete's sense of fair play, and a sense that we owe the world something in return when it has blessed us with good fortune or that the world owes us a life worth living when we have been born into poverty or suffering.

Michel Serres argues that before there is a social contract there is a "natural contract of symbiosis and reciprocity"[8] that finds expression in our sense that however much nature gives us, we must give that much back in return. While most social tracts, such as the Declaration of the Rights of Man, constitute citizens of one's own state as legal subjects, and exclude those beyond the pale of reason—so-called savages, the insane, women, criminals, aliens, and animals—the natural contract encompasses all humanity and all life forms. Though we are socialized to play down our sense of owing something to the world at large, this sense of obligation, Serres suggests, is never completely extinguished in any society or any mind[9] and often haunts us.

> What do we give back, for example, to the objects of our science, from which we take knowledge? Whereas the farmer in bygone days gave back in the beauty that resulted from his stewardship what he owed the earth, from which his labor wrested some fruits. What should we give back to the world? What should be written down in the list of restitutions.[10]

Let's take stock. First, everything hinges on what I shall call existential scarcity—the fact that there appears never to be enough of the wherewithal of life, whether material goods or spiritual qualities, to go around, and that one must go in search of what is lacking at home to make good this insufficiency. This search may precipitate quarrels in a family over who deserves what, conflicts between social classes over just apportionments of opportunities or wealth, and migration or expatriation as strategies for finding the kinds of satisfaction abroad that one could not find at home. Existential scarcity implies that something is felt to be missing in one's life and that one deserves a break, a better job, better weather, better health, more recognition, or more love. Second, the unequal distribution of luck or good fortune means that people are constantly imagining how a more equal distribution can be effected; how luck can come their way, even if it is at someone else's expense, and how life can be fairer. It also means that those who are best favored, whether by luck, inheritance, or hard work, often feel an urge to redress, through benevolent gifts and gestures, the situation that advantages them but disadvantages so many others. Welfare systems, and aid and development programs undoubtedly express the discomfort with inequality that informs the enlightenment writings of Jean-Jacques Rousseau, Thomas Paine, Robert Owen, John Adams, and Thomas Jefferson. And anthropologists are particularly susceptible to this impulse since their careers are conditional on the goodwill and gifts of those among whom they do their fieldwork—peoples who have often suffered the ignominy of colonial conquest and its legacies of poverty and powerlessness. But though we might answer the ethical call by keeping faith with those about whom we write, giving them voice, using their worldviews as a means of critiquing our own, we share with those in the business of foreign aid a troubling sense that in trying to do the right thing we may be doing the wrong thing, and that seeking to do the least harm only creates new and unforeseen problems.

On this cautionary note, consider the following story of a young Kuranko woman that I first met in a Freetown amputees' camp in January 2002 not long before the decade-long Sierra Leone civil war finally came to an end. Fina Kamara and her six-year-old daughter Damba both suffered the amputations of their hands and forearms during a rebel attack on their village three and a half years before, and in the course of our conversations, Fina Kamara told me that Damba had been taken to the United States, ostensibly for specialist medical treatment. Fina had no idea if or when Damba would return to Sierra Leone. All she knew was that eight to twelve children had been taken from the Murraytown camp and that the man who organized their trip to America went by the name of Uncle Joe.

After two years of inquiries, during which I wondered how this unidentified agency had justified such a prolonged separation of mother and daughter, I discovered that the child amputees, including Damba, had been flown to New York by a non-profit organization called Friends of Sierra Leone.[11] Its "Gift of Limbs" project had been co-sponsored by the Rotary Club of New York, and its purpose was to fit the amputees with prosthetic limbs and provide physical therapy. Damba, I discovered, was subsequently placed in the care of an expatriate Sierra Leonean family living in Virginia.

Between 2002 and 2003, Damba's "guardian," Amina Jah, phoned Fina on three occasions, twice sending $200 moneygrams to help her with medical expenses. Damba also phoned, saying she missed her mother and could not wait to see her again. As baffled by the events that had led to the loss of her only daughter as by the unspeakable events that had reduced her to the status of a refugee, Fina nonetheless accepted that her daughter would have opportunities in the United States that she would never have at home. Her only hope was that the Jah family would not change Damba's last name, and that Damba would return to Sierra Leone and meet her real family.

Fina's rationalizations reflected the widespread West African custom of fostering[12]—placing one's child in the care of kinsmen in order to give the child a better life (especially through schooling), "loaning" a child to a needy or childless couple, apprenticing a child to a Qu'ranic teacher, or even "pledging" a child to work off a debt. The radical departure from traditional practice in Fina's case was that Damba had not been freely given but taken and kept without full disclosure. I had the impression that Fina's separation from Damba was like another amputation. The phantom pain from her severed hand was now compounded by the loss of her daughter.

In mid-2003, Fina Kamara moved from Freetown to an amputees' camp in northern Sierra Leone so she could be closer to her home village and extended family. When I passed through Kabala in January 2008, I wanted to visit Fina to see how she was faring and to ask after Damba, but time ran out and it was not until I was back in the United States that I learned, through the mediation of a Sierra Leone friend, Kaimah Marah, what had happened to Fina since we last met in Freetown in January 2002. I emailed Kaimah, giving him guidelines and questions for an interview I wanted him to conduct with Fina Kamara in the Number Three Amputees Camp in Kabala. The following passages contain transcribed portions of this interview, which Kaimah conducted in Krio.

Kaimah began by asking Fina if she was well.

"I am alive, thank God, though I still feel pain in my arm and my health is poor. It is very hard for me, and I have difficulty taking care of my children."

"How many children do you have now?"

"Magba, my first-born, is in the Ahamadiyya Secondary School. He is in form three. Abdulai and Kunnah both attend the Ansaru Primary School. Abdulai is in class five and Kunnah is in class one."

"How do you manage to pay their fees?"

"The NarSarah clinic[13] pays Magba's fees. I pay for the other children."

"And Ferenke, is he there?"

"Yes, but he is still too young to attend school."

"What about your husband, is he there?"

"He is in Kondembaia. But he is old. He used to farm, but now he is unable to work. He lives with his other wives. I have to be father and mother to our children. I barely survive. The government provides shelter for us, nothing more. We depend on those who come to our rescue. It is really hard. My left hand is gone, so I cannot do farm work. I do a little soap making and *gara* dying. And I took out a micro-loan from the NarSarah clinic for sixty-eight thousand leones [\$25]. I used the money to pay other farmers to clear a farm for me, so I could plant groundnuts, peppers, onions and rice. But the interest after six months will be fifteen hundred leones [\$5], and this will be hard for me to pay."

After a long pause, during which Kaimah switched off his tape recorder and gave Fina the money I had sent for her, Kaimah inquired about Damba.

It seemed that when Fina left Freetown in the rainy season of 2003, she lost all contact with Damba and her "guardians" in Alexandria, Virginia.

"Was this because you had no way of communicating?"

"I had no cell phone then. They could not call me, and I could not call them."

In 2006, Fina was invited to the United States, all expenses paid, for a reunion with Damba on the Oprah Winfrey Show. It took the show's producers four months to locate Fina, secure a visa for her (in Guinea), and make the necessary travel arrangements. It was an extraordinary story, and it was not until I had done some research on the internet that I fully understood what had happened.

In 2006, Damba was fourteen and attending the Francis C. Hammond Middle School in Alexandria, Virginia. She sang alto in the choir, acted in school plays, and excelled in her academic work. She was also an anchor on the school's daily newscast. But she had never explained to her classmates why her left arm was missing. One morning she aired a video of herself in which she recounted the story of how rebels invaded Kondembaia in August 1998 and her "peaceful and normal life" came to an end. Men, women, and children were rounded up and made to stand beneath the two great cotton trees in the center of the village. Even though she was a six-year-old child, Damba was one of those selected to pay the price for those who had, in the rebels' view, recently voted into power a government that had vowed to destroy them. She was forced to the ground and her arm pinioned to the root of one of the cotton trees. "I could not hold the fear in me," she said. "I was cold and terrified. I felt a sharp pain running through my entire body. I was overwhelmed, and my whole body was shaking. When my mother asked if she could pick me up and tie my bleeding arm, the same rebel who had cut off my arm ordered her to lay by me, and he cut off my mother's left arm."

A school friend sent Damba's video to Oprah Winfrey, and in October 2006 Damba was invited to travel to Chicago and appear on Oprah's show. Oprah had told Damba that she was going to help her "dream come true," and Damba assumed this meant she would be going back to Sierra Leone to see her mother. Instead, Fina was brought to the United States and on 7 November, when the show aired, Damba found herself reunited with her mother and holding her baby brother Ferenke in her arms in front of a television audience of several million. Damba was in tears, unable to find words for the happiness she felt. As for Fina Kamara, she thanked Oprah, Oprah's mother, and the Jah family, and expressed through an interpreter her appreciation and joy.

It is in the nature of media spectacles, as it is in the nature of stories, to conjure the illusion of moral closure. And there is always a heroic agent or supernatural helper, like Oprah, who effects the closure and whose benevolent power makes possible the reunion, the happy ending, the miracle. But such stage-managed moments of truth may easily blind us to the vexed world in which we actually live and to which we return when the story has been told, the carnival over, and the spectacle done.

"So much happened to me in America," Fina said. "People were so friendly when they found out that I was Damba's mother. I was so happy when I met my only daughter again. Now I am praying that with the help of God, my other children will go to America too. My husband is too old to take care of them, and I believe that if my sons go to America all my difficulties, stress, and poverty will be over."

"But would you want to live in America?"

"I worried a lot when I was there, because my children were back here. There was no one to take care of them in my absence. That is why I wanted to come back as soon as I could."

"Do you know who Oprah Winfrey is?"

"She is a South African lady who took pity on Damba. She arranged for me to travel to America to meet Damba. Damba cannot travel to Sierra Leone because she has no green card. That is why I had to go there."

"Did Oprah offer you any help with your children's education or with your health problems?"

"She paid for my trip, that was all. I hoped someone would help me, but no one did."

I could not help but think that had Oprah funded a visit home for Damba, far more might have been accomplished than this brief reunion between mother and daughter before an audience of strangers. Damba could have spent time with all her siblings and restored a sense of continuity with her natal community.

"Where did you stay in America?" Kaimah asked.

"Amina Jah and her husband took care of me throughout my one month stay. On Sundays they took me to their church to pray. I visited Damba's school, and her friends and neighbors."

"Are the Jahs from Sierra Leone?"

"Yes. Amina Jah is Kono, her husband is a Kissy man."

Oprah is like a storyteller. In the theatrical arena of her show, she conjures a vision of life as deeply troubled yet ultimately open to renewal and resolution. Our efforts pay off. Virtue is rewarded. Adversity is overcome through confession, contrition, and compassion. The official Oprah website posted a report on the show in which Fina appeared. It was entitled "A Mother's Love." On the show, Oprah had told Damba, "You have an amazing mother. If all the mothers in the world were like your mother, this would be a different kind of world. We are honored to have you here." The implication was that a mother's moral duty was to sacrifice her own happiness for her daughter's well-being, and since well-being was synonymous with achieving the American Dream, Fina had made the right decision in giving Damba a chance of a life in the United States.

Sometimes we forget that the passage to modernity through education, money, and mobility is, despite appearances, often accompanied by grief and guilt. This gap between the simplicity of our idealizations and the complexity of our lived situations is the subject of one of Guy de Maupassant's most troubling stories.

The Adopted Son begins like a folktale: two peasant families live in neighboring cottages near a seaside resort, the parents struggling to make ends meet, the children of each family nonetheless happy.[14] One hot August afternoon a carriage stops in front of one of the cottages, and a well-born and wealthy young woman steps down to admire the peasant children playing in the road. Madame Henri d'Hubières, who is childless, becomes attached to Charlot the only son of the Tuvaches, and after several weeks of visiting the family she offers to adopt him. Monsieur d'Hubières draws up a contract to cover all eventualities. If the boy turns out well, he will in time inherit the d'Hubières estate. In any event, he will receive a handsome sum when he comes of age and his parents will be paid a pension of 100 francs a month until their death. However, the boy's parents are outraged by this suggestion, and refuse to give up their son for adoption. Madame d'Hubières then asks after the other boy who she had observed playing with Charlot and assumed to be his brother. On being told that this boy belonged to the Vallins family who lived next door, the d'Hubières took their proposition to the Vallins who, after some haggling, accepted it. The Vallins were now able to live comfortably on their pension while the Tuvaches, though miserably poor, consoled themselves with the thought that they had done the right thing in not selling their child. Years passed, and one day a brilliant carriage stopped again outside the peasant cottages. The young man who stepped down from the carriage was Jean Vallin, now twenty-one. Entering the house of the Vallins family, he greeted his astonished parents who later that day proudly introduced their successful son to the local mayor, deputy, curé, and schoolmaster. Faced with the good fortune of his erstwhile friend, Charlot Tuvaches reproached his parents for stupidly refusing to give him the opportunity that the Vallins had given Jean. "See what I should have been by now," he said. And he declared that he would never forgive his parents for depriving him of his one chance of happiness. On the night he walked out on his parents, he heard the sounds of celebration from the neighboring cottage. The Vallins were celebrating the return of their son.

This conflict between the bonds and obligations of kinship, traditionally conceived, and the freedom to embrace a life beyond the world into which one is born entails several moral quandaries. How, for example, can one fulfill one's filial obligations without compromising one's own ambitions, if to remain in one's natal village may doom one to the same poverty that oppressed one's parents and caring for them in their dotage may mean the abandonment of one's own dreams of improving one's lot? And how can a migrant reconcile the material gains he makes in his own life with the abandonment of his ancestral world and possible estrangement from kith and kin? Through remittances alone? And how can one decide the good, when local and global worlds seem so mutually antithetical, and the tug of tradition comes into conflict with the allure of modernity?

School fees for Fina's eldest son, Magba, were paid by the NarSarah clinic. This clinic was established in Kabala in 2002 by a Kuranko expatriate, Dorcas Kamanda, and her husband Dan. Born into a family of 26, Dorcas converted to Christianity in the late 1960s and moved to Colorado to study for a nursing degree under the auspices of the United Methodist Church. She recalls her Sierra Leonean childhood as a happy time.

We were hungry, but we were happy. Everybody took care of you. Everybody was your mother or father. It was simply life as we knew it [and] any missing creature comfort that we have become accustomed to in modern America was more than replaced by the undying support of family members and fellow villagers, each of whom did their share to make life just that much more comfortable. We were really, really happy.[15]

Dorcas speaks in equally glowing terms of her American life, her conversion to Christianity, and her commitment to a mini-medical and spiritual revolution in Sierra Leone. In the words of the NarSarah project, Dorcas is committed to "funding materials and personnel in areas such as prayer and worship, health, education, agriculture, transport and communications." But the irony is that utopia (ou-topos) is literally nowhere. And while the vision of a perfect world or a better place—whether in the distant past or the near future—helps us explain and escape our present reality, it remains a state of mind—a "heaven," in Dylan Thomas's words "that never was nor will be ever" yet is "always true."[16] In reality, life must always be lived within limits, and the difference between traditional and modern societies is simply a difference between the kinds of limits that people struggle against. If poverty, disease, and limited educational or employment opportunities define the limits in Sierra Leone, spiritual impoverishment, loveless marriages, stress, loneliness, and the struggle to lose weight are the things we struggle with most in the United States, at least in Oprah's worldview. Still, there are some limits that hold true for all human beings, such as the difficulty of reconciling the ontological security that comes from the bond between mother and child with the inevitable separation from home that initiates the beginning of our own adulthood. This difficult transition from attachment to autonomy constitutes the Oedipal project—the eternal struggle of the young to come into their own, frequently against the criticisms, constraints, and dictates of the old. In my view, this is the same struggle that is entailed in the passage from tradition to modernity, which is why every migrant, leaving home to make his or her way in the wider world, is Everyman, and why the attainment of new life inevitably means the severing of primary bonds, a departure from a natal place, and the symbolic death of the old.

When I first met Fina Kamara, I saw only her tragedy—her autonomy lost because of the loss of a limb, her life overshadowed by the loss of her only daughter. But I now ask whether it is not the destiny of a parent to sacrifice her own well-being for the well-being of her child, even at the risk of her own welfare—as Fina did, attempting to rescue her mutilated daughter from the bloody machetes of the

Revolutionary United Front boys. Is it not imperative that one give up one's own emotional claim on one's offspring in order that they flourish in the world, just as it is in the nature of every young life to break free from primary bonds and constrictive roots so that it may branch out, reach up, and find the sun? The choice between attachment and separation is never easy. Intimate bonds are as basic to our security as they are potentially inimical to our autonomy. And while separation is inevitable, it entails losses we may mourn forever. When Kaimah asked Fina Kamara to describe the hardest thing in her life, she replied, "It is the pain of losing my arm, of being unable to farm and provide for my children. It is the pain of struggling to improve their chances in life, to get them an education, so they can help me and their father who is old and almost blind." But like any good parent, Fina Kamara readily admits that her children's happiness matters more than her own. As for Damba, she describes the moment she left for America as "terrifying." "I was crying and my mom was crying. She had to let me go because she knew I'd get a better life." But will Damba ever lament the life she may never have in Sierra Leone, the extended family she may never know, the natal village to which she may never return? These are questions that an anthropologist cannot answer because culture never completely determines such matters and each individual, at different times in his or her life, will construe such existential dilemmas differently. Thus, while I sometimes rue the partial eclipse of my ties with my natal New Zealand, I am aware that in escaping the confines of a provincial upbringing I truly came into my own.

Still, the movement from a local to a global world, or from tradition to modernity, is as fraught as the journey of life itself. There are always losses as well as gains, and it is never possible to decide in retrospect which of our decisions, or our parents' decisions, were for the best. Rather than strive to do the maximum good, I prefer the Hippocratic principle of doing the least harm and hold to the existential tenet that every human being needs to have some hand in deciding his or her own destiny. This is why I remain troubled about the events that overwhelmed Fina Kamara's life, leaving her no option but to go along with the decisions of others, and why I find in her story uncanny echoes of a story that broke in late October 2007 when a group of seventeen European "charity workers" were arrested in Chad and charged with the attempted kidnapping of 103 local children.

According to parents and relatives of many of these children, the charity workers had visited villages in the Chad-Sudan border region, offering free schooling in the nearby town of Abeche. Marc Garmirian, a journalist traveling with the Zoe's Ark group at the time of their arrest, felt that the charity workers' judgment had been "clouded by idealistic zeal." "What struck me was their state of mind," he told a BBC reporter, "their conviction. They were sure they were doing good and had a mission to carry out." Indeed, one is struck, in remarks by one of the French detainees, by a total insensitivity to the wishes of the children (who believed their departure from home would only be temporary), not to mention the rights of the children's parents and relatives, many of who traveled long distances to Abeche after hearing of the alleged abductions.

Responding to a BBC journalist who asked Christine Peligat to explain the motives of Zoe's Ark, Peligat said that the team was "rescuing children from Sudan's Darfur region. And the only thing they wanted [was] to give these children a better life. That's it. This is the only aim of this operation."

"But what were they going to do with the children?" the journalist asked. "They were going to take them back to France?"

"Yes and find some families so that they can have these children. It was not like some people have said, that we were like an organization for adoption. That's not true. All we wanted was to save the children. There was no trafficking. We are not child traffickers."

A few days after the story broke in Europe, the BBC news service initiated an internet debate, asking, "Would you ever give up your child in hope of a better life?" Some respondents, imagining a life-threatening situation, said they would do anything to keep their child from mortal danger, even if this meant losing their child. Others were critical of the assumption that Europe was necessarily a better place to bring up one's children than Africa. Others spoke of the need to help Africa look after its own, rather than assume that the continent was a place of ignorance and savagery from which children had to be rescued. Still others made a case against adoption, arguing that the bond with one's biological parents is more important than anything else in life—educational opportunities, medical care, physical comfort. As I read through these various responses, many of them from people who had themselves been stolen or adopted as children in order to receive "a better life," I was reminded of Kuranko dilemma tales that sharpen one's awareness of life's aporias and suggest that accepting them may be preferable to the illusions of moral closure and intellectual certainty to which so many of us cling.

8

IDENTIFICATION TO DESCRIPTION
An Essay on Metaphor

> Metaphors can ... be foundational elements of philosophical language,
> "translations" that resist being converted back into authenticity or
> logicality.
>
> —Hans Blumenberg, *Paradigms for a Metaphorology*

So inured have we become to thinking of concepts as representations
of reality that it is necessary to remind ourselves that they are nothing
more than metaphors that have been given airs. The philosophical
illusion of abstraction that supposes that thought can withdraw or
distance itself from not only material objects and practical matters,
but also social conditioning, dates from the mid-fifteenth century. But
the etymology of even our most (allegedly) abstract words contradicts
the Cartesian view. Our word *time* is from the Latin *tempus*, originally
denoting a "stretch," and cognate with *tempora* ("temples of the head"),
possibly because the skin of the forehead stretches and corrugates as
a person ages. The Chinese character meaning duration, *chiu*, was
explained by the Han lexicographers as derived from the character
jen, man. *Chiu* was a man stretching his legs and walking "a stretch,"
just as a roof stretches across space, or time stretches from one event
to another.[1] In Central Australia, time is so deeply spatialized that
landforms are construed as the petrified forms of ancestral bodies,
tracks, ritual activities, campsites, viscera, excreta, sperm, and sweat.
By contrast with the aestheticized and spiritualized worldview of non-
Aboriginal Australians, who speak of "sacred sites," Aboriginal people
speak of "wombs" or "bellies" (Warlpiri, *miyalu*).

Even the concept of a society invokes images of the human body. In many Germanic and African societies, the joints of the arm, hand, and fingers provide a means of conceptualizing degrees of relationship, while in Central Australia different categories of kin are associated with different parts of the body (Warlpiri: breast/mother; chin/father; shoulder/junior sibling; chest/mother's brother).[2]

For Aboriginal people, different social groupings are associated with different areas of the desert, and intergroup alliances are spoken of as relations between places. In Indian Vedic hymns, all living things, including the sun, the moon, and the air, were created from parts of the body of *purusha*, a man offered up in sacrifice by the gods. Social groups had the same bodily origin: "The Brahmin was his mouth, his arms were made by the Rājanya [warrior], his two thighs the Vaisya [trader and agriculturalist], from his feet the Sudra [servile class], was born.[3] And in classical Chinese thought, the inner and outer worlds of experience were regarded "as having identical systems of physiology," and the aim of Chinese medicine and mysticism was to keep the two systems working in congruence, attuned to one another.[4] This metaphorical fusion of social body, personal body, and body of the land is as evident in traditional cosmologies as it is in modern positivist sociology.[5] These are "ontological metaphors"[6] in which being is never "pure being" but always a matter of being-with-others, being-embodied, and being-emplaced. Hence Heidegger's observation that in Old English and High German, "To be a human being means ... to dwell" (though dwelling is not a universal mode of being, as the Warlpiri verb "to be" [*nyanami*] immediately suggests, for it also means "to sit").

What remains invariant, however, is that, as Maurice Merleau-Ponty observed, "Our body, to the extent that it moves itself about, to the extent that it is inseparable from a view of the world and is that view itself brought into existence, is the condition of possibility, not only of the geometrical synthesis, but of all expressive operations and all acquired views which constitute the cultural world."[7]

If abstraction is a misnomer, and all thought is mediated by our sense of being embodied and socially grounded in the world, then our tendency to distinguish between prescientific and scientific thought on the basis of the latter being immanent and the former transcendent is questionable. That most thought consists in likening one thing to another goes without saying. But that thought may sometimes possess an identity relationship with its object is a figment of our imagination. Metaphors can have real effects without our positing an identity relationship between the terms that are brought together in the image.

Indeed, just as it is more convivial to converse with others instead of impose one's own views on them, it is more edifying and enjoyable to generate figures of speech without pretending that any one of them captures the essence of reality.

The Particular and the General

A recurring problem for human thought is how the particular is related to the general, for instance, a relationship between individuals and groups, parts and wholes, microcosm and macrocosm, ethnos and anthropos. While identity thinking tends to valorize the more encompassing term, subsuming the particular under the general, metaphorical thinking tends to make each term reciprocal to the other. As such it echoes both hermeneutics and fractal theory. While the hermeneutic circle implies that the whole can only be understood by reference to the individual, and the individual can only be understood by reference to the whole, fractal theory proposes a "self-similarity" between large scale and small scale phenomena without, however, assigning higher value to the former. Just as a single fern frond or snowflake contains miniatures of itself, so kinship relations become metaphors of all relations. Writing on the relationship between *ambwerk* and *tuman* (elder and younger siblings of the same sex) in Tangu, Kenelm Burridge notes that the terms "are categories of more general understanding, as well as categories of specific relationship."[8] Similarly, in Iatmul society, "Everything and every person has a sibling and the polysyllabic names are so arranged in pairs that in each pair one name is the elder sibling of the other. Throughout the whole field in which direct dualist thought is recognizable, it is accompanied by the concept that one of the units is senior to the other."[9] In many human societies, fraternal relations are reiterated in such generalized notions as the brotherhood of man or blood brotherhood, while the paterfamilias becomes a model for paternalistic authority in the state (the "fatherland") or in heaven (God). Not only is the world replete with recursive patterns; it also exhibits recursive processes. Thus, processes of gestation and giving birth are reiterated in rituals of initiation, images of nation-building, the rhetoric of revolutionary action, creation myths, and concepts of creativity (conceiving a new idea).[10]

Whether we theorize these relations as metaphorical or fractal, they reveal deep resemblances between the structure of the world and the structure of thought. But this relationship is recursive, not reductive, for while structures and processes are roughly similar, one is not the cause or origin of the other. Neither do they replicate themselves exactly or entail the same effects from one situation to another. It is this unpredictability, this openness to new combinations and permutations, that makes it impossible to claim a relation of identity between these disparate phenomena. According to Heraclitus's famous aphorism, "everything is in flux" (*panta rhei*). One cannot step into the same river twice, for neither self nor river stay the same over time.

Through Throats Where Many Rivers Meet

I now turn specifically to metaphorical connections between the human body, the social body, and the body of the cosmos in order to explore the potentialities for thought and action that reside in these presumed continuities between person and world.

Consider the opening lines of Dylan Thomas's poem, "In the White Giant's Thigh" (1950):

> Through throats where many rivers meet, the curlews cry,
> Under the conceiving moon, on the high chalk hill,
> And there this night I walk in the white giant's thigh
> Where barren as boulders women lie longing still
>
> To labour and love though they lay down long ago.
>
> Through throats where many rivers meet, the women pray,
> Pleading in the waded bay for the seed to flow
> Though the names on their weed grown stones are rained away,
>
> And alone in the night's eternal curving act,
> They yearn with tongues of curlews for the unconceived
> And immemorial sons of the cudgelling, hacked
>
> Hill.

Here, the confluence of several rivers is likened to a throat or cervix, a bay to a womb, a chalk hillside to a thigh, while fecundity and poetic fluency alike are linked to phases of the moon, tides in a bay, and seasonal rhythms of the weather or animal life. Physiological, meteorological, geographical, and poetical processes are condensed into unifying images whose ambiguity is expressed semantically by such key phrases as "conceiving moon" and "curving act." As Thomas puts it later in the poem: "All birds and beasts of the linked night uproar chime."

Let us now turn to an ethnographic analogue of this embodied worldview. Two hundred miles north of San Francisco, the Redwood Highway enters a region of evergreen forest, sea fog, and mountain rain. Just before it reaches the Oregon border, the highway crosses the estuary of the Klamath River, the traditional center of the Yurok lifeworld. The Yurok conceived of this world as a great disk, divided by the Klamath River and surrounded by the sea. Yet they took no interest in whence the river came, or in the ocean beyond the river's mouth. Their cultural and economic life was concentrated on the river itself, and on the annual salmon run that supplied enough food for the entire year. The river was both the source of their livelihood and the focus of their social existence, and in the Yurok worldview ideas pertaining to the river and its environs, to the salmon and its biology, and to human physiology and anatomy, were coalesced. Thus, the periodic affluence of the waterway had "a functional interrelation with the periodicity of vital juices in the body's nutritional, circulatory, and procreative systems," and the main concern of Yurok magical activity was to ensure "that vital channels be kept open and that antagonistic fluids be kept apart."[11]

This Yurok theory of correspondence is vividly illustrated by an anecdote told by Erik Erikson, who worked among the Yurok during the 1930s. When he first arrived on the Klamath, Erikson met an elderly female healer who treated somatic disorders and did psychotherapy with children. Erikson discovered that the principles of Yurok therapy were not unlike the principles of psychoanalysis, and he began to "exchange notes" with the old woman. He noticed, however, that despite her willingness to talk, she seemed melancholy and withdrawn. It soon became apparent that her gloominess stemmed from an incident some days before. She stepped out into her vegetable garden and, glancing down the hundred-foot slope to where the Klamath enters the Pacific, she saw a small whale enter the river's mouth, play about for a while, then disappear. Since the Creator (Wohpekumeu; the widower across the ocean) had decreed that only salmon, sturgeon, and similar fish should cross the freshwater barrier, the episode portended that the world disk was slowly tilting from the horizontal, that saltwater was entering the river, and that a flood was approaching that might destroy all humankind. The old woman's anxieties not only reflected her Yurok cosmology but her profession as a healer.

A healer must have superb control over the oral-nutritional canal because he or she has to suck the "pains" from a patient's body and then, having swallowed two or three of these "pains," vomit them up. The "pains" are visualized as slimy, bloody stuff resembling tadpoles, and the healer is able to spew them forth without bringing up food as well. In preparing for such a healing session, a healer must abstain from drinking water because water and the bloody substances extracted from the patient's body are mutually antagonistic. The same reasoning explains why, after eating venison—a "bloody" meat—one should wipe one's hands clean and not wash them in water. The underlying principle is that contrasted fluids such as blood and water, semen and water, or urine and water should never meet in the same aperture or channel. Thus, salmon, which are water-born, must be kept away from the house of a menstruating woman; money, which originates in another "stream," must not be brought into association with sexual intercourse; a person must never urinate in the river; and oral sex is banned because cunnilingus prevents money flowing, and interferes with the salmon run in the Klamath. All such inappropriate conjunctions are thought to lead to impoverishment and weakening of both people and the natural environment.

We can now understand how a saltwater whale entering the freshwater stream signaled a more general disturbance of the geographical-anatomical environment. Something alien and inedible has entered the mouth of a river that only edible things like salmon and sturgeon should enter. This suggests an inversion of the oral scheme of things in which control of the mouth is fundamental to social and ethical integration. It is because the Yurok healer is preeminently a master of oral-nutritional processes—sucking, vomiting, avoiding the use of "dirty" words—that such an inversion affects the healer more deeply than others, and requires his or her skills to redress the ecological imbalance. This may explain why, when the old woman saw the whale in the mouth of the river, her first reaction was to keep quiet about it, possibly hoping that by controlling her mouth she might induce some change in the external world.

In both Yurok cosmogony and the poem by Dylan Thomas the world of things is merged with the world of being. Consequently, non-human entities like stones, hillsides, and whales assume the status of signs whose decipherment mediates understanding and action in the human world. This corporeal and sensible way of reading what the world means presupposes an identity relationship between language, knowledge, and bodily praxis, though this relationship is one of reciprocity, and does not imply the superiority of language over life, persons over non-persons, or intellectual knowledge over practical savoir-faire.[12]

Metaphor exemplifies this embodied theory of knowledge and speech. When the Dogon equate word and seed, or speak of the ripe millet being pregnant,[13] the metaphors disclose vital relations between proper knowledge, productive activity, correct speech, and socio-physical well-being. Metaphor is not merely a figure of speech. Nor is it merely a "concrete" mode of thinking that fails to achieve abstraction. Rather, it posits connections between different forms of life without making any one of these forms all-encompassing, fundamental, or transcendent. If identity thinking is always at the service of hierarchical distinctions between the knower and the known, or subject and object, metaphorical thinking is egalitarian; it places the terms compared on a par. That this mode of thinking is not unique to "primitive" thought is suggested by the poetry of Dylan Thomas.

> Thomas stressed that all ideas and actions began in the body. As a result, he insisted, the best way to render a thought or action, however abstract, was to express it in as physical a way as possible. Every thought, for him, could find an equivalent in blood, flesh, or gland. He saw it as his particular task to find and express all the equations between body and world, between body and idea.[14]

Thus, Thomas speaks of the rain wringing "out its tongues on the faded yard" much as the old Yurok healer speaks of the social repercussions of the whale entering the mouth of the Klamath River. The Dogon too scrutinize the natural world for auguries that bear upon the human condition so that, for example, should a tree be found that bears fruit without first flowering, this may be said to be a sign that a woman could well conceive a child without having resumed menstruating after the birth of a previous child. The metaphor is founded on the correspondence that the Dogon say exists between flowering and fruiting in the vegetable world and menstruating and giving birth in the human world.[15]

Metaphor and Embodiment

Identity thinking is so insistent on privileging mind over matter that it readily makes the mistake of defining metaphor in terms of a contrast between tenor and vehicle—where tenor is the "underlying idea or principal subject which the vehicle or figure means."[16] This intellectualist bias toward subjugating empirical reality to abstract concepts not only explains why Enlightenment thought is intolerant of myth and metaphor; it reveals its blindness to its own barely disguised analogical character.

Vernacular language is conspicuously anthropomorphic. We habitually speak of an angry sky, of the sun rising and setting, of stars looking down, of the wind blowing, of a brooding landscape, of social ills, and of economic depression and recovery as if these natural or social phenomena were themselves possessed of consciousness and will. Reciprocally, we speak of the shoulder or brow of a hill and the foot of a mountain, of being petrified with fright, of having roots, of being turned on, switched off, and burned-out, of a person reacting automatically or behaving mechanically as if the body of the earth, the actions of a machine, and the human body were organically interconnected. By contrast, Enlightenment reason insisted on a series of separations that elevated thought to the same powerful position over nature that dictators are given over all other human beings.[17]

In both cases, the power relationship is illusory. Dictators are fallible and mortal. And even the seemingly most abstract words in our language are based on universal features of the human body. In all Indo-European languages, the verb "to know" is cognate with words meaning "king," "kin," "kind," "generation," "knee," and "can." Indeed, the embodied intentionality of human Being seems to be inextricably tied up with our views about the world, and "I think" (*cogito*) is inseparable from "I can" (*practico*). As for the world of scientific theory, one has only to consider the mechanistic imagery of eighteenth-century philosophy, the arboreal metaphor in nineteenth-century paleography, the topographical and archaeological imagery in psychoanalysis and structuralism, the organic analogies in functionalist sociology, and the metaphors of the mirror, the fountain, and the lamp in literary theory to agree with Jorge Luis Borges that the history of ideas may be nothing more than the history of a handful of metaphors.[18] Moreover, if, as Stephen Pepper argues, world theories are so often generated by drawing analogies from the immediate sensible world, might not adequacy in explanation be seen as a matter of choosing the right metaphor rather than a question of epistemological correctness?[19] For, by suggesting correspondences between the world of ideas and the world of things, a well-chosen metaphor may reveal an underlying link that makes common sense and so avoids the fallacy of misplaced concreteness. An excellent example of this kind of theory-building is given by Gregory Bateson, who, in trying to visualize and understand processes of social control among the Iatmul of Papua New Guinea, compared Western and Iatmul societies in terms of a contrast between radically symmetrical animals (such as jellyfish and sea anemones) and animals with transverse segmentation (such as earthworms, lobsters, and people).[20] The biological analogy got Bateson's thought moving in a new direction and revealed fractal relations between the form of social and natural worlds.

Ludwig Wittgenstein famously argued that a philosopher has nothing to say, but only something to show, and that showing depends on analogies rather than propositions.[21] Adorno characterized Walter Benjamin's thought in the same way: "The rebus is the model of his philosophy."[22] In a similar vein, Richard Rorty observes, "It is pictures rather than propositions, metaphors rather than statements, which determine most of our philosophical convictions ... With the notion of the mind as mirror, the notion of knowledge as accuracy of representation would not have suggested itself."[23]

The very word "picture" suggests that the European intellectual tradition has always reified vision as a primary and unitary metaphor for knowing. Even the later and more technical term for sight, the one adopted by Plato and Aristotle for philosophical contemplation, *theorein* (Θεωρείυ),was not originally a verb but a noun, *theoros* (Θεωρός), meaning "to be a spectator," from which it derived its later meaning of "looking at," ultimately "to contemplate." Here, clearly, the same word was used to designate in a confused way both seeing (the optical phenomenon) and intellectual comprehension, and this is even more clear with the term *noein* (υοείυ),which in early Greek "stands for a type of seeing which involves not merely visual activity but the mental act that goes with the vision." It was probably through the use of this word, *noein* (υοείυ, υóος), that the Greeks were first enabled to distinguish clearly the experience of "thinking" as such. Then, through the process of analogy so important in the evolution of language, the classical word for sight, *idein*, also came to designate (especially in the form *eidenai*, ειδεναι) the process of thinking, since the word for thought, *noein*, also meant, in its primary sense, "to see."[24]

Metaphorical Instrumentality

Making a case against identity thinking is not merely an exercise in demystification that calls into question the view that thought can attain the kind of omnipotence ascribed to God or science. It is, more imperatively, a way of treating thought, not as a technique for mastering and manipulating the world but for making our lives more personally and socially fulfilling. William James summarizes this pragmatic argument in these words: "The truth of an idea is not a stagnant property inherent in it. Truth happens to an idea. It becomes true, is made true by events."[25] Ideas become true not when they meet some abstract moral or logical standard, but when they make our lives more worthwhile.

This test applies equally to ideas that we deem scientific and ideas that we call religious, to cosmology and philosophy. Rather than enforce distinctions between these discursive regimes, declaring some to be intrinsically true or false, it is more edifying to regard them as potential truths whose value for us will depend on the situations we face in life. In a secular society that sets greater store by scientific knowledge than religious belief, religion provides a stock of "extra truths"[26] that may be drawn on to cope with situations in which science provides no answers. In any society, these extra truths comprise a shadowy resource on which people can fall back in critical situations, or when the dominant discourse fails them. In sum, no one mode of thinking, feeling, being, or behaving will see us through all the situations we face in life.

In this vein, let us reconsider the ameliorative potential of the metaphorical conflation of personal body, social body, and world body that I explored at the beginning of this chapter. Among the Songhai of Mali, pathways not only connect different parts of a village or chiefdom but serve as a metaphor for social relations as well as internal human anatomy. Movements of "blood," "heat," and "breath" take place along pathways in the body (*fondo*, pathway, road). Vital organs such as the heart, liver, lungs, and stomach are likened to crossroads where blood or heat is concentrated and then diffused. When these movements of blood, heat, or breath are flowing unimpeded in the right direction a person is healthy; if the flow is reversed or obstructed, illness occurs. Illness signifies that blood, heat, or breath has become blocked, withdrawn, or forced to flow backward.[27]

The Songhai view rests on the ontological assumption that the fate of any individual is linked to the quality of his or her social relationships, as well as the economic and political state of his or her society. Like the riverine metaphors of the Yurok, African metaphors of pathways coalesce social, economic, political, and anatomical elements into a single image that expresses their interdependence. Thus, the Songhai regard the circulation of people, goods, and services along paths in the village as vitally connected to the circulation of blood, heat, and breath in the individual body.

Among the Kuranko, the metaphor of paths is also significant. The adage *nyendan bin to kile a wa ta an segi* describes the way a particular species of grass (used for thatching) bends one way as you go along a path through it and bends back the other way as you return along the path. This movement to and fro of grass along a pathway is used as a metaphor for the movement of people, goods, and services within a community; it is a metaphor for reciprocity. Thus, in Kuranko one often explains the reason for giving a gift, especially to an in-law, with the phrase *kile ka na faga*, "so that the path does not die." If relations between affines or neighbors are strained, however, it is often said that "the path is not good between them" (*kile nyuma san tema*), and if a person disappoints a friend then people may comment *a ma kile nyuma tama a bo ma* (he did not walk on the good path with his friend).

When there is a loss of trust between people, Kuranko often speak of the path being obstructed or darkened. Diviners may say that "the gates are closed," though a gift can "open" the path, just as a sacrifice to the ancestors "clears" or "purifies" the path between members of a lineage and their forebears. Similarly, if a person confesses a grudge or ill will toward a neighbor, it is thought that this can clear the path between them.

The metaphor of walking along paths is also central in many Kuranko oral narratives. A key metaphor for impeded social communication is lameness or difficulty in walking, as when an eldest son is loath to grow up and assume his father's position or when a girl is loath to marry and bear children. While the first failure leads to an interrupted succession that jeopardizes the continuity of a lineage, the second implies a breakdown in the system of marital exchanges on which alliances are built among different clans in the village. Limping, like halting speech, is thus an expression of psychophysical ambivalence in which a deeply regressive urge prevents a person coming of age and standing on his or her own feet.[28] Just as Kuranko speak of sociality in terms of people moving together as one, so the Kabyle (Algeria) speak of a "measured pace" (neither lagging like a sluggard nor running ahead like a dancer) as a metaphor for a person's attunement to the collective rhythms of work "which assign each act its particular moment in the space of the day, the year, or human life."[29]

These ethnographic examples suggest that metaphorical thought is deeply linked to a concern for social skillfulness, and for the practical knowledge on which social life depends—farming, raising children, building a house, etc. Humanitas is consummated in one's everyday relations with others, rather than in one's capacity for espousing moral values. In dealing with personal or social crises, therefore, diagnosis and treatment may call for apposite metaphors as much as abstract knowledge.

Coping with Crisis

A critical situation involves an unbearable conflict between two or more ideas ("being in two minds"), between two or more practical possibilities ("being pulled or torn in two directions"), or between conceptual and practical alternatives ("knowing what one ought to do but not being able to do it"). In all these "double bind" situations an impasse is reached that may be manifest mentally or verbally as a "dilemma" or "contradiction," or physically and energetically as a "bind," "knot," "spasm," "tearing," or "splitting."

Since metaphors coalesce social, personal, and natural aspects of Being, as well as unifying ideas and practices, it is only to be expected that metaphors should often be called upon in resolving these double binds. Indeed, it is because anthropomorphic metaphors bring these domains together in a single unitary image that they can facilitate movement from one domain to another. In particular, a movement is facilitated from the domain where the double bind is manifest and where, therefore, anxiety is most intense, to another domain that is relatively free from anxiety and accordingly still open to control and manipulation. Religion provides a good example. Because an analogy is drawn between earthly and heavenly spheres, it is possible for believers to transfer "anxiety-arousing internal and interpersonal conflicts to the vaults of heaven" and achieve some "distance from the problems besetting [them] and to speculate about them with some measure of objectivity."[30]

That walking or running help us with mental depression may be because fluency of body movement induces fluency in thought. Activating the body can therefore alleviate the tendency toward immobilization and depression in the mind. Among the Kuranko, diviners are consulted when a person falls ill. By addressing river pebbles (neutral objects) laid out on a mat, the diviner is able to discern the cause of the illness. Bodily sickness is often attributed to a social event, such as a spouse's infidelity, an unresolved feud with a neighbor, or a failure to make sacrifices to one's ancestors. Appropriate social actions—a spouse's confession, a neighbor's apology, a sacrifice to one's ancestors—have a correspondingly beneficial effect on the body and mind of the ailing individual. And, as we have seen, a Yurok shaman responds to a geographical crisis, such as a whale entering the mouth of a salmon river, by asserting control over a corresponding zone of his or her anatomy—the oral-nutritional canal.

It would be a mistake to disparage metaphorical instrumentality as a primitive mode of thought, or a magical or primary-process activity. In my view, differences in modes of thought across cultures are idiomatic rather than formal, and if we take care to relate thought to context of use when we make cross-cultural comparisons this becomes quite obvious. If crisis be considered one such context, we find that metaphorical instrumentality is just as typical of modern societies as preindustrial ones. For instance, Erik Erikson observes that the phenomenon of transference is as clearly understood and utilized by Yurok healers as by modern psychotherapists.[31] It can also be argued that recourse to jargon and "experience-distant" concepts in the human sciences indicates how anxieties that arise in the course of research are alleviated through a shift to quantification, or to a neutral and abstract language that supposedly corresponds to the domain of human events. Moreover, modern consumerism and branding suggest that the manipulation of commodities such as cars, clothes, cosmetics, foodstuffs, and houses mediates a displacement of affect from the domain of personal relationships to a neutral domain where the consumer can conjure an illusion of being in control.

Poetry as Therapy

Dylan Thomas's "In the White Giant's Thigh" involves two transformations. The first is a transference from the domain of individual anatomy to the comparatively neutral domain of landscape: the "waded bay" at the mouth of the river Towy and a cemetery on the side of a chalk hill. The second transformation is a corollary of the first. It involves a scale reduction in which the individual body and the body of the earth assume the same proportions. These transformations render the world of subjectivity thinkable and graspable. In sum, metaphor has therapeutic power. It transports us conceptually and affectively from our inner preoccupations into a parallel universe where our immediate concerns are transfigured.

A remarkable instance of this therapeutic power of poetry is recorded by John Stuart Mill in his *Autobiography*. When he was fifteen, Mill read Jeremy Bentham for the first time and at once decided to devote his life to reforming the world. But five years later, in the autumn of 1826, he began to suffer serious misgivings about this project, and he put a question to himself, the answer to which plunged him into despair:

> Suppose that all your objects in life were realized; that all the changes in institutions and opinions which you are looking forward to, could be completely effected at this very instant: would this be a great joy and happiness to you? And an irrepressible self-consciousness distinctly answered, "No!" At this my heart sank within me: the whole foundation on which my life was constructed fell down. All my happiness was to have been found in the continual pursuit of this end. The end had ceased to charm, and how could there ever again be any interest in the means? I seemed to have nothing left to live for.[32]

Mill's crisis had been partly precipitated by the realization that his education under his father's hand had given him the means of attaining happiness, yet these means were not in themselves strong enough to "resist the dissolving influence of analysis" and actually make him happy.[33] "For I now saw, or thought I saw, what I had already before received with incredulity—that the habit of analysis has a tendency to wear away the feelings: as indeed it has when no other mental habit is cultivated, and the analyzing spirit remains without its natural complements and correctives."[34] He saw that his intellectual upbringing had made "precocious and premature analysis the inveterate habit of [his] mind," "undermining" and "weakening," as he put it, a feeling for nature and for the "pleasure of sympathy with human beings."[35]

This profound disconnectedness of personal, social, and natural aspects of his Being immobilized him for more than two years, during which he lived in a state of "dry, heavy dejection," performing his intellectual tasks "mechanically." But gradually his malady lifted, first through a resolve not to make happiness a direct goal or necessary precondition of his existence, and second through cultivating what he calls "passive susceptibilities." In this endeavor, William Wordsworth's poetry, which he first read in the autumn of 1828, was a revelation, reawakening a lost love of "rural objects and natural scenery" and helping him recover that disposition of mind that John Keats called "negative capability." Mill describes Wordsworth's poems as "a medicine." "They seemed to be the very culture of the feelings, which I was in quest of ... I needed to be made to feel that there was real, permanent happiness in tranquil contemplation. Wordsworth taught me this, not only without turning away from, but with a greatly increased interest in, the common feelings and common destiny of human beings."[36]

That there are modes of thought that alienate us from others and from the natural world may be more significant than the commonplace observation that digital devices foster narcissism and undermine sociality. Metaphorical thinking counters intellectual estrangement by returning us to the world of what G. B. Vico called common sense (*sensus communis*). By this term Vico turns from "the abstract universality of reason" to "the concrete universality represented by the community of a group, a nation, or the whole human race,"[37] where what is held in common is "not a knowledge based on argumentation," but a practical knowledge (*phronesis*) based on knowing how to live.

Almost a hundred years later, Robert Graves, traumatized mentally and physically by his experiences in World War I, rediscovered how to live through poetry, which he came to regard as "a form of psychotherapy," a mode of homeopathic healing.[38] In his critical essays, Graves emphasizes the bodily aspect of metaphor, stressing how poetic rhythms can induce trance and so move a poet into those unconscious areas of being where healing occurs of itself. It is interesting in this respect that Graves is one of the few writers on prosody who relate poetic meter to human activity and movement within the *habitus*. He plays up the practical role of the Nordic *scop* in shaping charms for the protection of king and realm, and in performing such mundane tasks as "persuading a ship's crew to pull rhythmically and uncomplainingly on their oars against the rough waves of the North Sea by singing them ballads in time to the beat."[39] The slap of oars, the rattle of rowlocks, the ring of hammers on an anvil in a forge, the beat of feet around altar or tomb, or the ploughman turning at the end of each furrow (from *versus* to verse) all indicate the practical environment of speech, sound, and movement in which poetry originated. Because he gives such accent to the pragmatic and therapeutic power of poetry, it is not surprising that Graves's early poems frequently refer to walking, the relaxed momentum of which is, as we have already seen, often served as a metaphor for social mobility and adequacy.[40]

In forging links between personal, social, and natural worlds and in reforging these links when they become broken, poetry fosters wholeness of being. But poetic metaphor also accomplishes this act through a scale reduction in which social, natural, and personal worlds are placed on a par, so allowing us to feel equal to the world around us. In this sense, poetry may be likened to the art of miniature painting. Here, as Claude Lévi-Strauss observes, "the intrinsic value of a small-scale model is that it compensates for the renunciation of sensible dimensions by the acquisition of intelligible dimensions." Reduction in scale and objectification extend our power over a homologue of a thing, so allowing it to be grasped, assessed, and apprehended at a glance. "A child's doll is no longer an enemy, a rival or even an interlocutor. In it and through it a person is a made into a subject."[41]

For many Westerners, the romantic appeal of traditional societies and Eastern religions is possibly the scale compatibility between the individual and the cosmos. In an ashram or a village, a person can, it is imagined, comprehend the universe as a whole, orienting himself within it by extrapolating from self to world, near to far. In the modern world, however, such facile synecdochism breaks down. As George Devereux points out, there ceases to be any overall pattern one can grasp. Complexity, diversity, and change disorient the individual, and extrapolation from his own backyard to the wider world does not work. The whole symptomatology of schizophrenia, Devereux argues, is an attempt to overcome this scale incompatibility between the individual and the world, and "neutralize the dysphoria resulting from disorientation" by withdrawing into make-believe backyards.[42] The same search for scale compatibility may explain why increasing numbers of Kuranko people have embraced Islam. Baffled by sociopolitical changes that impinge upon their lives, yet unable to grasp or decide these changes, Kuranko villagers experiment with the seemingly straightforward practices of Islam as a way of magically regaining a sense of control—for Islam, like modernity, belongs to the world beyond their horizons, yet, in its elementary demands, lies well within their grasp. Synecdochism has both a temporal and a spatial dimension. To magically narrow the distance between "here" and "elsewhere" has similar existential implications to collapsing the present into the past through an abolition of history.[43] Contriving to make the present continuous with the ancestral past, like making the individual appear to be continuous with the cosmos, brings the wider world within a person's grasp in the here and now. In effect, remote and "abstract" realms like the past are concretized. Tallensi ancestors become embodied in shrines of clay or stick; in Aboriginal Australia, dreaming-tracks and song-lines are visible, tangible forms of ancestral presence in the contemporary landscape; in Northern Luzon, the Illongot map mythological events onto the landscape rather than the calendar;[44] among the Nuer, "the tree under which mankind came into being was still standing ... a few years ago";[45] and among French alpine peasants, anecdotes about the past often have the force of events recently experienced. "Once I was walking in the mountains with a friend of seventy," John Berger recalls. "As we walked along the foot of a high cliff, he told me how a young girl had fallen to her death there, whilst haymaking on the *alpage* above." "Was that before the war?" I asked. "In 1833," he answered.[46]

This immediatization and concretization of space-time effectively brings the world back home. Working with a common fund of accessible images—trees, paths, houses, the human body—and making personal, social, and natural domains a seamless, unified, coextensive whole, places self and world on the same scale. Not only does this make the universe coherent and comprehensible; it enables people to act upon themselves in the conviction that such action will have repercussions in social and even extrasocial realms. Conversely, this view enables people to manipulate external objects and words—as in divinatory, healing, and cursing rites—in the conviction that such actions will have repercussions on themselves or on others. Thus, mastery of the external world is linked reciprocally to mastery of self, and people act as if the universe were extensions of themselves and they of it.

It may be an exaggeration to claim that identity thinking is incompatible with social equality, environmental sustainability, and humanitas. To be sure, no form of human thought is not interested, partial, and biased. But thought that claims to be abstract—a view from afar that has liberated itself from social conditioning and historical context—is as deluded as a person who absents himself from society, claiming to have a mind of his own. In seeking to distance itself from myth and metaphor, the senses and the body, reason achieves neither purity nor universality nor social justice, but simply reveals the historical lengths to which the European bourgeoisie has gone in establishing its sovereignty over all others while disguising its dependency on the disempowered masses by claiming they are devoid of reason.

✎ 9

ISLAM AND IDENTITY AMONG THE KURANKO

Yesterday and today are not the same. Whatever sun shines, that is the sun in which you have to dry yourself.
— Mamina Yegbe Marah

According to successive Sierra Leone censuses, Muslims comprised 35 percent of the population in 1960, 60 percent in 2000, and 71 percent in 2008. But what motivates such affiliations? What do they connote in individual experience? And what exactly do they entail in practice?

When people in any society identify themselves as Muslim, Christian, Hindu, Buddhist, agnostic, or atheist, it is unclear how that identification translates into everyday experience or, for that matter, what experiences are encapsulated by or compressed into the category term. In other words, totalizing labels, whether political or religious, racial or social, signify different things to different people at different times, and cannot be assumed to be internally coherent or constant, either at the level of consciousness or behavior. This point is well made by Naveeda Khan in her work on "Muslim becoming" in Pakistan, where Islam is less an entrenched ideology, repeatedly realized in practice and reiterated in doctrine, than a set of possibilities that are aspired to and subject to continual debate.[1] In northeast Sierra Leone, where lip service to Islam has steadily increased during the half century I have been doing fieldwork among the Kuranko, the meaning of "conversion" remains ambiguous. In 1979, when I asked an elderly man, Fore Kande, to explain the spread of Islam in his village, Fore compared "conversion" to "this ferensola business," alluding to the wave of political enthusiasm then sweeping through the Kuranko area for electing a scion of the ruling house of Barawa, S. B. Marah, to the national parliament and thereby improving the economic fortunes of an isolated region of Sierra Leone. "We are all in this ferensola business," Fore said, "we are all one (*be ara kanye*); it is our cause (*ma l koinya*)." Referring to both the push for political representation and the increasing popularity of Islam, Fore added, "Where everyone goes, there you will go also. Would a person with any social intelligence (*hankilimaye*) turn his back on what everyone else is doing? Would he invite snubs and ill-feeling, or risk losing the help that neighbors give in times of need?" Interestingly enough, Fore spent much of his life working for Christian missionaries in Guinea. During this period, he was as comfortable with calling himself a Christian as he was now comfortable with calling himself a Muslim. Another elderly informant, Mamina Yegbe Mara, captured this spirit of religious pluralism very well. "Yesterday and today are not the same. Whatever sun shines, that is the sun in which you have to dry yourself."

I will return to this notion of conversion as a form of social pragmatism rather than personal conviction. For the moment, however, I invoke Fore's remarks as a reminder that we cannot infer how people experience the world from the way they represent it to themselves and to others. As another informant, Saran Salia Sano, put it, "There are many ways that a bird can fly in the sky."

There is clearly a danger in deploying category terms as if they covered an established, abiding, and internally consistent reality and, by implication, marked significant discontinuities between different ontologies, epistemologies, or cosmologies. Yet the academic study of religion often depends on intransitive categories and downplays transitional phenomena such as becoming, in-betweenness, and intersubjectivity, as if substantives provide a more gratifying sense of intellectual mastery over mercurial and diverse modes of lived experience. Prioritizing the study of sacred texts and identifying religious life with liturgy or with institutions like mosques, churches, temples, or sacred sites reinforces an intellectual bias toward the graspable rather than the evanescent, and risks reducing lived experience to procrustean forms and pre-established rubrics.

At the same time, a literate bias makes it difficult if not impossible to do justice to forms of religious life in non-literate communities where no sui generis conception of "religion" exists, scripture is not the basis of belief, and personal faith is less imperative than conforming to communal norms. Historically, the scholastic bias that finds its ultimate expression in theology has led us to ignore vast numbers of human beings, not only in tribal but in urban-industrial societies, for whom religious literacy is peripheral to their lives. Rather than invoke pejorative terms like paganism, animism, anthropomorphism as place holders for people outside the so-called great traditions, or for experiences that cannot be assimilated to extant category terms, it may be edifying to approach the core questions of religiosity without using the word religion at all.

But how are we to do justice to the complexity and fluidity of life-as-lived without falling back on substantives that give an impression of seamlessness, simplicity, and immutability? Scarcely have I begun this essay than my writing is circumscribed by a set of substantives—Islam, West Africa, animist, pagan, Muslim, Kuranko, literate, preliterate— often couched as mutually exclusive binaries that preemptively define the phenomena I wish to explore without prejudice. Is my only option to deploy these terms as means of entering a field, only to critique or abandon them as empirical investigation reveals their limitations? In anticipating my conclusions, I confess that forty-five years of intermittent fieldwork in Sierra Leone has given me to understand that people's allegiances, like their memories, are subject to continual revision, not only from generation to generation but from one situation to another. People opportunistically experiment with new technologies and cosmologies in much the same way that they code switch between mother tongue and krio, shift their affections, change their allegiances, and expand their horizons.

One thing remains constant. The space one identifies as "other" is at once a source of regeneration and danger. Just as powerful Mande medicines like *korte* were in great demand in regions beyond the Mande area, Kuranko have long regarded foreign imports like salt and cloth, roofing iron, kerosene, Islamic charms, Arabic literacy, Western education, and cellphones as having transformative potential, partly because they come from elsewhere. If the bush has always been regarded as a source of vitality, so too have Islamic and European cultures. But foreign influences and commodities can undermine rather than augment the autonomy one already possesses, and the struggle to strike a balance between conserving what one has and seeking to possess what others have is as existentially fraught for the Kuranko as it is for any human beings. Perhaps this explains strategies to have it both ways, like the increasing number of Sierra Leoneans who prefer the appellation "ChristMus" to signify an allegiance to both Christian and Muslim traditions, the Bible and the Koran, and freedom to worship in both mosques and churches.

Islam in West Africa

In his magisterial study of Islam in West Africa, Ousmane Oumar Kane makes a distinction between superficial and deep Islam, the former associated with preliterate rural communities that either resisted Islamization or adopted Islam on their own terms, and the latter with communities in which formal Qur'anic schools, Muslim clerics, Arabic literacy, and mosques became not only central to community life but involved scholarly, political, and economic networks that connected them to other communities throughout Arabia and the West Sudan (Bilad al-Sudan). Although the influence of Islam on West African cultural life can be traced back to the eighth century—the key elements of the new epistemology—"the belief in God, the prophets, the Day of Judgment, angels, and rewards and punishments"[2]—were assimilated into local worldviews and practices to very different degrees.[3] At the same time, Islam "adapted to local environments by emphasizing its ritual and magical elements rather than its legal elements,"[4] and Muslim clerics "played similar roles to those of traditional priests ... transcendental mediators and ritual experts."[5]

While Kane's critique of the colonial gaze, that regarded Africa "essentially as a continent of orality, and obscured its literary tradition,"[6] is entirely justified, his focus on Islamic scholarship and Arabic literacy leads him to neglect communities that assimilated elements of Islamic thought, accommodated Muslim "strangers," yet resisted or remained largely indifferent to the new epistemology, its proselytizers, and its institutionalized forms. My aim in this chapter is to explore this movement from informal influence to institutional presence among the Kuranko from the early seventeenth century to the present day, and to show the value of complementing Kane's historiographical and intellectualist approach to Islam in West Africa with an ethnographically based understanding of Islam in quotidian life and consciousness.

The Kuranko

Arriving in the West Guinea Highlands as warriors, hunters, migrants, or refugees after the collapse and fragmentation of the Mande Empire in the late sixteenth century, the Kuranko still confidently trace their origins to Mande. When asked whence they came, Kuranko invariably reply, "From Mande, from up" (*teliboi*, lit. sun comes from, i.e., the east). The first Kuranko incursions into the forested region between present-day Guinea and Sierra Leone, were by the Mara, a clan whose name derives from the verb *ka mara* (to subjugate, conquer, place under one's command). According to a Kuranko adage, "a clan might be older than the Mara, but it is under a cotton tree[7] planted by the Mara that they were raised" (*morgo sikina yan mara kode, koni l ma ku l ta maran ku l finyan bandan koro*).

Avowedly non-Muslim, the Mara may have migrated from the plains of the Upper Niger and Sankaran Rivers to escape Islamic jihads, hence the folk etymology that derives the word Kuranko from *kure n'ko*, literally, "I am [like] the kure tree" (whose hard bark signifies the invincibility of warriors or resistance to forced conversion). Though the Mara trace their ancestry back to Mansa Yilkanani, who is described as "the first father" or "the first ancestor" whose son, Saramba, "came down" from Mande, occupied the West Guinea Highlands, and apportioned fiefdoms among his fifteen sons,[8] the name Yilkanani derives from the Arabic Dhul-Quarnein (the two-horned, i.e., Alexander the Great), and in myths I collected from Mandinka *jelibas* (praise-singers) associated with Kuranko rulers, Yilkanani was a contemporary of Muhammad and Suleiman (Solomon), and Allah appointed the prophet as Yilkanani's mentor.[9]

That allusions to the Qur'an should figure in the myths and genealogies of a ruling family whose members declare themselves to be *suniké* (non-Muslim), brings us to consider the reasons for these juxtapositions of Muslim and non-Muslim elements in Kuranko history, myth, ritual, and consciousness.

Throughout this book I have argued that identity is a representation, and only partially or arbitrarily a lived reality. As with an iceberg, where more lies beneath the ocean than is projected above it, so with the relationship between ostensibly Muslim and supposedly "animist" elements in Kuranko social life. Different elements become foregrounded or backgrounded in different historical and social contexts.

It is important to note, however, that many elements that a scholar might identify as Islamic are not recognized as such by Kuranko informants. Moreover, customs that a Westerner might identify as religious, ritual, or spiritual are not glossed by the Kuranko with equivalent terms, since for them these usages are simply "duties" or "work" (*wale*), on a par with working a farm, caring for a child, greeting a neighbor, clothing one's body, or making offerings to one's ancestors. Just as many English speakers are ignorant of the etymology of the words they use every day, so Kuranko identify Arabic borrowings as *Kuranko kan* (Kuranko language) even though they date as far back as the thirteenth century when Islamic culture infiltrated every aspect of Mande life. Thus sacrifice (*saraké*) is cognate with the Arabic *sadaqa*, Allah is known as Altala, or simply referred to as *Dale Mansa* (creator chief), guardian angels are called *malaika* (from the Arabic *malik*), and the genii loci of the land are called *nyenne* (*jinn*). Islamic culture influences chronology (New Year, Ramadan, and the beginning of initiation rites), as well as funerary practices, notions of the afterlife (*lahira*), the use of protective charms (*sebé*), and mythology (the first people in the world were M'bimba Adama and Mama Hawa—ancestor Adam and ancestress Eve). Typically, however, pre-Islamic and Islamic forms coexist. Thus, while villagers divide the day into three parts—morning (*sorgoma*), midday (*teli ro*, in the daytime, or *teli la fe*, sun is full), and evening (*teli ko kere*, sun back breaks or *wure*), people are well aware of the Islamic division of the day into the times that prayers are offered (*walha, sanfana, lansaran,* and *fitire,* all non-Kuranko terms). Sometimes, portmanteau words reveal the fusion of indigenous and imported elements, as in the general word for teacher, *karamorgo* (Arabic *qara'a*, read, and Mande *morgo*, person), and remind us that Kuranko themselves often do not distinguish between these elements, though the term *sundan*[10] is frequently used of non-indigenous varieties of rice, visitors, or guests. Yet there are many situations in which people are not only conscious of the difference between indigenous and exogenous elements but regard this difference with some ambivalence.

I allude here to a pan-human paradox. While openness to others, and to the outside world, is as essential to human sociality as it is to individual vitality, it carries the risk of psychological uncertainty and uncontrolled change and may prove to be a sordid boon. Gifts are potentially poisons.[11] An alliance with a djinn may bring a person wealth and renown, but he or she may have to pay the price of such favors by sacrificing the life of a child. Kuranko relations with whites were similarly vexed. Villagers who worked for the colonial administration and learned to read and write were often said to have given up their lives (*ka a wakale ka nie fili*) to the *tubabu*.

This ambivalence also characterized non-Muslim relations to Muslims. The critical issue is existential control—how one can monitor and manage relations between one's own-world and the world of others in such a way that, on balance, one gains as much as, or more than, one loses from the relationship. Thus, when Fula jihadists conquered Solima in northern Sierra Leone in the early nineteenth century, many Solima rejected Islam and placed an embargo on building mosques, even though other elements of Islamic influence were retained. As C. Magbaily Fyle observes, "the hostility was against Islamic political control," not Islamic prayers, the Arabic language, or Muslim traders.[12]

One strategy for preserving one's autonomy without sealing oneself off completely from the world is to create a "permeable reactive barrier" between self and other that allows some elements to pass through while filtering out the rest. In Firawa, the village where I did my first fieldwork in 1969–70, five clans were designated *sunike* or *tontigi* (rulers and law-owners). They were ostensibly non-Muslim and occupied thirteen of the eighteen lineage compounds (*luiye*) in the central and eastern quarters of the village. Three other Muslim clans (*morenu* or *moris*)—Sano, Dabu, and Sise—occupied four *luiye* at the western end of the village. The mosque was also located here—a fenced-off prayer ground in the Sano *luiye* that was upgraded to a small mud-brick building in the 1990s.

This physical segregation was not imposed on the Muslim clans by the local ruling clan (the Mara), nor did it imply a prejudice or prohibition against intermarriage between Muslim and non-Muslim families.[13] Indeed, intermarriage suggests an emphasis on engagement and exchange between Muslim and non-Muslim estates.

In return for hospitality and protection from the Mara, the *moris* officiated in life crisis rituals, were a source of protective charms, and helped expand if not internationalize the Kuranko worldview. In offering sacrifices to lineage ancestors, more distant ancestors would be asked to pass on the offerings to Allah, and Qur'anic divination (using water, mirrors, or readings of the Qur'an) complemented traditional pebble divination. Perhaps the most critical of these relations of complementarity was between chief and imam—between the court *gbare*, where the chief and his council of elders met to administer the law, and the village mosque where Muslims congregated for prayers. But what exactly did each estate stand to gain from this arrangement, and how did each preserve its rights and privileges against encroachments from the other side?

The Dynamics of Openness and Closure

Oral traditions confirm what scholars have frequently attested—that Islam was disseminated throughout west Sudan by Mandinka and Fulani traders and travelers. It has also been suggested that the appeal of Islamic monotheism lay in its power to provide a centralized cosmology that transcended the cultural heterogeneity of indigenous communities, divided by estate, clanship, and history.[14] The image of the ummah overcame the insularity and isolation of local polities, and gave individuals a sense of having a place in the wider world. At the same time, Muslim traders mediated interregional trade and provided local rulers with means for consolidating their power and increasing their wealth. When the Scottish explorer Alexander Gordon Laing visited the Barawa capital of Kulakonke in 1822, Kuranko were eager to engage in trade, offering ivory and gold in exchange for salt, tobacco, and Manchester cloth.[15] One may presume that Kuranko rulers were equally open to Muslim traders, offering Islamic medicines, divinatory techniques, and literacy well before the nineteenth century.

But an opportunistic openness to the outside world does not imply a readiness to subject oneself to its influence. On the contrary, traditional rulers hoped to take advantage of new forms of wealth and new technologies of communication without conceding power or radically revising their worldviews. Often, however, the traders and travelers from the outside world sought not reciprocal exchange, but to subjugate, colonize, and convert. These were the terms under which the British sought to impose their will on the Sierra Leone hinterland, and to a lesser extent this same "civilizing mission" increasingly came to inform the Muslim presence in the country from the time of the Colonial Office's approval of the role of *alimanis* (Muslim headmen, from the Arabic *al-imam*) in court hearings and schools.[16] Driving upcountry today, Ahmadiyya schools and mosques stand alongside Evangelical, Mormon, and Seventh-Day Adventist churches, and the slogans painted on vehicles proclaim a spirit of religious eclecticism (Allah Is One, God Is One, God Is Great, Thank the Lord, Allah Is My Provider, God's Time Is Best), as well as offer paths to prosperity (Enter a New Level of Plenty).

Because of its remoteness and inaccessibility, as well as the agnosticism of many Kuranko rulers, the Kuranko heartland remained largely peripheral to institutional Islamic influence for hundreds of years, despite Fulani Muslim invasions and incursions.[17] But assessing the degree of Islamic influence from Kuranko oral traditions is extremely difficult, if for no other reason than the keepers of these traditions (the *finas* and *jelis*) were expected to praise their lords by exaggerating their virtues and casting them in an entirely positive light.

According to Barawa traditions, the tenth ruler of Barawa, Marin Tamba Mara, was visited in the mid-nineteenth century (circa 1862–84) by a Fula *karamorgo* (literate teacher) or *mori* (Muslim) called Karakome Alfa Ibrahim, who "converted" the pagan Mara to Islam, a conversion that so pleased Marin Tamba that he became known as Sewa, meaning "happy." A Fula clan—the Thoronka—were subsequently given the chieftaincy in the neighboring chiefdom of Kalian.

We must exercise caution in how we interpret "conversion" in this context, for though the word roughly translates the Kuranko verb *yelama*, "to change or exchange," as in changing one's clothing, changing places with another person, or undergoing change from childhood to adulthood, it does not carry the Euro-Christian connotations of revelation or rebirth, suggesting a complete psychological transformation of a person's life and worldview. Indeed, "conversion" to Islam among the Kuranko may be a euphemism for military conquest followed by vassalage, or simply suggest that Islam disseminated "downward" from a ruler to his subjects. Marin Tamba's "conversion" to Islam may have reflected a reciprocal arrangement, independently reached by his successors, to offer pastoral Fulani grazing rights for their herds in return for the cattle needed for chiefly sacrifices or as gifts to seal political alliances (often involving intermarriage and cattle bridewealth) with neighboring polities. But other oral histories suggest a different story. Not long after Marin Tamba's alleged conversion, he rebelled against submission to Fula military forces from Solima in the north.[18] Barawa was invaded by Fula and their Solima allies, and the defeated Marin Tamba (alias Sewa), took his own life.[19] Despite becoming a tributary state to Solima in the late eighteenth century, Barawa had an ambivalent and vacillating relationship with Islam that has continued to the present day.

When the Barawa chief, Tala Sewa Mara, passed away in 1992, people became, in the words of one informant, "hostage to the rebel war." Village elders fled to Freetown, leaving a power vacuum that was provisionally filled by the appointment of a man called Konkoro Mara who did not belong to the ruling lineage. Konkoro had a Muslim mentor, Alhaji Suleiman Faro, who hailed from Mongo, a chiefdom to the east of Barawa. Alhaji Faro, like his father before him, was a *mori*, and as a leader of the Gbangbane witch-finding association, had occult powers that he was prepared to use to get his way. Despite the fact that a son of the ruling house, Abdul Mara, was appointed chief when the civil war ended in 2002, the appointment was facilitated by his brother, S. B. Marah, right-hand man to President Alhaji Ahmad Tejan Kabbah. Abdul subsequently came under suspicion of hoarding local gold for his own benefit. Despite pressures from ardent Muslims for Alhaji Faro to become chief, a prominent expatriate, Bockarie Mara returned home from London to ensure that his lineage would continue to rule over the newly amalgamated Barawa and Woli chiefdoms. In May 2017, Abdul was appointed section chief of Barawa.

While material or political advantages might accrue from striking a deal with Fula or Mandinka Muslims, and a chief's charisma might be increased by being in possession of the magical medicines, occult powers, divinatory skills, and talismanic objects purveyed by Muslims, his power could be undermined from these same quarters. Kuranko villagers bemoan the dung left by Fula herds, and Mara informants often told me that Fula cattle herders would stay clear of Mara chiefdoms lest they be attacked by leopards—the totem of the Mara into which some clansmen could shape-shift in order to prey on livestock or attack enemies.

Despite historiographical and ethnographic evidence of a frequently antagonistic relationship between Kuranko agriculturalists and Fula pastoralists, or between agnostic chiefs and Muslim proselytizers, political alliances, economic exchange, and a spirit of tolerant coexistence are equally evident. One could declare oneself a Muslim without embracing the five duties or "pillars" of Islam, acquiring Arabic literacy or rote memorizing the Qur'an. *Moris* could officiate at sacrifices and prayers addressed to Allah without diminishing the central role of ancestors. And in paying lip service to Allah, communities that comprised many different hereditary clans, including rulers, commoners, Muslims, or *nyemakale* (cobblers, praise-singers, blacksmiths, keepers of chiefly traditions), and slaves, could transcend historical differences and hierarchical distinctions, although joking relations (*sanakuiye*) between clans and the sharing of totemic animals could also overcome exclusive clan, chiefdom, and even tribal boundaries and create the semblance of universal brotherhood or fictive kinship, similar to the Islamic ummah. As for literacy, it was regarded as having magical efficacy long before it became a means for the acquisition of Islamic knowledge. Even today, villagers often wash *suras* from a slate (or pulp written prescriptions from a clinic) and drink the decoction as Europeans might swallow a pill. Tightly folded pages of Qur'anic text, stitched into leather sachets, and worn around the neck, provide protection from sorcery, and similar sachets attached to country-cloth gowns were used by hunting militias (*tamaboros*) during the civil war to fend off bullets, just as they were used in the past to fend off arrows.

All these borrowings from Islam were adopted for various reasons, and to a greater or lesser extent, by Kuranko rulers and commoners alike. In the Mara family to which I am affiliated, one brother and three sisters were fervent Muslims married to Muslims, three brothers had a more non-committal relationship with Islam, while the youngest brother, Noah, repudiated both Islam and Christianity, once declaring to me, "I have never embraced any moral system, and I hope I never will."[20]

From Barawa to Diang

I now turn from Barawa to the neighboring chiefdom of Diang in order to explore further the strategies whereby Kuranko chiefs formed relations with Islam that did not compromise their power but promised to augment it. While suspicious of outsiders, including English administrators, Muslim clerics, and state officials, Kuranko rulers have sought to strike a balance between insularity and openness—calculating the risks of new alliances, and hedging their bets when faced with new avenues for development and new forms of power.

The Diang chief Sheku Magba Koroma II died in 1995 after forty years in power. In my frequent visits to Kondembaia,[21] the principal town of Diang, I would almost always find chief Sheku Magba on the high porch of his house, his sandals shucked off, a fly whisk draped over his shoulder, a kettle of water and furled umbrella (which he used as a walking stick in both dry and wet seasons) close at hand. It was, however, only after his death, when I became close friends with his son Sewa Magba, that I learned how Sheku Magba had become a Muslim and a chief.

When Sheku Magba was a small boy, a Mandinka Muslim called Sori, who hailed from Karina in northern Sierra Leone, came to Diang chiefdom to recruit boys for his Qu'ranic school. Though Sheku Magba's lineage had been "pagans" for as long as anyone could remember, the boy's father's elder brother decided that he should go with the Qu'ranic teacher. Sheku Magba was not present when the fateful decision was made; he was in the bush with his age-mates, searching for wild fruit. But when he was summoned and told what had been decided, he declared himself happy to go with the stranger and learn whatever there was to be learned from him.

On arriving in Karina, Sheku Magba was introduced to a second *karamorgo* who told Sori, "This small boy that you have brought with you is a star. You must take special care of him." And so it was that Sheku Magba received special treatment and, unlike the other boys, was not beaten if he was careless or dilatory in his Qur'anic studies.

Twenty-five years passed, and Sheku Magba's *karamorgo* gave his eldest daughter Mami Ami in marriage to his star pupil, and with his teacher's blessing Sheku Magba traveled with his new wife to Kono where he went into business selling native tobacco. At about this time, Sheku Magba's father Chief Sama Magba Koroma died, and a new chief was installed in Diang. The new incumbent, Mansa Bala, belonged to a rival ruling house, had many wives, but proved to be an ineffectual ruler. The real power in Diang was wielded by his brother, Mamadu Sandi, who was given to assaulting people without provocation, abducting other men's wives, and stealing people's property with impunity.

A certain Alhaji Magba Kamara, who had received some education and was connected to Diang through his mother, saw a way of resolving this situation. Pretending to be Mansa Bala, he wrote a letter to the British District Commissioner, resigning the chieftaincy on the grounds that he was weary of the burden of his numerous responsibilities. The letter was taken to Mansa Bala, who was told it was from the colonial administration regarding some improvements that were about to be made in the chiefdom. These required his warrant. Mansa Bala signed and sealed the letter, and a week later the District Officer arrived in Kondembaia to take the staff from him.

When elections were called for his successor, the rivalry between the two ruling houses—known as the Magbas and the Ferenkes—resurfaced with a vengeance. Although Mansa Bala had accepted the loss of the staff, his brother Mamadu Sandi had not. And when a section chief, whose name was Ma Ferema Kona, suggested that Sheku Magba be nominated as a candidate for the chieftaincy (because some diviners had predicted that the new chief would be a Muslim), the Ferenkes drove the Muslim Mandinkas from Kondembaia.

Sewa recalls what happened next.

> Ma Ferema Kona and some other elders, like Pa Bunkure, went to Kono to look for my dad. He was in Tankoro by then. He was living there. They said to him, "We have come to get you." My dad said, "What for?" They said, "We want you to be our candidate in the elections at Kondembaia." He said, "How could I be chief? I'm just a poor man, just doing my business, selling this tobacco leaf to make a living. I'm poor, and my brothers are there." They said, "No, this is not about money. You are going to be our chief. We are going to elect you." He said, "All right, let's go." So they went to Kondembaia. Some of his elder brothers were not happy about this. They said, "What! Over our dead bodies! How can you people come and crown our junior, junior brother Sheku, small, small Sheku?" One of my uncles poisoned himself because of this. There were eight of them contesting for the chieftaincy. By the time of the election, four were dead.[22] But the elections were held and my dad became Paramount Chief. He brought stability. He built a mosque. He started converting people to Islam.

Religious Pluralism

Sewa's father was not just a role model for Sewa; in many ways Sewa became his father. As a small boy, he had been nicknamed "walking stick" because of the way he followed his father everywhere, dogging his heels, head down, concentrating on placing his feet exactly where his father placed his, literally walking in his father's footsteps. But Sewa had inherited more than his father's way of walking; he had inherited the right to rule and it was his ambition to emulate the political even-handedness and incorruptibility for which his father was known during forty years as Paramount Chief of Diang.

That Sewa was sustained emotionally in exile by the "belief" he had inherited from his father (by which he meant both Islam and a sense of what in Kuranko is known as *bimba che*—ancestral legacy or birthright) was made very clear in the way he responded to my question: "Do you think of yourself as a Muslim?"

"I am a Muslim. I was raised in a Muslim home. My father was a Muslim, just as I told you, and my mother too. But I am first and foremost a Kuranko man."

Sewa's response is illuminating. It shows that a nominal identification with Islam may reflect idiosyncratic affections and collective affiliations to very different degrees, and that ethnic, religious, national, or familial allegiances are given very different emphases in different social contexts.

Sewa's mother Tina Mara, hailed from Barawa, and her marriage to Sheku Magba Koroma II cemented a longstanding alliance between Barawa and Diang. While Tina's conversion to Islam was partly a condition of her marriage, her father, Tina Kome Mara, who enlisted in the Sierra Leone Battalion of the West African Frontier Force and fought the Germans in Neu Kamerun in World War I, was agnostic, though married into a Muslim Mandinka family. When I asked his sons whether their father converted to Islam, I would receive answers not unlike the answer Sewa gave to the same question. Tina Kome's son Abdul, himself an observant Muslim, confided to me that his father's dying words were "God the chief," but whether he meant the Christian or Muslim God was not clear. Abdul's agnostic younger brother Noah said that their father embraced Islam to help him stop drinking alcohol. Tina Kome's second-born son, Sewa Bokarie, rose to prominence in Sierra Leone's post-independence government, but during his forty years as a senior politician with the Sierra Leone People's Party (SLPP) and despite his personal agnosticism, he opportunistically paid his respects to both Christian and Muslim constituencies and allied himself with a Mandinka Muslim praise-singer, Faraba Demba Gibate, who on public occasions would trace Sewa Bokarie's illustrious ancestry back to Yilkanani (Alexander the Great), Solomon, Muhammad, and the rulers of Mande.

In all these instances, one cannot speak of dual or competing identifications, or even of syncretism. Rather, one has to think of tradition as a fund of potential ways of praising a ruler, giving legitimacy to a high office, appealing to different constituencies, or dealing with personal issues such as impotence, ill health, family feuds, and alcoholism.

What is brought to the fore in one context will be thrust into the background in another, and this oscillation will be played out in both consciousness and behavior. Throughout the 1970s, I worked closely with an elderly medicine-master (*besetigi*) called Saran Salia Sano. Though born into an ostensibly Muslim clan and living in the Muslim quarter of Firawa, Saran Salia was a reluctant Muslim who only attended mosque to appease his classificatory sons. Despite this gesture, Saran Salia's leadership of the Kome association and his use of traditional medicines put him at odds with his two classificatory sons, both of whom made the hajj in the early 1970s and returned to Firawa as fervent proselytizers. Too old to farm, and dependent on Abdulai and Hassan for food, a roof over his head, and a proper burial when he died, Saran Salia faced a dilemma. Although the *alhajis* insisted he not only desist practicing medicine but also renounce "jujus."[23] Saran Salia was willing to share his experiences with me, even though Abdulai and Hassan insisted on monitoring our conversation. Fortunately for me, Abdulai proved less dogmatic than his brother, and even took some pride in his "father's" career as *kometigi* and *besetigi*. Indeed, on one occasion, as our conversation was coming to an end, and Hassan was out of earshot, I asked Abdulai why he and his brother had obliged Saran Salia to renounce Kome.

"I like it," Abdulai mumbled defensively. "It's the elders who told him to give it up. And I cannot go against them."

"Do you use the medicines yourself?" I asked.

"Yes. Even Hassan does."

"Alhaji Hassan?" I asked, surprised.

"Yes," Abdulai said. "If they shoot an *alhaji* with *korte* he'll fall to the ground and die just like any other man unless the antidote is supplied."

"Is Islam unable to protect him?"

"If Alhaji Hassan offended a man who owned *korte*, and that man used *korte* against him, then Hassan would die. The *korte* does not care where it goes when it dies! Hell and heaven are all the same to it."

One could cite numerous examples of religious opportunism and pluralism. Of how people hedge their bets, or proclaim one thing while doing another, or how people vacillate between different identifications as their interests change and social fashions dictate. When I first lived and worked in Firawa, people would speak to me about djinn without embarrassment, cite instances of people who had profited from alliances with them, and declare that a farmer would be foolish not to make sacrifices to the genii loci before bush-felling. Forty-five years later, one villager whose father was a renowned storyteller, his stories replete with djinn, told me that "the imams don't like this devil business. Islam has changed people."

"So if a person wants to improve his life, what do the imams say?"

"They speak not of this world but the next."

Yet even though new epistemologies and dogmatic pronouncements make their presence felt, an eclectic spirit persists. Stories of djinn are still told on moonlit nights, Shar'ia law had made no impact in traditional courts and moots, associations like Kome still exist, children attend both Qur'anic and Western schools, Qur'anic and traditional medicines and divinatory techniques still figure in people's lives, and both God and Allah are acknowledged in public ritual and popular culture alike. Despite Islamic pressures to abandon female genital cutting, traditional initiation (*biriye*) rites are still crucial to community life.

It would be all too easy for an educated, literate individual to regard the traditional practices as animist or magical, and to celebrate either Islamic or European scholarship as rational—as foundational to Africa's future as the "old" beliefs and practices were fundamental to its past. But who are we, who write arcane essays few will read, to judge any worldview as intrinsically reasonable or unreasonable? Is there any difference between Imam Hassan's dogmatism, a jihadist's violent implementation of his religious vision, and Europe's civilizing mission? And if we turn from these ideological assertions of what is true and good and focus on the opportunistic way in which we all lead our lives, focusing on the existential quest for well-being, then what holds true for one person, or for an entire society at a given time, will not necessarily hold true for another person, or another society, at another time. Circumcision rituals once served to shape moral adults and create community cohesion; now these imperatives have given way to other imperatives, including schooling, and the freedom to define one's own path through life. Islam was once anathema to many Kuranko; now it is embraced as a way of feeling that one is part of a wider world, a shared humanity. Traveling far beyond the borders of one's village was once deemed reckless, even though broadening one's horizons might bring new benefits to one's natal community in the form of new commodities and life-giving medicines. Nowadays, many prefer migration to countries beyond their own national borders to a life that repeats the time-honored routines of their forefathers. Once a thatched roof served to keep one's house dry, and wattle and daub was sufficient to build strong walls; now only tin roofs and cement walls will suffice. *Plus ça change, plus c'est la même chose.*

In Defense of Existential Anthropology

> Necessity compels philosophy to operate with concepts, but this necessity
> must not be turned into the virtue of their priority—no more than,
> conversely, criticism of that virtue can be turned into a summary verdict
> against philosophy. On the other hand, the insight that philosophy's
> conceptual knowledge is not the absolute of philosophy—this insight, for
> all its inescapability, is again due to the nature of the concept.
> —Theodor Adorno, *Negative Dialectics*

To speak of existential anthropology is to declare an intellectual commitment to engage directly with lived situations, in all their empirical diversity, intersubjective complexity and open-endedness. Rather than discard concepts, one seeks to demystify them, seeing them as potentially no more or less useful to making our lives manageable and meaningful than caring friends, first aid kits, palatable food, and labor-saving devices. Against the idealist tradition of Plato, Emmanuel Kant, and Claude Lévi-Strauss, one resists the assumption that ideas have revelatory power, whether to mirror the nature of being or uncover the structures of the unconscious mind. In this respect, negative dialectics and existential anthropology are invitations to explore what lies on the margins of thought, and why human beings are moved to venture beyond what is conventionally knowable and thinkable.[1]

Existential anthropology and negative dialectics are philosophically skeptical. They doubt that either thought or life can achieve final meaning, complete certainty, or intellectual closure. But while there is always more to any human situation than can be encapsulated in a concept or summarized in a single word, concepts and words remain some of our most potent, if sometimes magical, means of gaining some purchase on the world.

Ideas are like tools or coping mechanisms. The measure of their worth lies in their capacity to help us achieve everyday goals, such as personal or communal well-being, rather than realize metaphysical ideals, such as truth and goodness. Yet means tend to become ends. Fetishized, ideas take on a life of their own, or become appropriated as shibboleths by the powers-that-be. As Georg Simmel observed, though born of the life-process, these reified forms—languages, religious doctrines, political ideologies, philosophical systems, and moral laws—come to have such a hold over us that "life often wounds itself upon the structures it has externalized from itself as strictly objective."[2]

The focus of existential anthropology is this vexed relationship between what Simmel called "life processes" and the forms of "more-than-life" that are surplus to our social needs and often obstacles to their satisfaction. Jean-Paul Sartre sees this relationship dialectically, as a tension between what is already constituted as custom, tradition, or habit, and what human beings actively endeavor to constitute as the conditions for a viable life.[3] Although the Sartre of *Being and Nothingness* (1943) focuses on the free acts of human subjects, for the Sartre of *Critique of Dialectic Reason* (1960) freedom has become a synonym for "certain routes [through life] which were not initially given," and for "the small movement which makes of a totally conditioned social being someone who does not render back completely what his conditioning has given him."[4]

Just as Theodor Adorno, Pierre Bourdieu, and Claude Lévi-Strauss identified existentialism with Sartre's early work, so many anthropologists regard "existential anthropology" as a reactionary attempt to turn a social science into a bourgeois form of subjectivism focused on individuality, interiority, and intuition. In view of anthropology's infatuation with a concept of culture that has its roots in German idealism, this is perplexing. For in its emphasis on situations, critical events, and lived experience, existential anthropology has resisted the reification of culture and offered anthropology a way out of the impasse of idealism without reverting to material determinism.

The fatal flaw of bourgeois idealism is its tendency to deploy thought and language as magical means of transcending reality rather than engaging with it. As Theodor Adorno notes of Kierkegaard, his invocation of spiritual inwardness reflected the décor of nineteenth century bourgeois homes, offering "a refuge from an increasingly unpleasant world"[5]—the very world, in fact, that provided the material underpinnings of bourgeois privilege and power. In his own critique of the "idealist cult of inwardness," Herbert Marcuse points out that that the bourgeois oppositions between body and soul, love and sex, or thinking and doing, that underwrote social divisions between the allegedly refined "upper classes" and the so-called lower orders,[6] were echoed by academics for whom the world of thought became increasingly alienated from lived reality. In privileging logos over life and generating jargons to create an air of authority and omniscience, the intellectual not only distanced himself from the world of those who lacked time to think, leisure to read, or money to burn; he deployed thought and language as bulwarks against that world. In turning a blind eye on areas of experience that were fraught, unfathomable, or unspeakable, the intellectual could blithely write off vast numbers of people on the grounds that they were beyond the pale of reason.

As I understand it, the mission of anthropology is to write against these habits of dismissing other lives and other life forms as if one's own lifeworld were the measure of all things. To do ethnography is to engage with the lives of others in their worlds, in their languages, in their time, and on their terms. But this immersion in another lifeworld finds its ultimate justification neither in a desire to bear witness to how the other half lives (and dies), nor in a desire to improve the other's lot, nor in a desire to avoid parochialism, but in a commitment to discover or recover a sense of what goes beyond one's own singularity, whether cultural or personal, and constitutes, for good or for ill, our common humanity.

Ethnography exemplifies this venture. But it would not be possible unless it presumed some common ground—some capacity, phylogenetically given if not culturally acknowledged, for recognizing the other in oneself and oneself in the other. Such pan-human capacities include a mimetic capacity for learning languages, acquiring practical skills, forming affective bonds, and surviving separation and loss. These capacities are predicated on universal human needs, for recognition, respect, food, water, shelter, and affection, and reflect universal struggles, to reconcile one's own needs with the needs of others, to act rather than simply be acted upon, to cope with the fact of one's finitude, and to work out ways of dealing with the existential paradox of being singular and different in a world one shares with millions of the same species whose brains and behaviors reflect a common evolution and whose lives are interconnected with the life of the earth itself.

Despite the practical advantages of reaching out to others—taking spouses from outside one's family or local community, trading with strangers, forming alliances with potential enemies—what existential satisfaction comes from venturing beyond the lifeworld into which one was born? What drives one to remake and rethink oneself elsewhere, and through others, *as well as through concepts that allegedly enable one to transcend immediate empirical reality*? This broaches the question of critique. Of an anthropology whose raison d'être is to understand others from their own points of view and, as a corollary, reflect on one's own lifeworld from the standpoint of theirs.

Reification and Violence

I began writing this book within days of the inauguration of Donald Trump, and I bring it to a close with a renewed caution against the political dangers we face in becoming slaves to abstract generalizations and obedient to orders from above. In invoking the law to justify the separation of parents and children who have crossed the southern borders of the United States in a desperate hope of asylum, the Trump administration ignored the existential circumstances that drove these illegal migrants to embark on their harrowing journeys north and absolved itself of any human responsibility for their welfare. Whereas ethics evokes images of our common humanity—such as the categorical imperative to act only according to that maxim whereby you can will that it should become a universal law—the invocation of what is legal and illegal effectively subordinates the humanity of aliens to their national, racial, material, or ethnic identities, which are by definition not ours.

But what are laws except the momentarily reified expression of decades and often centuries of negotiation and revision based on individual cases, specific circumstances, and changing social contexts? To treat laws as if they were holy writ, and therefore beyond the power of mortals to amend, is to act in bad faith.

Laws, like customs and beliefs, change in accordance with the empirical situations in which human beings find themselves and to which they respond. Such changes are the net effects of a myriad of individual actions and reactions and only rarely the result of conscious collective coordination. Yet we readily fall into thinking that the whole is not only the sum of its parts but possesses a greater causal power and exerts a fateful influence over us. Consider flocking behavior. "A single bird's tendency to align and remain close (but not too close) to her peers can create a swirling flock that appears to be moving with a collective mind."[7] But a murmuration of starlings, a crowd of people, or cloud formations are inadvertent consequences of micro-behaviors that are the real prime movers. In exploring this phenomenon, Thomas Schelling asks why individuals tend to occupy seats in an auditorium from the middle rows to the rear before filling the front rows. For Schelling, all we need to know is that "people entering an auditorium have a sociable desire to sit near somebody but always to leave one empty seat between them," though other seating preferences are also at play, such a desire not to be too conspicuous or to be in a position to observe others entering the auditorium. The unintended result of these micro-behaviors is a patterning that is determined neither by an explicit policy of the theater management nor some collective consciousness of the audience. Not only is "the aggregate ... merely an extrapolation from the individual,"[8] but one cannot infer individual experience from collective phenomena.

This is also true of such conceptual aggregates as Race, Culture, Society, History, or Law. They are by-products of seeing the world from afar. But, like other collective nouns, they mask a vast variety of individual motives, understandings, and purposes. But distancing distorts. It creates forms of false-seeming, including the attribution of will and consciousness to concepts, objects, and social groups. Rather than act and speak as though such abstractions as "migrants" or "Africans" mirrored real groupings in which every individual was as identical to the others as they were collectively different from "us," we need detailed descriptions of social reality as it actually unfolds and is experienced.

If concepts, clouds, crowds, and paradigms do not bring into being the activities we spuriously explain by reference to them, what function do they serve? If a concept such as "recipe" is, as Michael Oakeshott observes, an abridgement of an activity—a post-facto shorthand for a process—cooking—that cannot be comprehensively accounted for, what value does a recipe have for us?

In arguing that the recipe is not the parent of the activity but its stepchild, Oakeshott[9] is suggesting that abstract concepts give us a sense of having some purchase on the world even though they do not themselves cause things to happen. Functioning as coping mechanisms, they foster the consoling illusion that our lives can be comprehended and controlled, and that we can share our experiences with others.

The Willing Suspension of Disbelief

When we lose the conceptual or physical props on which we have come to rely in navigating our way in the world, we will initially mourn what we have lost, and seek to recover it. Inevitably, however, we begin to cast about for new concepts, images, or practical skills that will restore our sense of existential equilibrium. Although new ideas and skill sets may come to provide the same satisfaction the old ones gave us, experience teaches us that we cannot expect any one concept, any one technique, or any one person to help us deal with every critical situation we encounter in life. A degree of doubt and uncertainty inheres in our relationships to practices, beliefs, and others, so that no matter how fervently we espouse our faith in them or express the hope that they will remain constant, we are aware that things change, and that our attachment to what has worked for us in the past is no guarantee that it will work for us in the future.[10] When Judith Sherman was thirteen, she was transported in a cattle wagon, along with countless others, from Kurima, Czechoslovakia, to "resettlement" in the east. Her father and mother, and her brother Karpu, would perish in concentration camps, though she would survive Ravensbrück to marry, bring children of her own into the world, become a grandmother, and remember her parents when they were younger than her own offspring and her brother who would "forever be nine." In her Holocaust memoir,[11] Judith Sherman speaks of the impact of her experiences in Ravensbrück on her faith.

Are You not tempted,

Lord,

To intervene

lend a hand,

prevent a scream?[12]

Although it is not for us to write the Holocaust, Judith once told me, because this is God's work, I can never forget that in our darkest hour, beaten and abused by the SS, we were so visible to them and so invisible to Him. Judith is prepared to wait for all eternity, if necessary, for God to account for his absence, and her memoir reads not only as a testimony to man's inhumanity to man but as an epistle to God, for while we, at a distance, can place the blame for the genocides and pogroms of the Nazi period squarely on Hitler and his minions, Judith Sherman will not excuse God for His part in allowing such things to happen.

The loss of concepts, of faith, or a way of life may be temporary or permanent. It may come upon one gradually or befall one like a bolt from the blue—an experience that the Apsálooke chief Plenty Coups, speaking of the catastrophic collapse of his people's traditional way of life, summed up in the compelling phrase, "After this, nothing happened."[13] But we are often free to conspire in this process, and in exploring the interplay between losing a belief and willingly suspending disbelief, I deploy Karl Jaspers notion of border-situations (*Grenzsituationen*)[14] in which concepts lose their vitality, cannot be formed, or are deliberately rejected, though old ideas may be charged with new life or, in the case of Judith Sherman's belief in God, coexist with endless questioning.

For many anthropologists, the initial phase of fieldwork is a deeply unsettling experience and may be compared with an ordeal or rite of passage. Like a neophyte undergoing traditional initiation, the novice fieldworker is abruptly cut off from his or her familiar lifeworld and cast into a transitional space in which physical discomfort and culture shock combine to destabilize one's habitual sense of self. Not only does one not know how to behave, one does not know what to think. This has nothing to do with fathoming the inner workings of another lifeworld, though theoretical conjectures may provide a consoling, if illusory, sense that one understands the world into which one has been thrown. Most urgently, however, one seeks to recover one's existential footing, and to this end one will often unconsciously or quite opportunistically avail oneself of anything that comes to hand or springs to mind.

Let me illustrate what I mean by sharing something of my own experiences of embarking on fieldwork in a remote Kuranko village in northern Sierra Leone in the dry season of 1969. During my first few weeks in the village of Firawa, I found myself so captivated by the things I heard and saw around me that it was all too easy to believe I intuitively understood them. In piecing together the "kinship system," I assumed that a conceptualization of the phenomenon "kinship" (*nakelinyorgoye*, lit. mother-one-relationship) would magically enable me to grasp the lived experiences encapsulated in the abstract term. It was similar to the way that Kuranko evoked witchcraft when confounded by mysterious deaths or inexplicable catastrophes. Naming one's fears was the first step to mastering them.

For Kuranko, initiation is not a matter of conceptual understanding but of undergoing direct experience; learning how to endure the social and emotional pain of adult life through learning how to withstand physical pain. Attaining this new understanding (*hankili kura*) entails suffering the eclipse of everything you know, all that you have, and all that you are. It is, as the Kuranko say, like the gown you put on when you are initiated. To don this gown, you must first be divested of your old garb, stripped clean, and reduced to nothingness.

As I struggled to find my footing in Firawa, the dry season initiations were in full swing. I was told of the neophytes' vulnerability to witches and of the dangers attending the surgical operations they would undergo. I heard of fearful encounters with bush spirits and arduous hazings. And I wondered how the young girls would fare, returning after weeks of sequestration in the bush, not to the security of their parental homes but to the uncertainties of life as newlyweds in the houses of strangers.

If I empathized with the neophytes, it was because I was also like a child, and the shock of too many new experiences—a language I could not speak, food I often found unpalatable, customs I could not understand, afflictions I could not cure—was beginning to erode my own self-confidence and make me vaguely paranoid. As the days passed, I began to miss and worry about my wife, who was living in the provincial town of Kabala, some thirty miles away.

One evening I walked out to the latrine that stood in the grassland behind the house where I had been lodged. For a while, the silence around me was broken only by the repetitive piping of a *sulukuku* bird. Suddenly, I was startled by the presence of several Senegalese fire finches flitting around me. Aware that for Kuranko these small, crimson birds embodied the souls of children who have died in infancy, I became convinced that something was amiss in Kabala—that my wife, who was pregnant with our first child, had had a miscarriage, that her life was in danger.

That night I slept badly, and in the morning confided my anxieties to my field assistant, Noah Marah. He too was missing his children and wondering about his wives in Kabala. Perhaps it was time for us to return. But I was determined to stay, at least until the initiates entered the *fafei*—the bush house where they would live for several weeks after their operations, receiving instructions from older women.

It was at this time that I consulted my first Kuranko diviner. His name was Doron Mamburu Sisé. Noah had sought his advice, and he allowed me to sit in on the consultation. So, a couple of days later, on the spur of the moment, I asked if I might follow suit. I have elsewhere described this consultation, in which the diviner assured me that my wife was in good health and would safely deliver a baby daughter.[15] I have also written of how I shared my dreams with Kuranko elders, receiving the same assurances that Doron Mamburu had given me, that my path in life would be clear, though this would be conditional on my making prescribed sacrifices—something I conscientiously did. These experiences informed my pragmatic interpretations of Kuranko divination and oneiromancy as modes of what Hubert Dreyfus calls "skillful coping."[16]

Beliefs are resources. They have no reality until brought from cold storage and put to work by a particular person in relation to a particular situation. One can never predict when and how a "quiescent" belief will be drawn upon, or by whom, or when it will be bracketed out. The "belief" that dead infants may be reincarnated and Senegalese fire finches provide their souls a temporary home is simply one of many possible resources, some conceptual, others practical, that a Kuranko woman may use in coping with the loss of an infant or, in my case, an anthropologist could use in articulating his inchoate anxieties. As Meyer Fortes observes in one of his most illuminating essays on everyday Tallensi life, "Fate, which in theory is irresistible and irrevocable, is in practice taken to be controllable ... It is thus recognized that it is not in the nature of man to submit blindly to what purports to be mystically inevitable."[17]

What made it possible for me to "go along with" Kuranko conceptions of divinatory and dream analysis was a capacity for suspending disbelief that comes naturally to human beings, enabling us to play with possibilities of thinking and acting that are not always consistent with normative prescriptions or approved by conventional wisdom. Despite one's espoused commitment to a faith, to reason, or to a particular worldview, one will readily place it in abeyance if it proves inefficacious. Our ability to suspend disbelief, like our capacity for dissociation, is an expression of a phylogenetic capacity for practical and imaginative play, and may be compared with the phenomenological epoche, in which extant concepts are bracketed out in order to open one's mind to possibilities that moral codes, social norms, and customary beliefs preclude. In such instances, one operates in a subjunctive (as-if) mode rather than prescriptively and dogmatically.

How we retrospectively rationalize our actions may bring us back to the question of belief, as we affirm or revise received ideas in the light of our experience, but whatever form our post-facto reflections and understandings take, there will be no guarantee that they will predetermine our future actions.[18] A corollary of this view is that philosophy itself is less a matter of forming new concepts or seeking absolute truth, than a question of inventing new metaphors, images, and ways of writing that speak directly to our changing life-situations—a view that Richard Rorty speaks of as a search for edification rather than systematization.[19] Hannah Arendt makes an even stronger claim, arguing that, "All philosophical terms are metaphors, frozen analogues, as it were, whose true meaning discloses itself when we dissolve the term into its original context."[20]

Ethnographic Realism

Writing of the difference between idealism and realism, Jorges Luis Borges cites Samuel Taylor Coleridge's view "that all men are born Aristotelian or Platonist. The latter know by intuition that ideas are realities; the former, that they are generalizations; for the latter, language is nothing but a system of arbitrary symbols; for the former, it is the map of the universe."[21] My own preference, however, is to think of conceptual reality and lived reality as complementary and not existentially incompatible, and the same goes for our conventional distinctions between the theoretical and the empirical, beliefs and practices, map and territory, idea and image. This is a pragmatist argument that places thinking and doing on a par, construing them as alternative means (*techne*) for achieving existential ends. If a concept or practice carries us into a more fulfilling relationship with others, or enables us to achieve a life goal, it is true, as William James would say, insofar as it has helped make this outcome possible. However, a satisfactory result does not mean that the concept or the practice has thereby acquired the status of a truth that holds good whatever the situation at hand. What has worked or proven to be edifying in one particular instance, may prove unhelpful or unenlightening in another. This is as true of the rules of thumb we apply in everyday life as it is of the explanatory models we deploy in science. Nor is there much point in insisting on a distinction between magical and real effects, since what really matters is whether a concept or a coping skill raises our spirits, bolsters our confidence, renews our faith, and improves our well-being. Yet, despite the fact that every person's sense of what is at stake will be different, from one day to the next, from one society to another, or one situation to another—getting in touch with God or the ancestors, dealing with pain, raising a child, or earning a living—life everywhere consists, as Baruch Spinoza put it, in a struggle to persevere in one's being. In this struggle for a viable life, different beliefs and actions will be tried and tested, regardless of whether convention dismisses some as weird, wrong, or impractical and deems others to be real, reasonable, or true.

Something similar is true of our psychological capacity for shape-shifting. There is always more to a person than meets the eye. There are lost selves or souls that seldom see the light of day, shadowy existences, hidden histories, closeted stories, faces concealed by masks. Philosophically, the suspicion that we are several rather than consistently the same often finds expression in the polarization of appearance and reality, or conscious and unconscious life. In his history of dynamic psychiatry, Henri Ellenberger characterizes this "unmasking trend" as a systematic search for underlying truth.[22] It bears comparison with what Paul Ricœur calls "the hermeneutics of suspicion" and is reminiscent of Claude Lévi-Strauss's deployment of geological and archaeological metaphors to argue that "understanding consists in reducing one type of reality to another," since "true reality is never the most obvious" and "the nature of truth is already indicated by the care it takes to remain elusive."[23]

Rather than draw a sharp distinction between a constant underlying reality and changing surface appearances, why not simply speak of multiple realities—or appearances—each one of which may have a part to play in our lives? As Fernando Pessoa, puts it:

> I've created various personalities within. I constantly create personalities. Each of my dreams, as soon as I start dreaming it, is immediately incarnated in another person, who is then dreaming it, and not I.
>
> To create, I've destroyed myself. I've so externalized myself on the inside that I don't exist there except externally. I'm the empty stage where various actors act out various plays.[24]

Consider the case of Mohammed Fofona, "the man who could turn into an elephant."[25] At a period in his life when his political fortunes had fallen and his self-esteem was at a low ebb, Mohammed invoked his clan's totemic association with the elephant and imagined that he could actually transform himself into an elephant at will. The potentiality of the totemic belief, like a belief in God or even a memory of better times, proves empowering. Not only does Mohammed embody a totemic ideal, but a hitherto theoretical possibility becomes, in his experience, a lived reality. A feeling of elephantine power and strength is translated into the conviction that he has actually become an elephant. For Alfred North Whitehead, Mohammed was guilty of the fallacy of misplaced concreteness—the all-too-human tendency to construe a subjective event—an inspired idea, an overwhelming emotion, a vivid memory, or intense sensation—as confirming an objective reality.[26]

The question is never whether such beliefs or concepts are intrinsically real or rational, but what kind of experiences bring beliefs and concepts into being. Our thoughts and actions do not necessarily proceed from an entrenched belief or fully formed point of view, but rather from a situation or event that confounds us. Beliefs are the retrospective, reified, and exaggerated courtesies we pay to practices or images that have helped us cope with such unsettling situations or critical events.

Countless examples could be cited from religion and anthropology of sensations, memories, or emotions re-imagined as spirits, ghosts, or "supernatural beings" with whom the living can converse, petition, ritually appease, summon as allies, impersonate, or become possessed by. Michael Puett has published edifying accounts of how, in early Chinese ritual practice, negative energies and volatile emotions were personified as ghosts or demons, so that in one instance a ruler's son would impersonate the ghost of his late grandfathers in order to bring about the proper disposition between the living and the dead.[27] There is, therefore, a direct comparison to be made between the reification of concepts—in which we act as if a word and the object it names are essentially one—and the ontologizing of experience, in which we act as if a mental event suggests the existence of an empirical being. In both instances, a metaphor is taken literally, and a word or idea is assumed to mirror an objective reality. It is important to emphasize, however, that though these attributions of life to concepts or this conflation of qualities and entities are "fallacious," they are basic cognitive processes and coping strategies. For in transforming a subjective experience of pain or pleasure, love or hate, into an objective form, we not only grasp that experience conceptually, we socialize our relationship with it and can thereby interact with as though it were a person.

Compelling examples of this phenomenon may be adduced from the medical field of allotransplantation in which anxieties over incorporating a foreign organ into one's body (and having to reconceive oneself) are alleviated by imagining the organ as possessing the donor's personality or as a newborn welcomed into one's life.[28] In a remarkable essay on a Suyá individual who received a kidney donated by an individual from another ethnic group, Nancy Scheper-Hughes and Mariana Leal Ferreira describe how the recipient had recourse to spirit helpers, moving from person to person in the form of birds, to overcome his resistance to the transplant and keep in touch with his family in a remote Xingu village. That "the Suyá world is implicitly multiple and fluid, a world in which human and animal, spirit and matter, lived and dreamed realities bleed into one another," undoubtedly helps explain why Dombá's experience of separation and loss was mitigated and the medical operation was successful.[29]

What Lévi-Strauss calls a science of the concrete, or *la pensée sauvage*, is not the preserve of primitive minds or unique to childlike reasoning but common to all humankind. The challenge is not to reject anthropomorphic thought or misplaced concreteness on the grounds that it is irrational but to evaluate all forms thought in terms of their effects and repercussion in our lives. Yet the danger of treating ideas as persons (or even equating them with transcendent or universal values) is that we risk subordinating real persons to moral abstractions and sacrificing human lives to high ideals. In the same way, treating an experience as if it were a living being risks estranging us from the real beings to whom we are beholden and whose lives should be the primary measure of our own humanity.

Not long ago, while waiting at a bus stop in Cambridge, Massachusetts, I fell into conversation with a man wearing dark glasses and carrying a folded white stick who had asked me if the bus that had just gone by was the Harvard Shuttle or the 77 to Arlington Heights. By the time the 77 did arrive and we both boarded it, Derek had confided that I was one of the few people he had spoken to that day whose tone of voice was neither condescending nor pitying. Surprised by this comment, I asked him to explain what he meant. "When I lost my sight," Derek said, "I began to see what life was like for women and for people of color whose slight difference in appearance is often sufficient grounds for others to demean or avoid them. When I went blind, I sensed immediately this change in people's attitudes toward me. My white stick was all it took to make me absolutely different in their eyes. I ceased to be Derek; I became a blind man."

Historically, there is no mystery about the process whereby thought becomes dissociated from being, and reason becomes sundered from the senses. As Maurice Merleau-Ponty observes, this Cartesian split not only entailed a radical separation of mind and body; it reinforced the doctrine of philosophical transcendence, creating a rupture between philosophical models "and the obscurity of the 'there is.'" Because thought is part and parcel of our embodied being, "it cannot, by definition, really be thought [conceived]. *One can only practice it, exercise it, and, so to speak, exist it; yet one can draw nothing from it which deserves to be called true.*"[30] This view not only calls into question the assumption that metaphors comprise tenor and vehicle or subject and object, for just as intersubjective relations involve one person's perception slipping or dissolving into the perception of another in "consummate reciprocity" so our relations with ideas and things often blur the lines we suppose to exist between them.[31] In this sense abstraction is a misnomer, or rather, yet another metaphor, since, as the etymology of the word suggests, abstraction is not a purely cognitive process but a social and physical action of "drawing away from," or withdrawing from someone or something.

Conceptual Limits and Existential Aporias

My final comments reiterate some of the leitmotifs in the work of Theodor Adorno, motifs that have been echoed throughout this book. In a key passage in *Minima Moralia* titled "Gaps," Adorno begins aphoristically: "The injunction to practise intellectual honesty usually amounts to sabotage of thought."[32] Adorno refuses to make distance from experience an acceptable price for rendering experience intelligible. He is critical of the academic conceit that words mirror the world, or that one can disclose all the steps whereby one reached some understanding or, for that matter, became the person one now is. One may contrive the appearance of such a movement from cause to effect, one thing leading inexorably to another, but this is simply an intellectual sleight of hand that produces systematic understanding at the cost of describing life in all its wavering, confusing, deviant and contradictory detail. "If life fulfilled its vocation directly," Adorno concludes,

> it would miss it. Anyone who died old and in the consciousness of seemingly blameless success, would secretly be the model schoolboy who reels off all life's stages without gaps or omissions, an invisible satchel on his back. Every thought which is not idle, however, bears branded on it the impossibility of its full legitimation, as we know in dreams that there are mathematical lessons, missed for the sake of a blissful morning in bed, which can never be made up. Thought waits to be woken one day by the memory of what has been missed, and to be transformed into teaching.[33]

What we miss, gloss over, censor out or artificially fill in when we impose narrative or intellectual order on our experience is what we might attempt, were we were trained otherwise, simply to describe. This would mean acknowledging the gap between precept and practice, the engrained habits that contradict our fantasies of freedom, the gulf between my reality and the reality of others, the difference between what can and cannot be said, the lived particulars that defy our generalizations, and the contradictions that point to "the untruth of identity" and "the fact that the concept does not exhaust the thing conceived." Adorno makes a case for a way of thinking and writing whose substance lies "in the diversity of objects that impinge upon it and of the objects it seeks, a diversity not wrought by any scheme." To these objects, he writes, "philosophy would truly give itself rather than use them as a mirror in which to reread itself, mistaking its own image for concretion."[34]

Adorno's "gaps" are reminiscent of what the Greeks called *aporiai*. Aporia literally means, "lacking a path" (*a-poros*), a path that is impassable. But unlike *odos*, *poros* connotes a sea lane or river road—passages that leave no permanent trace, surfaces "widowed of routes," where there are no stable landmarks and every trail must be blazed anew. An aporia is where we find ourselves out of our depth, in difficulties, all at sea. "The sea is … the aporetic space *par excellence*," writes Sarah Kofman, "and it is still the best metaphor for the aporia of discourse."[35] More generally, an aporia is a "puzzle," a "question for discussion" or "state of perplexity," and the aporetic method for broaching problems without offering immediate solutions is exemplified by the Socratic method, as well as the philosophical skepticism of thinkers such as Pyrrho, Timon, Arcesilaus, Diogenes, and Sextus Empiricus.

Sextus was quite explicit about the connection between skepticism and the aporetic method arguing that "the skeptic way" be embraced as a way of life (*agoge*) or disposition (*dunamis*), and that the suspension of judgment (*epoché*) helps us achieve inner tranquility or peace of mind (*ataraxia*).[36] Also influenced by Pyrrho, Michel Montaigne advocated that we accept both good and ill since both "are one substance with our life"—a life that is "composed, like the harmony of the world, of discords as well as of different tones, sweet and harsh, sharp and flat, soft and loud."[37] More recently, the aporia, defined as "an antinomy arising through the simultaneous existence of mutually exclusive entities, each irreducible to the terms of the other,"[38] has become a key postmodern trope, as in the writings of Samuel Beckett where logical absurdity and existential impasses combine to create overpowering images of human absurdity and indecisiveness. The last lines of *The Unnameable*, for example—"I can't go on, I'll go on,"[39] or the following from his *Three Dialogues with George Duthuit*: "The expression that there is nothing to express, nothing with which to express, no power to express, no desire to express, together with the obligation to express."[40]

The classical Greek aporia was primarily a logical conundrum that may be resolved through rational ingenuity—as in Zeno's paradoxes where motion seems to be both possible and impossible. As Kant observed, such aporias are artifacts of the way we think about the world and are not inherent in reality. My focus is, however, less on the aporias that arise from intellectual contemplation than on the enigmas, gaps and double binds that seem to inhere in the human condition itself, such as the fact that every individual is unique, yet shares most of his or her phylogenetic traits with every other member of his or her species, or the fact that every human being needs to act in relation to others and the world, yet is to the same extent acted upon, or the vexing gap between experience and expression that makes mutual understanding so fraught with difficulty. By describing how such perplexities are lived, I hope to paint a more compelling picture than if I simply analyzed the historical or social circumstances under which they made their appearance, or suggested how they might be resolved.

Some of the best examples of the limits of rational thought may be found in the beginning of the Sung dynasty in China (circa 960 BCE) when the "paradoxical words and strange deeds" of the Zen masters of the T'ang period were developed into the classic form of the koan Although the Chinese term *kung-an* signifies "public announcement," the koan's announcement takes the form of a puzzle that mystifies the listener or reader, inspiring him or her to abandon rational or habitual ways of responding to doubt, and become open to new forms of understanding, such as we might call lateral thinking, poetical thinking, or negative dialectics. Heinrich Dumouline refers to the koan as "a kind of spoof on the human intellect" and notes that its aim is to foster a sense of reality that is devoid of any sense of contending dualisms.[41] As one Zen master put it: "We have not to avoid contradiction, but to live it."[42] Accordingly, "Zen" is "not speculation at all but immediate experience of what, as the bottomless ground of Being, cannot be apprehended by intellectual means, and cannot be conceived or interpreted even after the most unequivocal and uncontestable experiences: one knows it by not knowing it."[43] "Consider the following from 1036 BCE, when the Rinzai school of Zen was entering its golden age. The koan takes the form of a play of question and answer.

Q: All people have their own native place owing to the causal nexus. Where is your native place?
A: Early in the morning I ate white rice gruel; now I feel hungry.

Q: In what way do my hands resemble the Buddha's hands?
A: Playing the lute in the moonlight.

Q: In what way do my feet resemble the feet of a donkey?
A: When the heron stands in the snow, its color is not the same.

One finds echoes of this oblique and disconcerting technique in many traditions and many places.[44] For example, the renowned Danish explorer and ethnologist Knud Rasmussen plied his Iglulik Eskimo informants with endless questions, expecting to get a coherent and consistent account of their worldview. But despite the fact that Rasmussen was fluent in Iglulik, his inquiries were met with "long and circumstantial statement[s] of all that was permitted and all that was forbidden" and his "why" questions were regarded as unreasonable and impertinent. One evening, as the light was fading and snow-filled wind gusts blew across the ground, one of Rasmussen's Iglulik informants, a man called Aua, impulsively invited the ethnographer to accompany him across the frozen landscape. First, Aua pointed to a group of bowed and exhausted men returning from their long vigils over blowholes on the ice. They had not killed a single seal, and their entire day of "painful effort and endurance had been in vain." Aua asked Rasmussen why this should be so. Aua then led Rasmussen to Kublo's house where a couple of children crouched, shivering, under a skin rug on the bench, the blubber lamp turned down low to conserve fuel. Why should the house not be warm and bright, the children enjoying life? Aua asked. He then led Rasmussen to a small snow hut where his sister Natseq lived alone; she was suffering from a malignant cough and had not long to live. "Why must people be ill and suffer pain?" Aua asked. "We are all afraid of illness. Here is this old sister of mine: as far as anyone can see, she has done no evil; she has lived through a long life and given birth to healthy children, and now she must suffer before her days end. Why? Why?" "You see," Aua went on. "You are equally unable to give any reason when we ask you why life is as it is. And so it must be. All our customs come from life and turn towards life; we explain nothing, we believe nothing, but in what I have just told you lies our answer to all you ask." Aua then listed for Rasmussen the things they feared—the capricious weather spirits, sickness, hunger, and death, the old woman of the sea, the vengeful souls of the dead, including the spirits of slaughtered animals. Against these perils, Aua said, we rely on

> the old rules of life which are based on the experience and wisdom of generations. We do not know how, we cannot say why, but we keep those rules in order that we may live untroubled. And so ignorant are we in spite of all our shamans, that we fear all the invisible things that are likewise about us, all that we have heard of in our forefathers' stories and myths. Therefore, we have our customs, which are not the same as those of the white men, the white men who live in another land and have need of other ways.[45]

For intellectuals, explaining rather than simply enduring life seems not only necessary but natural. Yet the kind of stoic acceptance of the limits of human understanding that is evident in Aua's conversations with Rasmussen should not be dismissed as an outmoded way of thinking that has no value in our modern world. Though we expand our scientific grasp of life, there are always limits beyond which we too are faced with the "invisible things" that Aua alludes to, and for which we require wit and wisdom rather than reason to address.

Throughout Africa there is a spirited tradition of riddles and dilemma tales that play up ambiguity as a way of inspiring debate on the recurring quandaries of everyday life. In one such Kuranko story that I collected in northern Sierra Leone in 1970, three brothers with the same father but different mothers, all of whom were born on the same day and initiated at the same time, claim the right to succeed their father as chief when the old man dies. Because the only way of evaluating the competing claims of the three brothers is in terms of their mothers' behavior, the storyteller appeals to his audience to remember how, in the early part of the story, each of these woman saved the life of her husband when he was a young man traveling the world in search of fame and fortune. The first woman saved the future chief from the murderous wrath of her father. The second woman sacrificed her only daughter to the djinn safeguarding a river crossing, so that the future chief could cross the river. The third woman told the future chief the answer to a conundrum that her father set every young man who came to his village. After considerable debate, the storyteller presented his own view by approving the argument of the first brother for why he should become chief in his father's stead.

> A man's fortune in life depends on his mother, and a man should never forget from whom he got his start in life, and with whom his life began. The brothers were all equal, in age and ability. But the brother whose mother first saved the life of the chief had the prior claim. If a person trips on a stone and falls down, he should not think first of the place he fell but of the place he tripped.[46]

I agree with both L.-V. Thomas, who writes that the whole point of such dilemma tales is to foster a "multiplicity of points of view and the sharpening of a critical sense,"[47] and J. Berry, who notes of Adangme tales that "no solution is suggested. Each of the audience must give his views and an *ad hoc* solution is accepted at each telling depending on the consensus of the opinion of those present and the weight of the arguments advanced."[48]

There are resonances here of William James' radical empiricism, where incompleteness and tentativeness are given the same analytical weight as the finished and the fixed. This is a philosophy that urges us not to subjugate the complexities and aporias of lived experience to the tyranny of reason or the consolation of order, but to cultivate that quality that John Keats called negative capability, the capability of "being in uncertainties, Mysteries, doubts, without any irritable reaching after fact and reason."[49] This view finds expression in Georg Groddeck's declaration in a letter to his friend and colleague Sándor Ferenczi that "the difference between us is that you are compelled to want to understand things, whilst I am compelled not to want to understand ... I am happy to remain in the dark, in the imago of the womb, which you wish to escape."[50] It bears a family resemblance to Michel Foucault's view that any "discursive formation" is not "an ideal, continuous, smooth text that runs beneath the multiplicity of contradictions, and resolves them in the calm unity of coherent thought"; nor is it "the surface in which, in a thousand different aspects, a contradiction is reflected that is always in retreat, but everywhere dominant. It is rather a space of multiple dissensions; a set of different oppositions whose levels and roles must be described."[51] It pervades Jacques Derrida's work, which moves from the impasse of age-old problems that admit of no solution to exploring the possibility of writing and living as if these problems were simply thresholds one has to cross, curtains one has to draw back, in order to enter a more edifying domain of existence.[52] And it is a view that finds expression in our idea of tragedy, as David Mamet so lucidly explains in his Arthur Miller obituary. Plays such as *Death of a Salesman* and *The Crucible* make us "feel fear," he writes, "because we recognise, in them, our own dilemmas ... We are freed, at the end of these two dramas, not because the playwright has arrived at a solution, but because he has reconciled us to the notion that there is no solution—that it is the human lot to try and fail, and that no one is immune from self-deception."[53]

I am not advocating a lapse into fatalism or nihilism. I do not regard existentialism as a philosophy of the absurd. I simply want to suggest that the intellectual rage for systematicity and totalization[54] is a magical compensation for our failed attempts to control the world or calm our anguish at the world's disorder. This does not necessarily mean that we give up on our attempts to change the way things are, or uncritically embrace any point of view; it is a case for a more sober sense of the limits of thought, and a reminder that we inherit, culturally and biogenetically, not an adapted or seamless nature but a set of incompatible and conflicted potentialities. Accordingly, no movement toward greater openness is without its gestures for closure. African dilemma tales, for all their tolerance of multiple points of view, foster a quest for ethically viable understanding. Zen practice, while dismissive of the idolatry of salvation, has its own agendas for deliverance from illusion. The case is, then, for recognizing the oscillations in everyday life between quite contradictory tendencies—logos and life, compliance and resistance, the transitive and the intransitive—without making special claims for one over the other or seeking a synthesis of them.

Notes

Notes for Introduction

Epigraph: Theodor W. Adorno, "Resignation," *Telos* 35 (Spring 1978): 165–68.

1. Hannah Arendt, *Men in Dark Times* (Harmondsworth: Penguin, 1973).
2. Hannah Arendt, "'What Remains? The Language Remains': A Conversation with Günter Gaus, October 28, 1964," in *The Portable Hannah Arendt*, ed. Peter Baehr, trans. Joan Stambaugh (New York: Penguin, 2003), 3–22, here 21. See also, video of this conversation, YouTube, "Hannah Arendt 'Zur Person,'" Munich 1965, https://www.youtube.com/watch?v=dso-ImQfVsO4 (last accessed 11 February 2019). Arendt's observations echo those of the Danish ethicist Knud Løgstrup, for whom trust is vital to what it means to be human. Without trust "human life could hardly exist … we would simply not be able to live." Knud Løgstrup, *The Ethical Demand* (Notre Dame, IN: University of Notre Dame Press, 1997), 8–9.
3. I cannot ignore the apparent contradiction here between, on the one hand, my call for an anthropology that complements a focus on cultural difference with a focus on human commonalties, and on the other hand, an ecological perspective that demands a similar complementarity between the human and the extra-human. Without arguing for the preservation of a Linnaean taxonomy or for reducing Homo sapiens to a biological species or for denying the relevance of arguments for the post-human, I deploy the concept of the human as a strategic rather than epistemological essentialism in an operationalist spirit. No exploration of the world can hope to encompass everything that is the case or completely dismiss abstraction as an intellectual strategy for comprehending the bewildering array of particularities that we encounter in everyday life.
4. "I doubt whether such ideas [natural trust as normal] could gestate in Løgstrup's mind once he … faced point-blank the realities of the world at war and under occupation, as an active member of the Danish resistance." Zygmunt Bauman, "The Liquid Modern Adventures of the 'Sovereign Expressions of Life,'" in *Concern for the Other: Perspectives on the Ethics of K. E. Løgstrup*, ed. Svend Andersen and Kees van Kooten Nieberk (Notre Dame, IN: Notre Dame University Press, 2007), 113–37, here 121.

5. Piers Vitebsky, *Living without the Dead: Loss and Redemption in a Jungle Cosmos* (Chicago: Chicago University Press, 2017), 2.

6. Hannah Arendt, *The Life of the Mind* (New York: Harcourt Brace, 1978), 6. In a 1972 essay on her own work, Arendt observed that "every human being has a need to think, not to think abstractly, not to answer the ultimate questions of God, immortality, and freedom, nothing but to think while he is living. And he does so constantly.

   "Everybody who tells a story of what happened to him half an hour ago on the street has got to put this story into shape. And this putting the story into shape is a form of thought." "Hannah Arendt on Hannah Arendt," in *Thinking without a Bannister: Essays in Understanding, 1953–1875*, ed. Jerome Kohn (New York: Schocken Books, 2018), 443–475, here 444.

7. Pierre Bourdieu, *Outline of a Theory of Practice*, trans. Richard Nice (Cambridge: Cambridge University Press, 1977), 1–9.

8. Napoleon Chagnon says to Timothy Asch, who is filming the ethnographer interacting with a Yanomamö friend, "We are looking here at ourselves … [we are] several times removed, but nevertheless ourselves."

9. Michael White, *Maps of Narrative Practice* (New York: Norton, 2007), 9.

10. Naveed Baig, Lissi Rasmussen, and Hans Raun Iversen, "Human First: To Be Witnesses to Each Other's Life; Twenty-One Years of Struggle for Equal Human Dignity," unpublished paper, Faculty of Theology, University of Copenhagen, 2017.

11. This point has been eloquently made by Devaka Premawardhana in his account of how the Makhuwa of Mozambique engage with Pentecostalism today only to distance themselves from it tomorrow or pay lip service to it in one context only to reject it in another. This existential mobility suggests an opportunistic and pragmatic attitude toward belief that calls into question a widespread assumption in the academic study of both anthropology and religion of an identity relationship between what people espouse and what they actually think and feel, such that we can understand a person's lived experience simply by asking what the person believes. Devaka Premwardhana, *Faith in Flux: Pentecostalism and Mobility in Rural Mozambique* (Philadelphia: University of Pennsylvania Press, 2018). See also Jonathan Haidt, *The Righteous Mind: Why Good People Are Divided by Politics and Religion* (New York: Vintage, 2012); and Kyle Roberts, "Riding the Moral Elephant: A Book Review of Jonathan Haidt's *The Righteous Mind*," *The Table*, 12 October 2015, retrieved from http: cct.biola.edu/blog/riding-moral-elephant-review-jonathan-haidts-righteous-mind/.

12. Theodor Adorno, "Why Still Philosophy?" in *Critical Models: Interventions and Catchwords*, trans. Henry W. Pickford (New York: Columbia University Press, 1998, 15–17, here 10.

13. Theodor W. Adorno, *Negative Dialectics*, trans. W.B. Ashton (New York: Continuum, 1973), 5, emphasis added.

14. Roland Barthes, *Camera Lucida: Reflections on Photography*, trans. Richard Howard (1980; New York: Farrar, Straus and Giroux, 2010), 32.

15. Michael Jackson, *Harmattan: A Philosophical Fiction* (New York: Columbia University Press, 2015).

16. Michael Jackson, *The Palm at the End of the Mind: Relatedness, Religiosity, and the Real* (Durham, NC: Duke University Press, 2009), xii.
17. William James, *Essays in Radical Empiricism* (Cambridge, MA: Harvard University Press, 1976), 35.
18. Ian McEwan, *Nutshell* (New York: Random House, 2017), 6.
19. Louis Menand, *The Metaphysical Club: A Story of Ideas in America* (New York: Farrar, Straus, and Giroux, 2001), 440.
20. Adorno, *Negative Dialectics*, 365.
21. Adorno, *Negative Dialectics*, 149.
22. With this term I am abbreviating what Adorno calls "rational identity thinking"; it assumes that an object possesses all the properties of its concept (*Begriff*) and is thus idealized without examination of its particulars. Gillian Rose, *The Melancholy Science: An Introduction to the Thought of Theodor W. Adorno* (London: Macmillan, 1978), 61.
23. Liisa Malkki, "Speechless Emissaries: Refugees, Humanitarianism, and Dehistoricization," *Cultural Anthropology* 11, no. 3 (1966): 377–404.
24. James Scott, *Seeing Like a State: How Certain Schemes to Improve the Human Condition Have Failed* (New Haven, CT: Yale University Press, 1998), 22–23.
25. João Biehl, *Will to Live: AIDS Therapies and the Politics of Survival* (Princeton, NJ: Princeton University Press, 2007), 203–31.
26. Martin Buber, *I and Thou*, trans. Ronald Gregor Smith (New York: Scribners, 1958), 9.
27. "All of the Western nations have been caught in a lie, the lie of their pretended humanism; this means that their history has no moral justification, and that the West has no moral authority." James Baldwin, *No Name in the Street* (London: Corgi, 1973), 59.
28. Hilda Kuper makes a similar observation in her study of race relations in Swaziland. While whites are compulsively preoccupied by color differences, "Swazi often discuss the European lack of manners, and I realised how sensitive Swazi were by the care with which I was instructed in etiquette." Hilda Kuper, *The Uniform of Colour: A Study of White-Black Relationships in Swaziland* (Johannesburg: Witwatersrand University Press, 1947), 40.
29. Max Horkheimer and Theodor W. Adorno, *Dialectic of Enlightenment: Philosophical Fragments*, trans. Edmund Jephcott (1987; Stanford, CA: Stanford University Press, 2002), 9. In anthropology, a similar line of critical thinking is evident in several important books: Michael Herzfeld, *Anthropology through the Looking Glass: Critical Ethnography in the Margins of Europe* (Cambridge: Cambridge University Press, 1987); Michael Herzfeld, *The Social Production of Indifference: Exploring the Symbolic Roots of Western Bureaucracy* (New York: Berg, 1992); Pierre Bourdieu, *Pascalian Meditations*, trans. Richard Nice (1997; Cambridge: Polity, 2000), chapters 2 and 3; Dominic Boyer, *Spirit and System: Media, Intellectuals, and the Dialectic in Modern German Culture* (Chicago: University of Chicago Press, 2005); Ghassan Hage, *Alter Politics: Critical Anthropology and the Radical Imagination* (Melbourne: Melbourne University Press, 2015).

30. Theodor W. Adorno, *Minima Moralia: Reflections from Damaged Life*, trans. E. F. N. Jephcott (1951; London: Verso, 1978), 132.
31. Hans-Georg Gadamer, *Truth and Method*, trans. Joel Weinsheimer and Donald G. Marshall (New York: Continuum, 2004), 17.
32. Friedrich Nietzsche, *Thus Spake Zarathustra* (1887), trans. Walter Kaufmann (Harmondsworth: Penguin 1978), 313.
33. Michael Allen Gillespie, "The Search for Immediacy and the Problem of Political Life in Existentialism and Phenomenology," in *A Companion to Phenomenology and Existentialism*, ed. Hubert L. Dreyfus and Mark A. Wrathall (Oxford: Blackwell, 2006), 531–44, here 532.
34. F. Scott Fitzgerald, *The Rich Boy* (1926; London: Hesperus Press, 2003), 3.
35. Aminatta Forna, "Don't Judge a Book by Its Author," *Guardian*, 13 February 2015.
36. Chimamanda Ngozi Adichie, "The Danger of a Single Story," TED talk, July 2009, https://www.ted.com/talks/chimamanda_adichie_the_danger_of_a_single_story.

Notes for Chapter 1

Epigraph: Judy Wieder, ed., *Celebrity: The Advocate Interviews* (New York: Advocate Books, 2001), 127.

1. Jiaying Ding, unpublished informal conversation, Fall 2016.
2. Maxine Hong Kingston, *The Woman Warrior* (New York: Knopf, 2005), 8.
3. Lila Abu-Lughod, *Writing Women's Worlds: Bedouin Stories* (Berkeley: University of California Press, 1993), 13.
4. John Berger, *The Sense of Sight* (New York: Pantheon, 1985), 266–67.
5. In linguistics, George Lakoff's experientialist approach to meaning explores the ways in which concepts are always embedded in changing fields of experience, embodied in sensory life, and generative of associations and images that cannot be reduced to a single stable definition of what the concept actually represents or really means. George Lakoff, *Women, Fire, and Dangerous Things: What Categories Reveal about the Mind* (Chicago: University of Chicago Press, 1987).
6. Michael Jackson, "Displacement, Suffering, and the Critique of Cultural Fundamentalism," in *The Politics of Storytelling: Variations on a Theme by Hannah Arendt* (Copenhagen: Museum Tusculanum Press, 2013), 117–33.
7. See Hannah Arendt on "the conscious pariah" in "The Jew as Pariah: A Hidden Tradition," *Jewish Studies* vol. 6, no. 2 (1944): 99–122, here 111.
8. Hannah Arendt, *Men in Dark Times* (Harmondsworth: Penguin, 1973), 27.
9. Hannah Arendt, "'What Remains? The Language Remains': A Conversation with Günter Gaus, October 28, 1964," in *The Portable Hannah Arendt*, ed. Peter Baehr, trans. Joan Stambaugh (New York: Penguin, 2003), 3–22, here 16.

10. "Those who succeed in a professional discipline are those who best absorb and apply its master narrative." Thomas Frank, *Listen Liberal, or Whatever Happened to the Party of the People* (New York: Picador, 2016), 37–38.

11. Martin Heidegger's notion of care (*Sorge*) as an existential a priori is relevant here, for in as much as care implies that one's very being-in-the-world is itself an issue, to be wondered at and thought about, the question of existence appears most sharply when one does not experience oneself as at home in the world—when timetables are interrupted, familiar spaces are destroyed, loved ones pass away, or one's lifeworld is threatened with extinction.

12. Kingston, *The Woman Warrior*, 8, 11.

13. There are echoes here of narrative therapy, where a client is helped recompose the story of her past life in ways that better enable her to find fulfillment in the present, much as a person might change the furniture in her living room to make the space more congenial. Michael White, *Maps of Narrative Practice* (New York: Norton, 2007).

14. Sunil Badami, "Of All Things Qualifying Us To Make Art, Where We 'Really' Come From Shouldn't Define Us," *Guardian*, 16 August 2017, retrieved from https://www.theguardian.com/global/commentisfree/2017/aug/16/of-all-things-qualifying-us-to-make-art-where-we-really-come-from-shouldnt-define-us, emphasis in text.

15. Sejal Patel, personal communication, 17 August 2017.

16. Ernesto Laclau and Chantal Mouffe, *Hegemony and Socialist Strategy: Toward a Radical Democratic Politics* (London: Verso, 1985). See also, Gayatri Chakravorty Spivak, *The Post-Colonial Critic: Interviews, Strategies, Dialogues*, ed. Sarah Harasym (New York: Routledge, 1990).

17. Zora Neale Hurston, "How It Feels to Be Colored Me," in *I Love Myself When I Am Laughing: A Zora Neale Hurston Reader*, ed. Alice Walker (Old Westbury, NY: The Feminist Press, 1979), 152–155, here 153.

18. Interview, Spring 2017.

19. Sidra Ali, untitled final paper for Reading and Research course, Harvard Divinity School, Spring 2017, 2–3. Sidra Ali completed an individual Reading and Research course with me at Harvard Divinity School in the spring of 2017, and the quotations are from her final paper for the course (reproduced here with her permission).

20. Alan Goodman, "Two Questions about Race," in *Is Race Real? A Web Forum Organized by the Social Science Research Council*, 7 June 2006, raceandgenomics.ssrc.org.

21. Hans-Georg Gadamer, *Truth and Method*, trans. Joel Weinsheimer and Donald G. Marshall (New York: Continuum, 2004), 405.

22. James Baldwin, *Nobody Knows My Name: More Notes of a Native Son* (New York: Dell, 1961), 17, emphasis in text.

23. James Baldwin, "Introduction," *Notes of a Native Son* (Boston: Beacon Press, 1984), 7.

24. Baldwin, "Introduction," 9.

25. Edmund White, "1983," in *Twenty-One Picador Authors Celebrate Twenty-One Years of International Writing* (London: Picador, 1993), 127.

26. David M. Amodio, "The Social Neuroscience of Intergroup Relations," *European Review of Social Psychology* vol. 19 (2008): 1–54.

27. C. Neil Macrae and Galen V. Bodenhausen, "Social Cognition: Thinking Categorically about Others," *Annual Review of Psychology* vol. 51 (2000): 93–120, here 94.

28. "The DNA Journey," retrieved 16 January 2019 from http://www.multi-media-english.com/videos/esl/the-dna-journey-letsopenourworld-6429.

29. Theodor W. Adorno, *Negative Dialectics*, trans. W.B. Ashton (New York: Continuum, 1973), 11.

30. Adorno, *Negative Dialectics*, 8.

31. Hannah Arendt, introduction to *Illuminations*, by Walter Benjamin, trans. Harry Zohn (New York: Schocken, 1968), 45.

32. Adorno, *Negative Dialectics*, 13.

33. Arendt, "'What Remains? The Language Remains,'" 19.

34. John Dewey, *How We Think* (1910; Buffalo, NY: Prometheus Books, 1991), 12.

35. Karl Jaspers, *Way to Wisdom: An Introduction to Philosophy*, trans. Ralph Manheim (1953; New Haven, CT: Yale University Press, 2003), 19–20.

36. Sartre's engagement with Marxism, prompted and inspired by Maurice Merleau-Ponty's critiques in the late 1950s, found expression in his "Question de Méthode," the prefatory essay in *Critique de la Raison Dialectique*, vol. 1 (Paris: Gallimard, 1960), published six years before Adorno's *Negative Dialektik* (Frankfurt am Main: Suhrkamp Verlag, 1966). For a full account of the development of Sartre's existential Marxism, see Mark Poster, *Existential Marxism in Postwar France: From Sartre to Althusser* (Princeton, NJ: Princeton University Press, 1975), ch. 4.

37. Adorno, *Negative Dialectics*, 5.

38. Jean-Paul Sartre, "The Itinerary of a Thought," in *Between Existentialism and Marxism*, trans. John Matthews (1972; London: Verso, 1974), 41 and 42.

39. Gregory Bateson, *Naven: A Survey of the Problems Suggested by a Composite Pictures of the Culture of a New Guinea Tribe Drawn from Three Points of View* (1936; Stanford, CA: Stanford University Press, 1958), 187–88.

40. William James, *Essays in Radical Empiricism* (1912; Cambridge, MA: Harvard University Press, 1976).

41. James Edie, "Notes on the Philosophical Anthropology of William James," in *An Invitation to Phenomenology: Studies in the Philosophy of Experience*, ed. James Edie (Chicago: Quadrangle Books, 1965), 110–32, here 119, emphasis in text.

42. George Devereux, *From Anxiety to Method in the Behavioral Sciences* (The Hague: Mouton, 1967).

43. William James, *Essays in Radical Empiricism* (Cambridge, MA: Harvard University Press, 1976).

44. Adorno, *Negative Dialectics*, 34.

Notes for Chapter 2

Epigraph: Veena Das, *Affliction: Health, Disease, Poverty* (New York: Fordham University Press, 2015), 1.

1. Hannah Arendt, "What Is Existenz Philosophy," *Partisan Review* vol. 13, no. 1 (1946): 34–56, here 36.
2. Arendt, "Existenz Philosophy," 37. Hugo von Hofmannsthal, "Moments in Greece," trans. Tania and James Stern, in *The Whole Difference: Selected Writings of Hugo von Hofmannsthal*, ed. J. D. McClatchy (Princeton, NJ: Princeton University Press, 2008), 80–100, here 87.
3. Hannah Arendt, introduction to *Illuminations*, by Walter Benjamin, trans. Harry Zohn (New York: Schocken Books, 1969), 1–55, here 11, 12, 13.
4. Theodor W. Adorno, "A Portrait of Walter Benjamin," in *Prisms*, trans. Samuel and Shierry Weber (Cambridge, MA: MIT Press, 1981), 237–41, here 229.
5. D. Miller, ed., *Goethe: The Collected Works*, vol. 12: *Scientific Studies* (New York: Suhrkamp, 1998). See also Carlos Cornejo's "From Fantasy to Imagination: A Cultural History and a Moral for Cultural Psychology," for a brilliant critique of Goethe's philosophy of life. Niels Bohr Lecture, Centre for Cultural Psychology, Aalborg University, 26 February 2015.
6. Godfrey Lienhardt, *Divinity and Experience: The Religion of the Dinka* (Oxford: Clarendon Press, 1961), 283, emphasis added, 291.
7. Previously published in Michael Jackson, *Allegories of the Wilderness: Ethics and Ambiguity in Kuranko Narratives* (Bloomington: Indiana University Press, 1982), 36–37.
8. Arundhati Roy, *The God of Small Things* (New York: Random House, 1997), 32–33. Echoes of this call to deterritorialize and disrupt master discourses are also found in G. Deleuze and F Guattari, *Kafka: Towards a Minor Literature*, trans. D. Polan (Minneapolis: University of Minnesota Press, 1986), 16, 26.
9. As Hannah Arendt notes, referring to Hofmannsthal's famous farewell letter to Stefan George and Edmund Husserl's "to the things themselves" phenomenology consistently celebrates "'the little things' as against big words, since precisely in these small things the secret of reality lies hidden." Arendt, "Existenz Philosophy," 36.
10. Caroline Heller, *Reading Claudius: A Memoir in Two Parts* (New York: The Dial Press, 2015), 10.
11. Heller, *Reading Claudius*, 184–85, emphasis added.
12. William James, *Essays in Radical Empiricism* (1912; New York: Dover, 2003).
13. Ted Hughes, *Birthday Letters* (London: Faber and Faber, 1998), 3.
14. von Hofmannsthal, "Moments in Greece," 87, emphasis added.
15. Jane Bennett, *Vibrant Matter: A Political Ecology of Things* (Durham, NC: Duke University Press, 2010), 3, 180, 182
16. William James, *The Varieties of Religious Experience: A Study in Human Nature* (New York: Signet, 1958), 382.
17. James Edie, *William James and Phenomenology* (Bloomington: Indiana University Press, 1987); Don Ihde, *Consequences of Phenomenology* (Albany:

State University of New York Press, 1986); Bruce Wilshire, *William James and Phenomenology: A Study of "The Principles of Psychology"* (Bloomington: Indiana University Press, 1968).

18. Michael Foucault, *The Use of Pleasure*, vol. 2 of *The History of Sexuality*, trans. R. Hurley (New York: Vintage, 1990), 8–9.

19. Mark Wrathall, "Existential Phenomenology," in *A Companion to Phenomenology and Existentialism*, ed. Hubert Dreyfus and Mark Wrathall (Oxford: Blackwell, 2006), 31–47, here 32.

20. Wim Wenders, dir. *Wings of Desire*. Berlin and Neuilly-sur-Seine: Road Movies Filmproduktion GmbH and Argos Films S. A., 1986.

21. Ibid.

22. Ibid.

23. Douglas Lockwood, *The Lizard Eaters* (Melbourne: Cassell, 1964), 8.

24. Lockwood, *Lizard Eaters*, 15–16.

25. Bennett, *Vibrant Matter*, 3.

26. von Hofmannsthal, "Moments in Greece," 87.

27. James Faubion coins the term "paranomic" (beside or parallel to the law) to suggest that ethical praxis often bypasses or bends rules without necessarily breaking them. In reinforcing this point, he notes that virtue is better understood in many practical contexts as a matter of virtuosity—a skill for getting around difficulties, for playing with possibilities, rather than slavishly following set rules or respecting conventional protocols. James D. Faubion, "Paranomics: On the Semiotics of Sacral Action," in *The Limits of Meaning: Case Studies in the Anthropology of Christianity*, ed. Matthew Engelke and Matt Tomlinson (New York: Berghahn, 2006), 189–209, here 205.

28. Veena Das, "A Gesture Was All There Was," *The Immanent Frame: Secularism, Religion, and the Public Sphere*, 18 October 2017, retrieved from https://tif.ssrc.org/2017/10/18/a-gesture-was-all-there-was/.

29. In a recent book, Marshall Sahlins tends to embrace a rather idealized conception of kinship amity. Marshall Sahlins, *What Kinship Is—And Is Not* (Chicago: University of Chicago Press, 2013). For a critique of this view and a discussion of the ways in which the reality of life among kin seldom conforms with the projected ideal, see Michael Jackson, *How Lifeworlds Work: Sociality, Emotionality, and the Ambiguity of Being* (Chicago: Chicago University Press, 2017).

30. For example, the "Samaritans" who help illegal migrants in the Sonoma Desert and the "Samaritans" who run hotlines for chronically depressed or suicidal individuals. See Ananda Rose, *Showdown in the Sonoran Desert: Religion, Law, and the Immigration Controversy* (New York: Oxford University Press, 2012), 81–84.

31. K. E. Løgstrup points out "that we do not become aware of the sovereign expressions of life until a failure or conflict or crisis disrupts our immediate preoccupation with the needs of the other." Kees van Kooten Niekerk, introduction to *Beyond the Ethical Demand*, by K. E. Løgstrup (Notre Dame, IN: Notre Dame University Press, 2007), ix–xxxii, here xx, xviii.

32. As Kess van Kooten Niekerk puts it, Løgstrup "does not deny that reference to general principles or norms may play a part in ethical argumentation.

But he stresses that norms and principles are subordinate to moral experience." van Kooten Niekerk, introduction to *Beyond the Ethical Demand,* xxiii.

33. K. E. Løgstrup, *Beyond the Ethical Demand* (Notre Dame, IN: Notre Dame University Press, 2007), 68.
34 Michael Jackson, *Allegories of the Wilderness: Ethics and Ambiguity in Kuranko Narratives* (Bloomington: Indiana University Press, 1982).
35. Emmanuel Levinas, "Ethics of the Infinite," in *Debates in Continental Philosophy: Conversations with Contemporary Thinkers,* ed. Richard Kearney (New York: Fordham University Press, 2004), 65–84.
36. ONUC is the acronym for the Organisation des Nations Unies au Congo established shortly after Congo's independence in June 1960 to keep the peace, prevent secessionist moves by the mineral-rich provinces of Kasai and Katanga, and supervise aid and development projects. I worked as a volunteer for ONUC and the Congolese Ministry of Youth and Sports.
37. I had, of course, been reading Joseph Conrad's author's note to *Heart of Darkness*—a story he describes as "the spoil I brought out from Africa, where, really, I had no sort of business."
38. This line, that passed through my mind at that moment, was from Blaise Cendrars's epic poem, *La Prose de Transsibérien et de la Petite Jehanne de France* (Paris: Éditions des Hommes Nouveaux, 1913).
39. George Orwell, "Reflections on Gandhi," *Partisan Review* vol. 16, no. 1 (January 1949): 5–12.
40. Pierre Bourdieu, *Pascalian Meditations,* trans. Richard Nice (Cambridge: Polity Press, 200), 207–9.
41. Lawrence Weschler, *Vermeer in Bosnia: A Reader* (New York: Pantheon, 2004), 17–18.

Notes for Chapter 3

1. Salome Karwah, who contracted Ebola while caring for her infected father, but survived it herself. Salome died in February 2017 after giving birth. Jen Krausz, "Salome Karwah Dies: Liberian Ebola Fighter Loses Life after Childbirth," *Newsmax,* 27 February 2017, retrieved from https://www.newsmax.com/thewire/salome-karwah-dies-ebola-fighter/2017/02/27/id/775880/.
2. B. McMahon, "Sierra Leone News: Sierra Leoneans Should Lead the Ebola Fight," *Awoko,* 13 October 2014, retrieved from https://awoko.org/2014/10/13/sierra-leone-news-sierra-leoneans-should-lead-the-ebola-fight-brig-mcmahon/.
3. When I discussed these events with Morowa forty years later, he reiterated these very words, adding that the killing of a witch was "our custom here." Michael Jackson, *Life within Limits: Well-Being in a World of Want* (Durham, NC: Duke University Press, 2011), 140.
4. When a confessed witch dies, his or her shade is known as *pulan*. The *pulan* haunts, oppresses, and terrorizes people, especially small children. It is

said that the *pulan* resembles a lizard or assumes the form of a lizard, and a *pulan*-catcher may show people a lizard wriggling inside a bag as proof that has caught a witch's shade. A *pulan*'s power enables it to lift heavy metal cooking pots or oppress people in their sleep. So terrified do some people become that they are paralyzed and have to be physically straightened out in the morning. Theoretically, a *pulan* will not enter a house that has white cotton over the lintel. If it does enter an unprotected house it counts people off in pairs, declaring "this and this are all right, this and this are all right," until it comes to a single and therefore vulnerable person, when it says, "this and myself are all right," whereupon it proceeds to oppress that individual. Since *pulan* cannot attack two people at once, one may take precautions against *pulan*-haunting by sleeping pairs.

5. Jean-Paul Sartre, *Critique of Dialectical Reason*, trans. Alan Sheridan-Smith (1960; London: Verso, 1976), 23.

6. If anyone disturbs the sleeping body of a suspected witch, or is witness to such an event, he will not make this publicly known lest the kinsmen of the alleged witch accuse him of murder. Kuranko point out that in such cases there is no real evidence of witchcraft. Furthermore, to accuse a person of witchcraft is a serious matter. Of all cases heard in the Native Court in Sengbe chiefdom between 1946 and 1967 only two cases of witchcraft accusation are recorded (the defendants were fined and ordered to "beg," i.e., apologize to, the plaintiffs). The sole cases of witchcraft accusation that came to my attention during fieldwork occurred in Kamadugu Sukurela in 1966. Two women, weeding a farm, quarreled. One said, "Now look, you are a witch!" The other rejoined, "Yes, I used to sit on your house." The case came before the chief's court and the accuser was ordered to withdraw her accusation and apologize (the women were not related). In a second case (from the same village), a woman was rumored to have confessed to killing her brother's daughter's son by witchcraft, but the confession was made within her family, and her husband was a "big man"; no one dared accuse her publicly of witchcraft or bring the matter to trial. Even *Gbangbane* does not make direct or specific accusations; the cult masters, like ordinary diviners, simply ascertain whether or not witchcraft is the cause of a person's illness or death. When I asked one informant to give me evidence that witchcraft really did exist, he said that his knowledge came from three sources: "it has a name and we have heard of it," "we have seen people die because of witches," and "witches confess."

7. B. Hallen and J. O. Sodipo, *Knowledge, Belief and Witchcraft: Analytical Experiments in African Philosophy* (London: Ethnographica, 1986), ch. 3.

8. Hallen and Sodipo, *Knowledge, Belief and Witchcraft*, 17.

9. E. E. Evans-Pritchard, *Witchcraft, Oracles and Magic Among the Azande* (1937; Oxford: Clarendon Press, 1972), 125, 118.

10. Examples include Effutu (R. W. Wyllie, "Introspective Witchcraft among the Effutu of Southern Ghana," *Man* vol. 8, no. 1 [1973]: 74–79); Banyang (M. Ruel, "Were Animals and the Introverted Witch," in *Witchcraft Confessions and Accusations*, ed. M. Douglas [London: Tavistock, 1970],

333–50); Ashanti (B. Ward, "Some Observations on Religious Cults in Ashanti," *Africa* vol. 26, no. 1 [1956]: 47–61; M. J. Field, *Search for Security* [London: Faber and Faber, 1960]).

11. Examples include the Dinka (G. Lienhardt, "Some Notions of Witchcraft among the Dinka," *Africa* vol. 21, no. 4 [1951]: 303–18, Mbugwe ("Some Structural Aspects of Mbugwe Witchcraft," in *Witchcraft and Sorcery in East Africa*, ed. J. Middleton and E. H. Winter [London: Routledge and Kegan Paul, 1969], 143–62).

12. S. F. Nadel, "Witchcraft in Four African Societies," *American Anthropologist* vol. 54, no. 1 (1952): 18–29.

13. P. Freire, *Cultural Action for Freedom* (Harmondsworth: Penguin,1972).

14. Ranajit Guha, *Elementary Aspects of Peasant Insurgency in Colonial India* (Delhi: Oxford University Press, 1983), 17.

15. Ruel, "Were Animals and the Introverted Witch," 334.

16. Evans-Pritchard, *Witchcraft, Oracles and Magic*, 37.

17. Jean-Paul Sartre, *Search for a Method*, trans. Hazel Barnes (New York: Vintage, 1968), 91.

18. Susan Buck-Morss, *The Origin of Negative Dialectics: Theodor W. Adorno, Walter Benjamin, and the Frankfurt Institute* (Hassocks, Sussex: Harvester Press, 1977), 54.

19. Monica Wilson, "Witch Beliefs and Social Structure," *American Journal of Sociology* vol. 56, no. 4 (1951): 307–13.

20. Theodor Reik, *The Compulsion to Confess: On the Psychoanalysis of Crime and Punishment* (New York: Wiley, 1966), 194, 199.

21. Cited in Jean-Paul Sartre, *Saint Genet: Actor and Martyr*, trans. Bernard Frechtman (New York: Braziller, 1963), 17.

22. In his study of Mohave suicide, George Devereux observes that witches often persuade themselves "by a retroactive self-deception of the 'opportune confabulation' type" that they actually bewitched someone who just happened to die at a time when they were experiencing strong suicidal impulses. Witchcraft confession is thus a kind of "vicarious suicide," an impulse that, Devereux notes, "is a human, rather than a specifically Mohave impulse." George Devereux, *Mohave Ethnopsychiatry and Suicide: The Psychiatric Knowledge and the Psychic Disturbances of an Indian Tribe* (Washington, DC: Smithsonian Institution Bureau of American Ethnology Bulletin no. 175, 1969), 387.

23. N. Katherine Hayles, *How We Became Posthuman: Virtual Bodies in Cybernetics, Literature and Informatics* (Chicago: University of Chicago Press, 1999); Rosi Braidotti, *The Posthuman* (Cambridge: Polity Press, 2013).

Notes for Chapter 4

Epigraph: Theodor Adorno, *Negative Dialectics*, trans. E. B. Ashton (New York: Continuum, 1990), 183.

1. Edourdo Kohn, *How Forests Think: Toward an Anthropology beyond the Human* (Berkeley: University of California Press, 2013).
2. Diana Coole and Samantha Frost, "Introducing the New Materialisms," in *New Materialisms: Ontology, Agency, and Politics*, ed. Diana Colle and Samantha Frost (Durham, NC: Duke University Press, 2010), 8–9.
3. Martin Heidegger, "The Thing," in *Poetry, Language, Thought*, trans. Albert Hofstadter (New York: Harper Colophon, 1975), 169. See also Heidegger's description of a table, not simply as a thing but as a vital part of a living space, mediating social relations and participating in our social life. Martin Heidegger, *Ontology—The Hermeneutics of Facticity* (Bloomington: Indiana University Press, 1999), 66–69.
4. Aristotle, *Physics*, Book II 3, trans. P.H. Wicksteed and F. M. Cornford, Loeb Classical Library 228 (Cambridge, MA: Harvard University Press, 1934).
5. "Object is no more than a subjectless residuum than it is posited by subject. The two conflicting determinations fit together: the residue, which science settles for as its truth, is a product of its manipulative procedures that are subjectively organized." Theodor W. Adorno, "On Subject and Object," in *Critical Models: Interventions and Catchwords*, trans. Henry W. Pickford (New York: Columbia University Press, 1998), 245–58.
6. Tim Ingold, "Introduction," *What Is an Animal*, ed. Tim Ingold (London: Unwin Hyman, 1988), 9.
7. Jean Piaget, "The Origins of Child Animism, Moral Necessity and Physical Determinism," in *The Child's Conception of the World* (Paladin: Frogmore, 1973), 236–81.
8. For a review of the voluminous literature on this topic, see Kristin Andrews, "Animal Cognition," The Stanford Encyclopedia of Philosophy (Summer 2016 edition), ed. Edward N. Zalta, revised 6 May 2016, retrieved from https://plato.stanford.edu/archives/sum2016/entries/cognition-animal/. Also see E. Sober, "Anthropomorphism, Parsimony, and Common Ancestry," *Mind and Language* vol. 27, no. 3 (2012): 229–38.
9. Wilfrid Bion, *Attention and Interpretation: A Scientific Approach to Insight in Psycho-Analysis and Groups* (London: Tavistock, 1975).
10. Peter Fonagy and Mary Target, *Psychoanalytic Theories: Perspectives from Developmental Psychopathology* (New York: Brunner-Routledge, 2003).
11. George Devereux, *From Anxiety to Method in the Behavioral Sciences* (The Hague: Mouton, 1967), 33–34.
12. Bruno Latour, *Politics of Nature: How to Bring the Sciences into Democracy*, trans. Catherine Porter (Cambridge, MA: Harvard University Press, 2004).
13. Jane Bennett, *Vibrant Matter: A Political Ecology of Things* (Durham, NC: Duke University Press, 2010), viii.
14. For example, it is sometimes said of an overbearing parent, *an dan miran bo a ma* (they have taken away the child's *miran*), and if intimidated by a person with commanding presence one might declare, *a yene miran bo ra ma* (When I saw him my *miran* went out of me).
15. Janet Hoskins, *Biographical Objects: How Things Tell the Stories of People's Lives* (New York: Routledge 1998), 3.

16. Hoskins, *Biographical Objects*, 3.
17. Jean-Paul Sartre, *The Emotions: Outline of a Theory*, trans. Bernard Frechtman (New York: Philosophical Library, 1948).
18. Jean-François Lyotard, *Libidinal Economy*, trans. Iain Hamilton Grant (1974; Bloomington: Indiana University Press, 1993).
19. D. W. Winnicott, *Playing and Reality* (Harmondsworth: Penguin, 1974), 17.
20. Bruno Bettelheim, "Joey: A 'Mechanical Boy,'" *Scientific American* vol. 200, no. 3 (1959): 117–27, here 117–118.
21. Bettelheim, 120.
22. Coole and Frost, "Introducing the New Materialisms," 27.
23. Keith Basso, "Wisdom Sits in Places: Notes on a Western Apache Landscape," in *Senses of Place*, ed. Steven Feld and Keith Basso (Sante Fe, NM: School of American Research, 1996), 55.
24. Jean-Paul Sartre, *The Philosophy of Jean-Paul Sartre*, ed. R. Cumming (New York: Vintage, 1965), cited by Keith Basso, *Wisdom Sits in Places: Language and Landscape among the Western Apache* (Albuquerque: University of New Mexico Press, 1996), 108.
25. The Kuranko word *wale* signifies both work and any forms of dutiful action such as raising a child, ruling a chiefdom, or performing a hereditary task.
26. Karl Marx and Frederick Engels, "The German Ideology," trans. C. Dutt, in *Karl Marx-Frederick Engels: Collected Works*, vol. 5 (Moscow: Progress Publishers, 1976), 19–608, here 43.
27. In many Aboriginal societies, sacred sites or story-places are said to recognize the sweat-smell of those who bear a kinship relationship to them. Illness or misfortune may come to those who trespass on a sacred site, but whose body odor cannot be unrecognized. Michael Jackson, *At Home in the World* (Durham, NC: Duke University Press, 1995), 181–83.
28. Charles S. Bird, with Mamadou Keita and Bourama Soumaoro, *The Songs of Seydou Camara*, vol. 1: *Kambili* (Bloomington: Indiana University Press, 1974).
29. Patrick R. McNaughton, *The Mande Blacksmiths: Knowledge, Power, and Art in West Africa* (Bloomington: Indiana University Press, 1988), 16, 69–70.
30. Anne Salmon, "Maori and Modernity: Ruatara's Dying," in *Signifying Identities: Anthropological Perspectives on Boundaries and Contested Values*, ed. Anthony P. Cohen (London: Routledge, 2000), 37–58, here 40. This touches on a complementary theme: under what conditions does a person become a thing? The same intersubjective logic whereby things take on the properties of persons explains why, when human actions are morally wrong or relationships in breach of convention (as in incest), images of immobilization and physical weakening are common tropes—the male factor turned to stone or wasting away.
31. Warren L. d'Azevedo, "Mask Makers and Myth in Western Liberia," in *Primitive Art and Society*, ed. Anthony Forge (London: Oxford University Press, 1973), 140.

32. John C. Messenger, "The Role of the Carver in Anang Society," in *The Traditional Artist in African Societies*, ed. Warren L. d'Azevedo (Bloomington: Indiana University Press, 1973), 101–27, here 109.
33. William R. Bascom, "A Yoruba Master Carver: Duga of Meko," in *The Traditional Artist in African Societies*, ed. Warren L. d'Azevedo (Bloomington: Indiana University Press, 1973), 62–78, here 33.
34. Lugwani, web documents, 2005, printouts on file with author.
35. Henry Glassie, *Turkish Traditional Art Today* (Bloomington: Indiana University Press, 1993), 103–4.
36. Warlpiri will speak of a deceased person as someone who has been lost or as *kumanjayi*—a word for a person whose name has been put out of circulation for a generation and whose living traces have been erased from the ground.
37. Coole and Frost, "Introducing the New Materialisms," 20, 21.
38. A. Irving Hallowell, "Ojibwa Metaphysics of Being and the Perception of Persons," in *Person Perception and Interpersonal Behavior*, ed. R. Taguiri and L. Petrullo (Stanford, CA: Stanford University Press, 1958), 63–85, here 65.
39. Michael Jackson, *Allegories of the Wilderness: Ethics and Ambiguity in Kuranko Narratives* (Bloomington: Indiana University Press, 1982), 17–18.
40. Bennett, *Vibrant Matter*, xvi, 122.

Notes for Chapter 5

1. Bronislaw Malinowski, *Argonauts of the Western Pacific* (London: Routledge and Kegan Paul, 1922), 6.
2. Bronislaw Malinowski, "The Problem of Meaning in Primitive Languages," in *The Meaning of Meaning: A Study of the Influence of Language upon Thought and of the Science of Symbolism*, ed. C. K. Ogden and I. A. Richards (1923; New York: Harcourt, Brace and World, 1946), 296–336, here 296.
3. Ludwig Wittgenstein, *Philosophical Investigations*, trans. G. E. M. Anscombe (Oxford: Blackwell, 1953), 109 (prop. 340), emphasis in text.
4. Ray Monk, *Ludwig Wittgenstein: The Duty of Genius* (New York: The Free Press, 1990), 306.
5. J. L. Austin, *How to Do Things with Words*, 2nd edition, ed. J.O. Urmson and M. Sbisá (Cambridge, MA: Harvard University Press, 1962).
6. E. E. Evans-Pritchard, *The Nuer: A Description of the Modes of Livelihood and Political Institutions of a Nilotic People* (Oxford: Clarendon, 1940), 12–13.
7. Evans-Pritchard, *The Nuer*, 12–13.
8. Evans-Pritchard, *The Nuer*, 11
9. Lawrence James, *The Rise and Fall of the British Empire* (London: Little Brown, 1994), 286.
10. Franz Fanon, *The Wretched of the Earth*, trans. Constance Farrington (New York: Grove Press, 1968), 264–67
11. Dominique Zahan, *The Religion, Spirituality, and Thought of Traditional Africa*, trans. Kate Ezra Martin and Lawrence M. Martin (1970; Chicago: University of Chicago Press, 1979), 112–18.

12. In an incisive review of anthropological studies of the formulaic, circumspective, and performative aspects of sociality in Central American societies, Kevin Groark argues that "intersubjective attenuation" should
not be read as evidence that subjective life is shallow but that it is conventionally consigned to the shadows rather than brought into the light.
Kevin P. Groark, "Toward a Cultural Phenomenology of Intersubjectivity:
The Extended Relational Field of the Tzotzil Maya of Highland Chiapas,
Mexico," *Language and Communication* vol. 33, no.3 (2013): 278–91.
13. George Steiner, *After Babel* (London: Oxford University Press, 1973),
224–25.
14. Michael Jackson, "Emmanuel," in *The Wherewithal of Life: Ethics, Migration,
and the Question of Well-Being* (Berkeley: University of California Press,
2013), 24–45.
15. Jean-Paul Sartre, *The Family Idiot: Gustave Flaubert 1821–1857*, vol. 2, trans.
Carol Cosman (Chicago: University of Chicago Press, 1987), 174; James
C. Scott, *Weapons of the Weak: Everyday Forms of Peasant Resistance* (New
Haven, CT: Yale University Press, 1987).
16. Herbert Marcuse, *Negations: Essays in Critical Theory* (London: Allen Lane,
1968), 129.
17. "To live on the surface, to take events of daily life with the meanings they
present rather than to seek their hidden purpose, to find happiness and joy
in what there already is, finds its easiest expression in a [premodern] age,"
write Hubert Dreyfus and Sean Dorrance Kelly, commenting on Ishmael's
view. Hubert Dreyfus and Sean Dorrance Kelly, *All Things Shining: Reading
the Western Classics to Find Meaning in a Secular Age* (New York: The Free
Press, 2011), 163.
18. Steven Sampson, "From Reconciliation to Coexistence," *Public Culture* vol.
15, no. 1 (2003): 79–184, here 180.
19. Hannah Arendt, *The Human Condition* (Chicago: University of Chicago
Press, 1958), 237.
20. E. Valentine Daniel, *Charred Lullabies: Chapters in an Anthropography of
Violence* (Princeton, NJ: Princeton University Press, 1996), 208.

Notes for Chapter 6

Epigraph: E. Valentine Daniel, "Suffering Nation and Alienation," in *Social
Suffering*, ed. Arthur Kleinman, Veena Das, and Margaret Lock (Berkeley:
University of California Press, 1997), 309–58, here 352.

1. Benedict Anderson, *Imagined Communities: Reflections on the Origins and
Spread of Nationalism* (London: Verso, 1983), 12.
2. David Gough, "Sect Promotes Village Values: Kenyan Group Sees
Salvation in Witchcraft and Circumcision," *Guardian Weekly*, 18–24
November 1999, 3.
3. Piers Vitebsky, *Living without the Dead: Loss and Redemption in a Jungle
Cosmos* (Chicago: Chicago University Press, 2017), 328.

4. Norman Davies, *God's Playground: A History of Poland*, vol. 2 (Oxford: Clarendon Press, 1981), 9.
5. Ghassan Hage, "The Spatial Imaginary of National Practices: Dwelling-Domesticating/Being-Exterminating," *Environment and Planning D: Society and Space* vol. 14, no. 4 (1996): 463–85, here 478.
6. Daniel, "Suffering Nation and Alienation," 352.
7. Bruce Kapferer, *Legends of People, Myths of State: Violence, Intolerance, and Political Culture in Sri Lanka and Australia* (Washington, DC: Smithsonian Institution Press, 1988), 209.
8. Arjun Appadurai, *Modernity at Large: Cultural Dimensions of Globalization* (Minneapolis: University of Minnesota Press, 1996); Paul Dresch, "Race, Culture and—What? Pluralist Certainties in the United States," in *The Pursuit of Certainty: Religious and Cultural Formulations*, ed. Wendy James (London: Routledge, 1995), 61–91; Akhil Gupta and James Ferguson, "Beyond 'Culture': Space, Identity, and the Politics of Difference," *Cultural Anthropology* vol. 7, no. 1 (1992): 6–23; Michael Herzfeld, *Cultural Intimacy: Social Poetics in the Nation State* (New York: Routledge, 1997); Verena Stolcke, "Talking Culture: New Boundaries, New Rhetorics of Exclusion in Europe," *Cultural Anthropology* vol. 36, no. 1 (1995): 1–24.
9. Nigel Rapport, "Post-Cultural Anthropology: The Ironization of Values in a World of Movement," in *Realizing Community: Concepts, Social Relationships and Sentiments*, ed. V. Arnit (London: Routledge, 2001).
10. Karen Fog Olwig and Kirsten Hastrup, eds. *Siting Culture: The Shifting Anthropological Object* (London: Routledge, 1997), 11.
11. National Inquiry into the Separation of Aboriginal and Torres Strait Islander Children from their Families (Australia), *Bringing Them Home: Report of the National Inquiry into the Separation of Aboriginal and Torres Strait Islander Children from their Families* Parliamentary paper / The Parliament of the Commonwealth of Australia, no. 128 (Sydney: Human Rights and Equal Opportunity Commission, 1997), 177, 178, 210.
12. Carmel Bird, ed., *The Stolen Children: Their Stories* (Sydney: Random House, 1998), 109.
13. Because it is the lost Aboriginal mother rather than the white father who figures in personal fantasies of reunion, narratives of Aboriginality and sovereignty tend to maternalize its key symbols of land and language.
14. National Inquiry into the Separation, *Bringing Them Home*, 242.
15. Bird, *The Stolen Children*, 77.
16. Coral Edwards and Peter Read, eds. *The Lost Children: Thirteen Australians Taken from Their Aboriginal Families Tell of the Struggle to Find Their Natural Parents* (Sydney: Doubleday, 1989), 191–93.
17. National Inquiry into the Separation, *Bringing Them Home*, 298.
18. Nancy de Vries, cited in Edwards and Read, *The Lost Children*, 193–94.
19. Hage, "The Spatial Imaginary of National Practices."
20. Edwards and Read, *The Lost Children*, 193.
21. National Inquiry into the Separation, *Bringing Them Home*, 239.
22. *New Zealand Women's Weekly*, 26 May 1997, 39.

23. Roy Wagner, *The Invention of Culture* (Chicago: Chicago University Press, 1975).

24. Franz Fanon, *The Wretched of the Earth* (New York: Grove, 1968), 29–30.

25. Liisa Malkki, *Purity and Exile: Violence, Memory, and National Cosmology among Hutu Refugees in Tanzania* (Chicago: University of Chicago Press, 1995), 52–63.

26. Kathy Irwin, "Maori Feminism," in *Te Ao Marama: Regaining Aotearoa: Maori Writers Speak Out*, vol. 2, *He Whakaatanga O Te Ao*, selected and edited by Witi Ihimaera (Auckland: Reed, 1993), 299–304, here 299.

27. Naomi Schor and Elizabeth Weed, eds. *The Essential Difference* (Bloomington: Indiana University Press, 1994).

28. E. Valentine Daniel, "Suffering Nation and Alienation," 351.

29. Ranginui Walker, "Immigration Policy and the Political Economy of New Zealand," in *Immigration and National Identity in New Zealand: One People, Two Peoples, Many Peoples?* ed. Stuart W. Grief (Palmerston North: Dunmore Press, 1995), 282–302, here 282. This confirmation of indigenous customary rights is based on British common law dating back to the sixteenth century—the law that underpinned colonial law and was invoked in the Australian High Court Mabo decision that overturned the doctrine of terra nullius and recognized Aboriginal native title rights.

30. Walker, "Immigration Policy and the Political Economy," 284.

31. Walker, "Immigration Policy and the Political Economy," 284

32. Walker, "Immigration Policy and the Political Economy," 286.

33. Walker, "Immigration Policy and the Political Economy," 286.

34. Walker, "Immigration Policy and the Political Economy," 302.

35. Walker, "Immigration Policy and the Political Economy," 283.

36. The title of this subsection, and its general theme, is anticipated by Arjun Appadurai's *Modernity at Large*.

37. Hannah Arendt, *The Human Condition* (Chicago: University of Chicago Press, 1958), 50–51. Arendt's ideas were taken up and explored by Elaine Scarry, *The Body in Pain: The Making and Unmaking of the World* (New York: Oxford University Press, 1985).

38. Maja Povrzanovic, "The Imposed and the Imagined as Encountered by Croatian War Ethnographers," *Current Anthropology* vol. 41, no. 2 (2000): 151–62, emphasis added.

39. E. Valentine Daniel, *Charred Lullabies: Chapters in an Anthropography of Violence* (Princeton, NJ: Princeton University Press, 1996), 142.

40. Bernie Kernot, *People of the Four Winds* (Auckland: Hicks, Smith, 197), 6–65.

41. Toonvan Meijl, "Historicising Maoritanga: Colonial Ethnography and the Reification of Maori Tradition," *Journal of the Polynesian Society* vol. 105, no. 3 (1996): 311–46; Evan S. Te Ahu Poata-Smith, "He Pokeke Uenuku i tu ai: The Evolution of Contemporary Maori Protest," in *Nga Patai: Racism and Ethnic Relations in Aotearoa/New Zealand*, ed. Paul Spoonley, David Pearson, and Cluny MacPherson (Palmerston North: Dunmore Press, 1996), 97–116.

42. Daniel, "Suffering Nation and Alienation," 311.

43. Daniel, "Suffering Nation and Alienation," 328–29, 343–44.

44. Ann-Belinda Steen Preis, "Seeking Place: Capsized Identities and Contracted Belonging among Sri Lankan Tamil Refugees," in Olwig and Hastrup, *Siting Culture*, 86–100, here 88, 96–98.
45. Dick Hebdige, *Cut 'n Mix: Culture, Identity and Caribbean Music* (London: Methuen, 1987), 158–59. Cited in Gupta and Ferguson, "Beyond 'Culture,'" 10.
46. Barbara Myerhoff, "Organization and Ecstasy: Deliberate and Accidental Communitas among Huichol Indians and American Youth," in *Symbols and Politics in Communal Ideology: Cases and Questions*, ed. Sally Folk Moore and Barbara Myerhoff (Ithaca, NY: Cornell University Press, 1975).
47. Liisa Malkki, "News and Culture: Transitory Phenomena and the Fieldwork Tradition," in *Anthropological Locations: Boundaries and Grounds of a Field Science*, ed. Akhil Gupta and James Ferguson (Berkeley: University of California Press, 1997), 86–91, here 93.
48. Liisa Malkki, "National Geographic: The Rooting of Peoples and the Territorialization of National Identity among Scholars and Refugees," *Cultural Anthropology* vol. 7, no. 1 (1992): 24–44, here 36, 37, 38.
49. René Devisch, "Frenzy, Violence, and Ethical Renewal in Kinshasa," *Public Culture* vol. 7, no. 3 (1995): 625–27.
50. Robert Orsi, *The Madonna of 115th Street: Faith and Community in Italian Harlem 1880–1950* (New Haven, CT: Yale University Press, 1985), 75, 78, emphasis added.
51. Radhika Mohanram, "(In)visible Bodies? Immigrant Bodies and Constructions of Nationhood in Aotearoa/New Zealand," in *Feminist Thought in Aotearoa/New Zealand: Differences and Connections*, ed. Rosemary Du Plessis and Lynne Alice (Auckland: Oxford University Press, 1998), 21–28, here 27.
52. Gary Younge, "Black, White and Every Shade Between," *Guardian Weekly* vol. 156, no. 222 (1997): 23.
53. Jane Freeman, "New Faces," *The Sydney Morning Herald*, 15 January 1997, 11.
54. Appadurai, *Modernity at Large*, 52.

Notes for Chapter 7

Epigraph: David Graeber, *Debt: The First 5,000 Years* (New York: Melville House, 2011), 89.

1. Emmanuel Levinas, "La Philosophie et l'éveil," in *Entre Nous: Essais Sur Le Penser-à-l-Autre* (Paris: Grasset, 1991), 103.
2. Ed Tronick, *The Neurobehavioral and Social-Emotional Development of Infants and Children* (New York: W. W. Norton, 2007), 292.
3. On the intersubjective grounds of ethical sensibility, Emmanuel Levinas observes that ethics begins in our face-to-face encounters with others and our responsiveness to the other's responsiveness to us. For Jean-Paul Sartre, "essentially, ethics is a matter of one person's relationship

to another" and that "ethical conscience" arises from one's awareness of always being, to some extent, in the presence of another and conditioned by this sense of being-in-relation with him or her. Emmanuel Levinas, *Time and the Other*, trans. Richard A. Cohen (Pittsburgh, PA: Duquesne University Press, 1987), 82–84. Jean-Paul Sartre and Benny Levi, *Hope Now: The 1980 Interviews*, trans. Adrian can der Hoven (Chicago: Chicago University Press, 1996), 68, 71.

4. K. E. Løgstrup points out "that we do not become aware of the sovereign expressions of life until a failure or conflict or crisis disrupts our immediate preoccupation with the needs of the other." Kees van Kooten Niekerk, introduction to *Beyond the Ethical Demand*, by K. E. Løgstrup (Notre Dame, IN: Notre Dame University Press, 2007), ix–xxxii, here xx, xviii.

5. K. E. Løgstrup, *Beyond the Ethical Demand*, (Notre Dame, IN: Notre Dame University Press, 2007), 68.

6. To capture the elusive and indeterminate character of an ethical sensibility, James Faubion has coined the term "paranomic" (beside or parallel to the law) to suggest that ethical praxis often bypasses or bends rules without necessarily breaking them. In reinforcing this point, he notes that virtue is better understood in many practical contexts as a matter of virtuosity—a skill for getting around difficulties, for playing with possibilities, rather than slavishly following set rules or respecting conventional protocols. James D. Faubion, "Paranomics: On the Semiotics of Sacral Action," in *The Limits of Meaning: Case Studies in the Anthropology of Christianity*, ed. Matthew Engelke and Matt Tomlinson (New York: Berghahn, 2006), 189–209, here 205.

7. P. R. Blake, K. McAuliffe, J. Corbit, T. C. Callaghan, O. Barry, A. Bowie, L. Kleutsch, et al., "The Ontogeny of Fairness in Seven Societies," *Nature* vol. 528, no. 7581 (2015): 258–61.

8. Michel Serres, *The Natural Contract*, trans. Elizabeth MacArthur and William Paulson (Ann Arbor: University of Michigan Press, 1995), 38.

9. Which is why murder and genocide are never straightforward and require extraordinary imaginative, discursive, and ritual preparation—transforming a person or persons who are manifestly human, like oneself, into radical others, alien objects, or mere beasts.

10. Michel Serres, *The Natural Contract*, trans. Elizabeth MacArthur and William Paulson (Ann Arbor: University of Michigan Press, 1995), 38.

11. I am indebted to Martha Carey for her help in this research.

12. Rather than the Eurocentric term "fostering," Esther Goody favors the more neutral term "pro-parenthood." Esther Goody, *Parenthood and Social Reproduction: Fostering and Occupational Roles in West Africa* (Cambridge: Cambridge University Press, 1982).

13. The NarSarah health clinic in Kabala is funded by CITA (Commission on International Trans-Regional Accreditation), a United Methodist Church organization based in Golden, Colorado.

14. Guy de Maupassant, *Collected Stories* (New York: Avenel Books, 1985), 234–237.

15. "NarSarah Clinic Beginnings: Serving Sierra Leone," retrieved 12 February 2019 from servingsierraleone.org/health/narsarah-clinic-beginnings/.
16. Dylan Thomas, "Poem on his Birthday," in *Collected Poems 1934–1952* (London: J.M. Dent 1952), 171.

Notes for Chapter 8

Epigraph: Hans Blumenberg, *Paradigms for a Metaphorology*, trans. Robert Savage (Ithaca, NY: Cornell University Press, 2010), 3.

1. Joseph Needham, "Time and Eastern Man," *Royal Anthropological Institute Occasional Paper*, no. 21 (1965), 1.
2. H. H. Meinhard, "The Patrilineal Principle in Early Teutonic Kinship," in *Studies in Anthropology*, ed. J. H. M. Beattie and R. G. Lienhardt (Oxford: Clarendon Press, 1975), 1–29; James Fernandez, *Bwiti: An Ethnography of the Religious Imagination in Africa* (Princeton, NJ: Princeton University Press, 1982), 88–89; Adam Kendon, *Sign Languages of Aboriginal Australia: Cultural, Semiotic and Communicative Perspectives* (Cambridge: Cambridge University Press, 1988).
3. E.J. Thomas, *Vedic Hymns* (London: John Murray, 1923), 122.
4. Philip Rawson, *Erotic Art of the East* (London: Weidenfeld and Nicolson, 1968), 231.
5. P. Brockbank, introduction to *Coriolanus*, Arden Edition (London: Methuen, 1976), 1–89, here 38.
6. George Lakoff and Mark Johnson, *Metaphors We Live By* (Chicago: Chicago University Press, 1980), 25–29.
7. Maurice Merleau-Ponty, *Phenomenology of Perception*, trans. Colin Smith (London: Routledge and Kegan Paul, 1962), 346.
8. Kenelm Burridge, *Tangu Traditions* (Oxford: Clarendon Press, 1969), 114.
9. Gregory Bateson, *Naven* (Stanford, CA: Stanford University Press, 1958), 243.
10. The best demonstration of the relevance of chaos fractal theory for ethnographic analysis is Quentin Gausset's *Constructing the Kwanja of Adamawa (Cameroon): Essays in Fractal Anthropology* (Berlin: LIT Verlag, 2010).
11. Erik Erikson, "Observations on the Yurok: Childhood and World-Image," *University of California Publications in American Archaeology and Ethnology* vol. 35, no. 10 (1943): 257–301, here 258.
12. Several pioneering explorations of this phenomenon can be cited, including Mary Douglas, *Natural Symbols: Explorations in Cosmology* (New York: Pantheon, 1982); Pierre Bourdieu, *Outline of a Theory of Practice*, trans. Richard Nice (Cambridge: Cambridge University Press, 1977); George Lakoff and Mark Johnson, *Metaphors We Live By* (Chicago: Chicago University Press, 1980); Nancy Scheper-Hughes and Margaret Lock, "The Mindful Body: A Prologemenon to Future Work in Medical Anthropology," *Medical Anthropology Quarterly* vol. 1, no. 1 (1987): 6–41.

13. Genevieve Calame-Griaule, *Ethnologie et Langage: La Parole Chez Les Dogon* (Paris: Gallimard, 1965), 28.

14. W. T. Moynihan, *The Craft and Art of Dylan Thomas* (Ithaca, NY: Cornell University Press, 1966), 48.

15. Calame-Griaule, *Ethnologie et Langage*, 28.

16. I. A. Richards, *The Philosophy of Rhetoric* (New York: Oxford University Press, 1936), 97.

17. Max Horkheimer and Theodor W. Adorno, *Dialectic of Enlightenment: Philosophical Fragments*, trans. Edmund Jephcott (1987; Stanford, CA: Stanford University Press, 2002), 6–7.

18. Jorge Luis Borges, "The Fearful Sphere of Pascal," in *Labyrinths: Selected Stories and Other Writings*, trans. Anthony Kerrigan (Harmondsworth: Penguin, 1970), 224–27, here 224.

19. S. C. Pepper, *World Hypotheses: A Study in Evidence* (Berkeley: University of California Press, 1957), 87, 91.

20. Gregory Bateson, *Steps to an Ecology of Mind* (Frogmore: Paladin, 1973), 50–51.

21. Desmond Lee, ed., *Wittgenstein's Lectures: Cambridge, 1930–1932* (Oxford: Blackwell, 1980), 35.

22. Theodor W. Adorno, "Portrait of Walter Benjamin," in *Prisms*, trans. Samuel and Shierry Weber (1967; Cambridge, MA: MIT Press, 1983), 227–41, here 230.

23. Richard Rorty, *Philosophy and the Mirror of Nature* (Princeton, NJ: Princeton University Press, 1979), 12.

24. James Edie, *Speaking and Meaning: The Phenomenology of Language* (Bloomington: Indiana University Press, 1976), 173.

25. William James, *Pragmatism* (1907; Indianapolis, IN: Hackett Publishing, 1981), 92.

26. James, *Pragmatism*, 93.

27. Jeanne Bisilliat, "Village Diseases and Bush Diseases in Songhay: An Essay in Description with a View to a Typology," trans. J. B. Loudon, in *Social Anthropology and Medicine*, ed. J. B. Loudon (London: Academic Press, 1976), 555–93, here 555–78.

28. A not untypical "conversion reaction" among neurotics who embody the contradictions of their familial environment is paralysis or pain in the legs and acute difficulty in walking. P. R. Miller, *Sense and Symbol: A Handbook of Human Behavioral Science* (New York: Harper and Row, 1967), 134–35.

29. Pierre Bourdieu, *Outline of a Theory of Practice*, trans. Richard Nice (1972; Cambridge: Cambridge University Press, 1977), 162.

30. George Devereux, *From Anxiety to Method in the Behavioral Sciences* (The Hague: Mouton, 1967), 4.

31. Erikson, "Observations on the Yurok," 261

32. J. S. Mill, *Autobiography and Literary Essays*, vol. 1, ed. J. M. Robson and J. Stillinger (Toronto: University of Toronto Press, 1981), 139.

33. Mill, *Autobiography and Literary Essays*, 145.

34. Mill, *Autobiography and Literary Essays*, 141.

35. Mill, *Autobiography and Literary Essays*, 145.

36. Mill, *Autobiography and Literary Essays*, 151, 153.
37. G. B. Vico, *On the Study Methods of Our Time*, trans. Elio Gianturco (Indianapolis, IN: Bobbs-Merrill, 1965). Cited by Hans-Georg Gadamer, *Truth and Method*, trans. Joel Weinsheimer and Donald G. Marshall (New York: Continuum, 2004), 21.
38. G. Stade, *Robert Graves* (New York: Columbia University Press, 1967), 12.
39. Robert Graves, *The Crowning Privilege* (London: Cassell, 1955), 72.
40. The therapeutic effects of walking may be understood phylogenetically. In discussing the soothing effects of rocking a baby, John Bowlby notes that the most effective rocking rhythm is sixty cycles a minute or above, i.e., "the rate at which an adult walks." John Bowlby, *Attachment and Loss*, vol. 1: *Attachment* (Harmondsworth: Penguin, 1971), 353.
41. Claude Lévi-Strauss, *The Savage Mind* (1962; London: Weidenfeld and Nicolson, 1966), 24.
42. George Devereux, *Basic Problems of Ethnopsychiatry*, trans. B. M. Gulati and G. Devereux (Chicago: University of Chicago Press, 1980), 202–3.
43. M. Eliade, *Cosmos and History* (New York: Harper and Row, 1959).
44. R. I. Rosaldo, *Illongot Headhunting, 1883–1974: A Study in Society and History* (Stanford, CA: Stanford University Press, 1980), 48.
45. E. E. Evans-Pritchard, *The Nuer* (Oxford: Clarendon Press, 1940), 108.
46. John Berger, *Pig Earth* (London: Writers and Readers Publishing Cooperative, 1979), 8.

Notes for Chapter 9

1. Naveeda Khan, *Muslim Becoming: Aspiration and Skepticism in Pakistan* (Durham, NC: Duke University Press, 2012), 5–10. In his magisterial exploration of "the sheer diversity of … those societies, persons, ideas and practices that identify themselves with 'Islam,'" Shahab Ahmed makes a similar point. "A meaningful conceptualization of 'Islam' as *theoretical object* and *analytical category* must come to terms with—indeed, be coherent with—the capaciousness, complexity, and, often, *outright contradiction* that obtains within the historical phenomenon that has proceeded from the human engagement with the idea and reality of Divine Communication to Muhammad, the Messenger of God. Shahab Ahmed, *What is Islam: The Importance of Being Islamic* (Princeton, NJ: Princeton University Press, 2016), 6, emphasis in text.
2. Ousmane Oumar Kane, *Beyond Timbuktu: An Intellectual History of Muslim West Africa* (Cambridge, MA: Harvard University Press, 2016), 58.
3. J. Spencer Trimingham, *Islam in West Africa* (Oxford: Clarendon Press, 1959), 21–46.
4. Sarah Eltantawi, *Shari'ah on Trial: Northern Nigeria's Islamic Revolution* (Berkeley: University of California Press, 2017), 45, emphasis added.
5. Nehemia Levtzion, "The Eighteenth-Century Background to the Islamic Revolutions in West Africa," in *Eighteenth-Century Renewal and Reform*

in Islam, ed. John Obert Voll (Syracuse, NY: Syracuse University Press, 1987), 21.

6. Kane, *Beyond Timbuktu,* 17.

7. Cotton trees were planted around villages on ridges or hills to provide protective palisades against attack.

8. E. F. Sayers, "Notes on the Clan or Family Names Common in the Area Inhabited by Temne-Speaking People," *Sierra Leone Studies* vol. 12 (1927): 14–108, here 80.

9. Michael Jackson, "The Migration of a Name: Alexander in Africa," in *Lifeworlds: Selected Essays in Existential Anthropology* (Chicago: Chicago University Press, 2013), 75–90, here 78–79.

10. *Sundan,* "stranger," is possibly cognate with "sudan" as in Bilad al-Sudan, "land of the blacks."

11. Marcel Mauss, *The Gift: Forms and Functions of Exchange in Archaic Societies,* trans. Ian Cunnison (London: Cohen and West, 1954), 62, 127.

12. C. Magbaily Fyle, *The Solima Yalunka Kingdom: Pre-Colonial Politics, Economics, and Society* (Freetown: Nyakon Publishers, 1979), 40.

13. Sometimes Muslims have elected to establish their own communities. Momori Sise was born in the village of Yusumaia, but as a young man went to Qur'anic school in Guinea. He returned home as an old man in 1964 with three wives and a married adult son. He founded a hamlet and planted an orange grove on land leased to him by the Sengbe chief. Michael Jackson, *The Kuranko: Dimensions of Social Reality in a West African Society* (London: Hurst, 1979), 42.

14. Sayers, "Notes on the Clan," 65; Robin Horton, "African Conversion," *Africa* vol. 41, no. 2 (1971): 85–108, here 100; Mohammed-Basiru Sillah, "Islam in Sierra Leone: The Colonial Reaction and the Emergence of National Identity," *Journal of the Institute of Muslim Minority Affairs* vol. 15, no. 1–2 (1994): 121–41, here 121.

15. Alexander Gordon Laing, *Travels in the Timanee, Kooranko and Soolima Countries* (London; John Murray, 1825), 405–6.

16. For a detailed account of institutionalized Islam in Sierra Leone through the twentieth century, including the Ahmadiyya Muslim Mission (established in 1927), see David Skinner, "The Influence of Islam in Sierra Leone History: Institutions, Practices, and Leadership," *Journal of West African History* vol. 2, no. 1 (2016): 27–72, here 37–49.

17. A. P. Kup cites evidence for the Islamization of the Kuranko from the early eighteenth century. A. P. Kup, *A History of Sierra Leone* (Cambridge: Cambridge University Press, 1961), 154.

18. C. Magbaily Fyle, *The Solima Yalunka Kingdom,* 62.

19. This is according to Kuranko oral traditions. It is possible, however, that the oral historians have conflated the Solima ruler, Manga Sewa, with the Barawa ruler, Manse Marin Tamba (alias Sewa). The Solima ruler, who came to power in 1862, subjugated Barawa and other Kuranko chiefdoms, but committed suicide in 1884 when Samori's Sofas besieged his capital and Sewa faced defeat. Samori went on to establish a theocratic Muslim state among the southern Mande-speaking peoples. C. Magbaily

Fyle, "Sewa," *Dictionary of African Biography*, vol. 2, Sierra Leone—Zaire (Algonac, MI: Reference Publications Inc., 1979), 144; Sayers, "Notes on the Clan," 70.

20. Michael Jackson, *In Sierra Leone* (Durham, NC: Duke University Press, 2004), 10.

21. Kondembaia was founded in the late 1880s, following the withdrawal of the Sofa invaders from Diang. The first chief, Kundembé, for whom the town was named, was succeeded by his first-born son Kerifa Do. Kerifa Do's younger brothers, Tina Ferenke and Sama Magba, followed. The rivalry between the two ruling houses reflects the fact that Tina Ferenke and Sama Magba were sons of the same father but different mothers (Tina and Sama), a notoriously vexed relationship known as *fadenye*.

22. In the factional fighting between the Ferenkes and the Magbas, the powerful *korte* medicines were allegedly used causing these deaths.

23. For Alhaji Hassan, the defining characteristic of jujus was that they were not made by Allah but by men. In conversations with him in 1979 and 2008, Hassan insisted, "Everyone who used jujus had been converted, and those who have resisted conversion and refused to pray have also given their jujus away. He also asserted that no Muslim would allow his daughter to marry a non-Muslim, and that this had been an incentive for many non-Muslims to convert. "In our grandfathers' day all was juju; in our fathers' day there was some conversion; now, in our day, we have seen a complete conversion to Islam." As my text makes clear, this is wishful thinking—a representation of a reality that is far more complex and pluralist.

Notes for Chapter 10

Epigraph: Theodor W. Adorno, *Negative Dialectics*, trans. E. B. Ashton (New York: Continuum Books, 1973), 11.

1. In his introduction to his commentary on Heidegger's *Being and Time*, Hubert Dreyfus writes, "The traditional misunderstanding of human being starts with Plato's fascination with theory. The idea that one could understand the universe in a detached way, by discovering the principles that underlie the profusion of phenomena, was, indeed, the most powerful and exciting idea since fire and language. But Plato and our tradition got off on the wrong track by thinking that one could have a theory of everything—even human beings and their world—and that the way human beings relate to things is to have an implicit theory about them." Hubert Dreyfus, *Being-in-the-World: A Commentary on Heidegger's Being and Time, Division 1*, (Cambridge, MA: The MIT Press, 1991), 1.

2. Georg Simmel, *The View of Life: Four Metaphysical Essays with Journal Aphorisms*, trans. John A. Y. Andrews and Donald N. Levine (1918; Chicago: Chicago University Press, 2010), 13.

3. Jean-Paul Sartre, *Search for a Method*, trans. Hazel Barnes (New York: Vintage, 1968), ch. 3.

4. Jean-Paul Sartre, "The Itinerary of a Thought," in *Between Existentialism and Marxism*, trans. John Matthews (1972; London: Verso, 1974), 35.

5. Martin Jay, *Adorno* (London: Fontana, 1984), 30.

6. Herbert Marcuse, *Negations: Essays in Critical Theory* (London: Allen Lane, 1968), 129.

7. Joshua Conrad Jackson, David Read, Kevin Lewis, Michael J. Norton, and Kurt Gray, "Agent-based Modelling: A Guide for Social Psychologists," *Social Psychological and Personality Science* vol. 8, no. 4 (2017): 1–9, here 3.

8. Thomas C. Schelling, *Micromotives and Macrobehavior* (New York: Norton, 1978), 1–3.

9. Michael Oakeshott, *Rationalism in Politics and Other Essays* (Indianapolis, IN: Liberty Press, 1991), 52.

10. Devaka Premawardhana makes this distinction between belief as "intellectual assent to propositional truths" and faith as "performance of trust in a relation of intimacy" pivotal to his understanding of Pentecostalism in northern Mozambique where pastors enjoin people "to have faith, don't believe." Devaka Premawardhana, *Faith in Flux: Pentecostalism and Mobility in Rural Mozambique* (Philadelphia: University of Pennsylvania Press, 2018), 148.

11. Judith Sherman, *Say the Name: A Survivor's Tale in Prose and Poetry* (Albuquerque: University of New Mexico Press, 2005).

12. Sherman, *Say the Name*, 62.

13. Jonathan Lear, *Radical Hope: Ethics in the Face of Cultural Devastation* (Cambridge, MA: Harvard University Press, 2008), 16.

14. Jaspers contrasts *Grenzsituationen* with *Altagsituationen* (everyday situations). While we are able to gain an overview of everyday situations and get beyond them, limit situations "possess finality"; "they are like a wall against which we butt, against which we founder." Karl Jaspers, *Philosophie, vol. 2, Existenzerhellung* (Berlin: Springer Verlag, 1932), 178–79. For an account of *Grenzsituationen* in English, see Karl Jaspers, *Basic Philosophical Writings*, ed. and trans. Edith Ehrlich, Leonard H. Ehrlich, and George B. Pepper (New York: Humanity Books, 2000), 97.

15. Michael Jackson, "From Anxiety to Method in Anthropological Fieldwork: An Appraisal of George Devereux's Enduring Ideas," in *Emotions in the Field: The Psychology and Anthropology of Fieldwork Experience*, ed. James Davies and Dimitrina Spencer (Stanford, CA: Stanford University Press, 2010), 35–54.

16. Hubert L. Dreyfus, *Skillful Coping: Essays on the Phenomenology of Everyday Perception and Action*, ed. Mark A. Wrathall (New York: Oxford University Press, 2014).

17. Meyer Fortes, "Coping with Destiny," in *Religion, Morality, and the Person: Essays on Tallensi Religion*, ed. Jack Goody (Cambridge: Cambridge University Press, 1987), 145–74, here 145.

18. John Dewey speaks of the pathos "of philosophies which think it their proper office to give an intellectual or cognitive certification to the

ontological reality of the highest values," a remark that could be taken as a critique of the ontological turn in anthropology. John Dewey, *The Quest for Certainty: A Study of the Relation of Knowledge and Action* (New York: Perigree, 1980), 34.

19. Richard Rorty, *Philosophy and the Mirror of Nature* (Princeton, NJ: Princeton University Press, 1978).

20. Hannah Arendt, *The Life of the Mind* (New York: Harcourt Brace, 1978), 104.

21. Jorge Luis Borges, "From Allegories to Novels," in *Other Inquisitions 1937–1952*, trans. Ruth L. C. Simms (New York: Simon and Schuster, 1965), 154–57, here 156.

22. Henri Ellenberger, *The Discovery of the Unconscious: The History and Evolution of Dynamic Psychiatry*, (New York: Basic Books, 1970), 537.

23. Claude Lévi-Strauss, *Tristes Tropiques*, trans. John and Doreen Wightmas (London: Jonathan Cape, 1973), 57–58.

24. Fernando Pessoa, *The Book of Disquiet*, trans. Richard Zenith (Harmondsworth: Penguin, 2001), 254.

25. Michael Jackson, "The Man Who Could Turn into an Elephant," *Lifeworlds: Essays in Existential Anthropology* (Chicago: Chicago University Press, 2013), 93–112.

26. Speaking of "the reality of the unseen," William James notes, "It is as if there were in the human consciousness a *sense of reality, a feeling of objective presence, a perception* of what we may call *something there*, deeper and more general than any of the special and particular senses by which current psychology supposes existent realities to be originally revealed." William James, *The Varieties of Religious Experience* (New York: Signet, 1958), 61, emphasis added.

27. Michael Puett, "Ritual Disjunctions: Ghosts, Anthropology and Philosophy," in *The Ground Between: Anthropologists Engage Philosophy*, ed. Veena Das, Michael Jackson, Arthur Kleinman, and Brighupati Singh (Durham, NC: Duke University Press, 2014), 218–33.

28. Michael Jackson, "Familiar and Foreign Bodies: A Phenomenological Exploration of the Human-Technology Interface," in *Lifeworlds*, 191–205, here 200.

29. Nancy Scheper-Hughes and Mariana Leal Ferreira, "Dombá's Spirit Kidney—Transplant Medicine and Suyá Indian Cosmology," *Folk: Dansk Etnografisk Tidskrift* (2003): 125–48, here 136.

30. Maurice Merleau-Ponty, "Eye and Mind," trans. Carleton Dallery, in *The Primacy of Perception: And Other Essays on Phenomenological Psychology, the Philosophy of Art, History and Politics* (Evanston, IL: Northwestern University Press, 1964), 159–90, here 177, 176. Emphasis added.

31. Maurice Merleau-Ponty, *Phenomenology of Perception*, trans. Colin Smith (London: Routledge, 1962), 354, 352.

32. Theodor Adorno, *Minima Moralia: Reflections from Damaged Life*, trans. E. F. N. Jephcott (London: Verso, 1978), 81.

33. Adorno, *Minima Moralia*, 81.

34. Adorno, *Negative Dialectics*, 5, 13.

35. Sarah Kofman, "Beyond Aporia," trans. David Macey, in *Post-structuralist Classics*, ed. Andrew Bejamin (London: Routledge, 1988), 7–44, here 10, 12.
36. Sextus Empiricus, *The Skeptic Way: Sextus Empiricus's Outlines of Pyrrhonism*, trans. Benson Mates (New York: Oxford University Press, 1996), 89.
37. Michel de Montaigne, *The Essays: A Selection*, trans. M. A. Screech (Harmondsworth: Penguin, 2004), 394.
38. C. J. Ackerly and S.E. Gontarski, *The Grove Companion to Samuel Beckett: A Reader's Guide to his Works, Life, and Thought* (New York: Grove, 2004), 16.
39. Samuel Beckett, *The Unnameable* (New York: Grove, 1958).
40. Samuel Beckett, *Proust, Three Dialogues: Samuel Beckett and Georges Duhuit* (London: Calder, 1987), 103.
41. Heinrich Dumoulin, *Zen Budhism: A History*, vol. 1: *India and China*, trans. James W. Heisig and Paul Knitter (New York: Macmillan, 1994), 245, 253.
42. Cited by Hubert Benoit, *The Supreme Doctrine: Psychological Encounters in Zen Thought* (New York: Inner Traditions International, 1984), 97.
43. Eugen Herrigal, *Zen in the Art of Archery*, trans. R. H. C. Hull (London: Routledge and Kegan Paul, 1972), 17.
44. Amartya Sen has pointed out that the "exaggerated focus on religiosity" by Western observers of India has led to a neglect or denial of scientific, secular, and skeptical traditions that date back to the second millennium BCE, such as the Lokayata tradition of skepticism, and the Carvaka system. Amartya Sen, *The Argumentive Indian: Writings on Indian History, Culture and Identity* (London: Allen Lane, 2005), 21–25. One might also mention the skeptical strain in Nagarjuna's doctrine of "emptiness," though Nakamura calls Sanjaya "the first skeptic in India." Haime Nakamura, *A Comparative History of Ideas*, rev. ed. (London: Routledge and Kegan Paul, 1986), 162.
45. Knud Rasmussen, *Intellectual Culture of the Iglulik Eskimos*, vol. 1: *Intellectual Culture of the Hudson Bay Eskimos* (Copenhagen: Gylden-Galske, 1929), 55–56.
46. Michael Jackson, *Allegories of the Wilderness: Ethics and Ambiguity in Kuranko Narratives* (Bloomington: Indiana University Press, 1982), 38.
47. Luis-Vincent Thomas, *Les Diola: Essai d'Analyse Fonctionelle sur une Population de Basse-Casamance* (Paris: Institut Française d'Afrique Noire, 1958–1959), 579.
48. Jack Berry, *Spoken Art in West Africa: An Inaugural Lecture delivered on 8 December 1960* (London: School of Oriental and African Studies, University of London, 1961), 10.
49. John Keats, *The Letters of John Keats 1814–1831*, vol. 1, ed. H. E. Rollins (Cambridge: Cambridge University Press,1958), 193.
50. Christopher Fortune, *The Sándor Ferenczi-Georg Groddeck Correspondence, 1921–1933*, trans. Jeannie Cohen, Elizabeth Petersdorff, and Norbert Ruebsaat (London: Open Gate Press, 200), 35.
51. Michel Foucault, *The Archaeology of Knowledge*, trans. A. M. Sheridan Smith (London Tavistock, 1972), 166.
52. Jacques Derrida, *Aporias*, trans. Thomas Dutoit (Stanford, CA: Stanford University Press, 1993), 12–13.

53. David Mamet, "Obituary: Arthur Miller," *New York Times*, 13 February 2005.
54. Derrida speaks of this tradition as logocentrism, or the "epoch of the logos. It assumes a universal logic and rationality, based on Western philosophical models, and a fixed, foundational principle which can be uniquely named … whether it be 'being' or 'God.'" Dermot Moran, *Introduction to Phenomenology* (London: Routledge, 2000), 448.

❧ Index

CPSIA information can be obtained
at www.ICGtesting.com
Printed in the USA
LVHW021330290422
716924LV00004B/117